DATE DUE

LIBERALS AMONG THE ORTHODOX

Unitarian Beginnings in New York City
1819–1839

LIBERALS AMONG

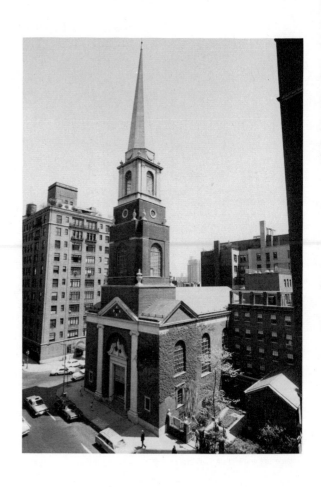

THE ORTHODOX

Unitarian

Beginnings in

New York City

1819-1839

WALTER DONALD KRING

BEACON PRESS BOSTON

This book is dedicated
to all of the souls, past and present, who have loved and labored
for ALL SOULS

Copyright © 1974 by Walter Donald Kring
Beacon Press books are published under the auspices
of the Unitarian Universalist Association
Simultaneous publication in Canada by Saunders of Toronto, Ltd.
All rights reserved
Printed in the United States of America

9 8 7 6 5 4 3 2 1

Library of Congress Cataloging in Publication Data

Kring, Walter Donald.
    Liberals among the orthodox: Unitarian beginnings
in New York City, 1819–1839.
        1. Unitarian Church of All Souls, New York.
2. New York (City). Community Church. 3. Unitarian
churches in New York (City). I. Title
BX9833.6.N49K74   288'.747'1   73–21275
ISBN 0–8070–1662–4

Contents

Preface

It has long been the hope of the members of the Unitarian Church of All Souls of New York City that an adequate history should be written about the church. Dr. Laurance I. Neale, the seventh minister of the church, told the congregation upon the announcement of his retirement in January 1955 that he hoped to devote the remainder of his life to writing such a history. Unfortunately Dr. Neale died a little over a year later, and his dreams about the history were never realized. This desire to have a history was renewed about ten years ago when the church was looking forward to the celebration of its 150th anniversary in 1969. I went through the church records, dipped into a few other sources, and produced a history of some 250 manuscript pages a year before the 1969 deadline.

But it was obvious to me and to all who read the manuscript that it was the "once-over-lightly" treatment typical of too many church histories. As we examined the history of the church and the people associated with it we realized that it contained a richness matched by few other churches in the country. The history of All Souls is in reality an important microcosm of the American liberal tradition in religion. Also, the original manuscript raised far more numerous questions than it answered. The book needed further research.

As a result, five years after the 150th anniversary, instead of presenting a book about the entire history of the church we offer a volume that covers the beginnings of the Unitarian movement in New York City from 1819, the year of the founding, to the end of Dr. Charles Follen's acting ministry in 1838. I have completed the story of Dr. Follen until his death in 1840. The book also contains the story of the founding of the Second Church (now the Community Church of New York) and the Brooklyn Church.

In *The Harvard Register* for February 1881, Edward Everett Hale, a Unitarian minister, but even more famous as the author of *The Man Without a Country,* wrote about All Souls Church: "The number of rare souls that have been connected with this society have been remarkable, and the weight its members have had in the life of the city and country is really exceptional." [1] As I studied the history of the church I realized what Edward Everett Hale meant. The history of All Souls is not just the history of the ministers but of a most remarkable group of laymen. As a result I have included a great amount of material, even genealogical material, on the founders and laymen of the early church period.

We are fortunate indeed to possess the complete minutes of every meeting of the society and the board of trustees from the very beginning of our history. The earliest records were written in the beautiful hand of Henry Devereux Sewall. The first entry refers to that Sunday afternoon, April 25, 1819, when the Reverend William Ellery Channing spoke to about forty persons in the home of his sister, Mrs. William W. Russel in Broome Street. Would that all of the minutes had been written in the flowing hand of the first entries. The writing becomes less and less legible as the years go by, until fortunately the typewriter was substituted for writing.

The various names of the church used in these pages may be confusing to persons not thoroughly acquainted with our history. When founded in 1819 the church was officially named, "The First Congregational Church in the City of New York." This remains the official and legal name to the present day. However, at various times, other names were given to the church. When the Second Congregational Unitarian Church was established in 1825, the early church was often called "The First Church," or "The Lower Church" (referring to its geographical position, not its ritual), and the daughter church was called "The Second Church," or "The Upper Church." When the second building was constructed in 1845 Henry Bellows suggested the name "The Church of the Divine Unity." When the third church building was dedicated in 1855, Bellows suggested a new name, "All Souls Church."

At various times since then the church has been known as "All Souls Church," "All Souls Unitarian Church," and "The Unitarian Church of All Souls." However, in this book in order to avoid confusion we have labeled all of the minute books, the "All Souls Minute Books," even though the church in the early days had not yet conceived of this name. It might be argued that the records ought to bear

---

[1] *The Harvard Register,* Cambridge, February 1881, p. 61.

the name "The First Congregational Church," but this is additionally confusing. Unlike many Unitarian churches in New England which were founded as Congregational churches and then became Unitarian in theology, All Souls Church has always been Unitarian in theology and Congregational in church polity.

In writing this volume of the history I have been greatly helped by many persons to whom I owe a debt of gratitude. Mrs. Lauck Walton at the outset of the project read all the minutes and gave me some good advice to enlarge the scope of the book beyond the usual church history. In the area of research I was fortunate to have the services of Jack Holzhueter in New York for several years. Now a research assistant at the Wisconsin Historical Society, Jack had an uncanny ability to find original source materials and to look into obscure matters. Without his help this book would not be what I hope it is, an in-depth treatment of early American religious liberalism. His support and encouragement have made this book possible.

I also owe a debt of gratitude to my wife, who continuously encouraged me to make the book the best I possibly could in the midst of a very busy life. I am also indebted to some of the members of the congregation who did some of the basic research and carding of material.

To Dr. Conrad Wright of the Harvard Divinity School, one of the most knowledgeable persons about early American Unitarian history, I am deeply indebted. He read the manuscript and made many valuable suggestions concerning facts and interpretation of Unitarian history. I am indeed sorry that Dean Richard Donald Pierce of Emerson College, a dear friend who read the manuscript and gave some suggestions before his untimely death, did not live to see the completion of this work.

My editor at the Beacon Press, the Reverend Carl Seaburg, has been a joy to work with, and his suggestions have always been apt. My special thanks to the members of the staff of the New-York Historical Society, the staff of the Massachusetts Historical Society, especially Miss Winifred Collins, and to the New York Public Library, especially the local history and genealogical rooms. I want to thank those who made the pictures for this book possible — acknowledgment is made in the text. I especially ought to thank the members of my church, the church staff, and my own secretary, Mrs. Rita Savides, who have been patient and understanding while I have been living in the early nineteenth century. I appreciate the help of the John Lindsley Fund and

Mr. Thayer Lindsley who helped make the publication of this book possible, and to the Beacon Press for their understanding and cooperation.

WALTER DONALD KRING

November 1973

Recessional at the 150th Anniversary Service, November 16, 1969.
Photograph by George E. Joseph

Prologue: All Souls Today

STANDING AT THE CORNER of 80th Street and Lexington Avenue in New York City and gazing up at the steeple of the Unitarian Church of All Souls, one is filled with a strong sense of solidarity and aspiration. The red-brick and sandstone church is impressive even amid the surrounding high-rise apartments. Lexington Avenue is a busy thoroughfare; the increasingly heavy traffic of today could not have been imagined by those who built the church on this spot in 1932. Yet somehow, the edifice dominates its bustling surroundings and stands as a concrete symbol of the aspirations of a group of men and women who seek God in truth and freedom within its walls. Despite rapidly changing times, this symbol has endured and is as relevant today as it was when the present church building was erected.

Entering the front doors of the New England Georgian building, one finds himself in the vestibule just outside the sanctuary; the vestibule is reminiscent of the Federal period of American architecture. From here one moves into the large, vaulted sanctuary itself with its rose-tinted walls and its long, red-carpeted, center aisle. The crisp white pews framed in mahogany seem to welcome the worshiper, and the high pulpit in the center of the chancel attests to the belief of those who built the church that the sermon is a significant weekly event. The tall windows, arched gracefully at the top, are filled with rippled antique glass to let in the light, so that the interior is joyful and bright as well as dignified and conducive to personal worship. The unmistakable aura of reverence within these walls is inspired, not by Byzantine ornateness and color, but by dignified simplicity. Around these walls various plaques attest to the ministers and laymen who have led the congregation, and who themselves worshiped here. Each of these memorials is of different design, many having been moved here

I

Coffee Hour in Fellowship Hall. Photograph by George E. Joseph

from earlier homes of All Souls; yet there is an aesthetic unity of design among them and a compatibility with the overall architecture of the present church.

On the basement level, beneath the church building, can be found Fellowship Hall, a huge, high-ceilinged room complete with a stage and an impressive array of theatrical equipment. Fellowship Hall is adjoined by a large semi-institutional kitchen beyond which is the much smaller Minot Simons Room. Fellowship Hall is the scene of the Sunday coffee hour which immediately follows the worship service. On most Sundays, a luncheon and speaking program conducted by the All Souls Guild follows the coffee hour. Congregational dinners are also held in this hall, as is a variety of other programs conducted by organizations both inside and outside the church. In 1968, Fellowship Hall underwent a "face-lifting"; adorning its now pale golden walls are twelve colored-glass windows designed and created by the present

2

minister. The Minot Simons Room, named for the sixth minister of All Souls, is also the scene of various supper programs and other activities, although of much-reduced proportions compared with those held in Fellowship Hall.

One can, if one wishes, enter the church building through the iron gate on Lexington Avenue which stands adjacent to the great doors to

Playroof on the Top of Wiggin House, All Souls Day School.
Photograph by George E. Joseph

3

the sanctuary. Descending the four red-brick steps just inside this gate, one is suddenly in a quiet rendezvous with nature, strangely incongruous with the concrete, brick, and glass city. A red-brick path picks up where the steps leave off and proceeds directly through the garden to the main entrance of Wiggin House, the parish building which connects with the church proper. This five-story edifice is topped by an enclosed playroof for little children — the pupils of the All Souls School, as well as the children enrolled in the Sunday-school classes.

Most of the rooms in Wiggin House are classrooms used from Monday through Friday by the preschool-age children of the All Souls School, and on Sunday mornings by the pupils of the church school. The rooms on the second floor, however, double as meeting rooms for adult activities in the afternoons and evenings. The Bellows Room, named for one of the most illustrious of the church's ministers, Dr. Henry W. Bellows (1814–1882), is a long, low-ceilinged room suitable for lectures, weekly meetings of the Bridge Club, and similar activities; it boasts both an electric organ and a piano. Adjoining the Bellows Room is the Sullivan Room — also named for a prominent minister of All Souls, a former Catholic priest, William Laurence Sullivan (1872–1935). Compared to the Bellows Room, the Sullivan Room is smaller and more intimate, having been attractively and comfortably furnished by the Parents Association. Here meet various discussion groups as well as the students of the high-school class of the Sunday church school.

The street floor of Wiggin House contains the main office of the church, the Ware Room, and the intimate chapel which was given by Mrs. Albert Wiggin in memory of her husband, for whom the parish building is named. More modern in architectural design than the church sanctuary, the little chapel is nonetheless of the same New England Georgian spirit: simple but dignified, and conducive to reverent worship. The chapel seats 60 persons and is the site of many weddings, memorial services, and children's worship services. A bronze bust of Albert Wiggin, at one time the president of the Chase National Bank and a leading citizen, rests modestly at the rear of the chapel. The bust of Mr. Wiggin was created by Mrs. Wiggin, whose hobby was sculpture. In the corridor outside of the chapel is another bust, this one in white marble of Mrs. Wiggin herself, created by the artist Victor Salvatore. The Ware Room — dedicated to William Ware, the

4

first minister of All Souls — stands next to the chapel, a gracious, formal reception room for entertaining wedding guests and others who attend services held in the chapel. Because William Ware was one of 19 children, a light-hearted custom at All Souls is for newly married couples to have their picture taken in the Ware Room just in front of William Ware's portrait. Handsomely and luxuriously furnished in a period style by the Women's Alliance, the Ware Room has its own tiny kitchenette and houses the Laurance Irving Neale Memorial Library — a collection of a wide range of religious texts and related nonfiction books which are available to all who care to come in and browse.

The Ware Room in Wiggin House, High School Seminar.
Photograph by George E. Joseph

Wiggin House, originally built in 1953, was then only three stories high. At that time it contained, in addition to the Ware Room and the chapel, mostly offices for the church staff and a few Sunday-school classrooms. Growing church school enrollments and other needs soon proved the inadequacy of the existing building, however; and it was decided to remodel Wiggin House, enlarging it to five stories. The

Wiggin House Chapel. Photograph by George E. Joseph

congregation also decided to establish the All Souls School for children of nursery-school and kindergarten ages. A campaign for funds headed by Mrs. Frederick Wappler raised over a third of a million dollars for the new addition. The enterprise was aided by a foundation grant of $200,000 made possible by Thayer Lindsley, a member of the church. The All Souls Day School, set up as a separate corporation apart from the church organization, functions independently from, but is ultimately responsible to, the church. At the same time, the church purchased an apartment in the adjoining building, 162 East 80th Street, where the church's executive offices are now located. The new Wiggin House was completed in the summer of 1965, and the following September opened its doors to the first pupils of the day school.

Now, children of all races and ethnic backgrounds trip gaily through Memorial Garden each weekday morning or afternoon for one of the school's two sessions. Here, in this oasis of greenery within the concrete desert of the city, English ivy, shrubs of privet, Japanese holly, and the indomitable black locust tree struggle for enough sunlight to grow. The persistent efforts of these plants to survive is perhaps not unlike the dedicated efforts of the All Souls congregation to find religious truth and deeper meanings in life. Perhaps, too, the very fact

6

that these plants do manage to get enough sun to sustain themselves as healthy organisms is also significant of the spirit that dwells within the church congregation and all for which it stands. In any case, for many church members, Memorial Garden epitomizes the spiritual essence of All Souls. Depending upon the season of the year, the garden is white with snow, red with tulips, or amber and orange with the turning of the leaves. At Yuletide, a giant, colorfully lighted Christmas tree presides; at Easter, white Easter lilies speckle the greenery as cheerful symbols of the rebirth of life.

But it is not just at Easter that Memorial Garden betokens the eternal renewal of life. All during the year its walks are filled with adults and, significantly, with children. In the nineteen-thirties, when it became clear that there were not funds enough to build a parish house, a small garden was planted next to the church and was called Friendship Garden in commemoration of Mrs. Alexander V. Fraser's devotion to the church. In 1955, after Wiggin House was completed,

The Memorial Garden in the Spring. Photograph by George E. Joseph

the area became the present Memorial Garden, and the memorial to Mrs. Fraser was made tangible in the lovely birdbath and plaque which now graces the garden. The present Memorial Garden was the gift of Mr. and Mrs. Samuel Ordway in memory of two of their three children, who died, one in infancy and one in his teens. A small plaque on the south wall of the church building contains the dedication:

Anna Hanson Ordway, Stephen Wheatland Ordway — I invite you to be friendly with my trees, my flowers, and my wild creatures.

Perhaps their spirits do reign, for the garden is indeed a friendly place for wild creatures. Various species of birds chirp among the leaves and pigeons eagerly pick up the rice from weddings. In fact, some years ago, people who happened to be at the church on Saturday afternoons became intrigued with what seemed to be a unique ritual. Every Saturday afternoon at about two o'clock, with predictable reliability, two rather unusually marked pigeons would enter, *on foot,* through the iron gate, proceed with great pomp down the brick steps and along the walk to join the other pigeons who had arrived more conventionally by air for the feast of wedding rice. So regular was this ritual that it soon became known to the human observers as "Luncheon at All Souls."

If Memorial Garden could tell us of all the scenes and episodes of life it has witnessed, not all would be happy ones. On a Monday in February 1958, for example, Frederick May Eliot, then president of the American Unitarian Association, died almost instantly of a heart attack upon reaching the gate. Miss Myrtle Crooks, the administrative assistant, saw him fall and reached him just as he breathed his last. Only the day before he had preached at the church, the last sermon of a distinguished man. A few days later, his mourners filed sorrowfully out into the garden after the memorial service conducted in his memory. The brick garden walk has also been trod by many a pathetic victim of the city's dread diseases: alcoholism, drug addiction, poverty, dissolution of age, and abject loneliness.

In the main, however, Memorial Garden is a happy spot in the midst of a trouble-ridden city. Dedicated to children and bearing the light-hearted, eager quality of childhood, the garden's mood is kept alive by the spirit of the children who daily dance on its walks among the ivy. In keeping with this spirit, a bronze sculpture — given anon-

8

ymously — was installed several years ago on the west wall of the chapel. Created by Euphemia Glover, the figures represent three small girls carrying balloons. The children are happily at play; their bronze balloons waving gaily in the breeze, or at least one imagines so. Each of the girls faintly resembles one of the three main human races, symbolizing that the family of man is divided into three racial groups but that basically all people are one.

The present Church of All Souls is actually the fourth house of worship built by the congregation. The first three buildings were farther downtown. As New York City expanded northward the congregation found it expedient to move with the expansion of the city. The site of the first church building was on Chambers Street and was occupied from 1821 until 1844. During a Sunday morning service a large piece of cornice fell and almost hit the minister, Dr. Bellows. The congregation moved farther uptown to a new building, which fronted on both Broadway and Crosby streets. When the Broadway church had been occupied for less than a decade the congregation decided to move again, to 20th Street and Fourth Avenue (now Park Avenue South). For 75 years the congregation occupied this basilica, which was often referred to as the "Beefsteak Church" or "The Church of the Holy Zebra." Despite the engaging of the expensive and prestigious English architect Jacob Wrey Mould, it was public consensus that because of the layering of limestone and red brick the building resembled a piece of raw steak more than a church.

The population kept expanding northward on Manhattan Island, and the 20th Street church lacked an adequate Sunday-school building. By 1928 the economic outlook of the church was bright, and it was decided to sell the old property and to move a third time, to 80th Street and Lexington Avenue. The story of the financial near-disaster as the congregation built the present edifice in the depths of the Great Depression will be told in a subsequent volume. Suffice it to say that the congregation almost lost the new building, but through a successful "Burn the Mortgage Campaign" the church was saved in 1945.

A church is more than a building or a series of buildings; a church has a distinctive personality. This is particularly true of All Souls Church as is illustrated by a rather consistent pattern in the one hundred and fifty years of history. The church was founded largely by New Englanders who had moved to New York City in the decade between 1810 and 1820. That the church has kept its New England flavor is evident immediately when one steps into the present New England Georgian building. All but two of the eight "settled" ministers have had a Harvard education, having been graduated from either Harvard College or the Harvard Divinity School or both. The only two exceptions were Dr. Thomas Slicer, who came from a Methodist background, and Dr. William L. Sullivan, who was a former Roman Catholic priest. The only acting minister (aside from Dr. Neale for a year) was Dr. Charles Follen, who was a member of the Harvard faculty.

The point of view of the congregation and its ministry has been a stable one. Only one minister of the eight retired (Dr. Neale in 1955), three died in office (Dr. Bellows in 1882, Dr. Slicer in 1916, and Dr. Minot Simons in 1942), and three resigned to enter other fields of endeavor after having served a successful ministry (William Ware in 1836 to write historical novels, Theodore C. Williams in 1896 to become the first headmaster of Hackley School, and William L. Sullivan in 1922 to become a national preacher for the Unitarian Laymen's League). The length of ministry has been consistently long. There has not been a single minister who has not done a creditable job in the work of the parish even though several left to enter fields other than the parish ministry.

The church has also steered a rather independent course in regard to trends within the Unitarian denomination. Sometimes the congregation followed the lead of the national Unitarian Association, as in the early years; sometimes it has taken the lead, as when Henry Bellows founded the National Conference of Churches in 1865 and established many churches in the Midwest; and sometimes it has not been too enthusiastic about its relationship to the denomination, as when headquarters was very reluctant to let the congregation ordain Mr. Laurance I. Neale, a layman, to be their minister in 1942. Radical theological trends within the denomination have never had much of a place in the All Souls picture, and yet the attitude of the members has seldom been what could be called reactionary. The interest has been largely in religious matters rather than political ones.

What characterizes the beliefs of a church such as All Souls? These beliefs were originally stated in the first covenant of the church, which was written in 1821. This statement proved to be far too conservative for the growing fringe of Unitarian ideas in New York, and the original covenant fell into disuse by 1846 when Henry Bellows was the last to sign it. There is no evidence that there was a covenant or bond of union in use at all from this time until the year 1922 when the Annual Meeting voted that the bylaws of the society should be amended to provide a "Bond of Fellowship for active membership in a book kept for that purpose." In 1922 there were 276 living members of the society. A letter was sent to each of these persons, asking each one to assume that his or her assent was given to this Bond of Fellowship "unless an express dissent therefrom is transmitted in writing to the undersigned on or before April 1, 1922." The names of four ladies who expressed their dissent are listed in the membership book.[1]

After this matter of a bond of union had been established, there was inscribed in a large hand in the membership book the new Bond of Union which now appears on the slate tablet on the outside of the church building.

In the freedom of the truth and in the spirit of Jesus
We unite for the worship of God and the service of man.[2]

Other Unitarian churches about the same time were adopting similar statements of purpose. Many of these have been dropped by the churches in the same way that the original covenant fell into disuse at All Souls. But this church has retained its statement of purpose, and it is repeated each Sunday morning at the beginning of the service to remind the members of the positive aspects of their faith and their commitment.

Although complete freedom is given to each individual to interpret the words of the Covenant or Bond of Union, there has been a basic common ground apparent in the opinions of the members of the congregation. Stripped of all specific and confining creeds, the Bond of Union embodies four religious principles which are far more significant than a casual reading would indicate. These ideas, which are so easily professed in the United States in the twentieth century, have a long and difficult history of human struggle behind them. Insofar as these ideas have been advanced at all in the process of civilization, they have come into being only through continuous effort and suffer-

[1] Register of the First Congregational Church in New York, p. 42.
[2] *Ibid.*, p. 43.

*The Covenant or Bond of Union
Inscribed on Slate on the
Front of the Church.
Photograph by George E. Joseph*

ing, beginning at least as far back as the reign of the Pharaoh Akhenaten in the early part of the fourteenth century B.C. Let us examine their meaning, especially as they apply to All Souls Church.

Truth and freedom have been ideas particularly acceptable to man, but always very elusive in their realization. At All Souls, the word *truth* is usually interpreted to mean that man lives in a Cosmos — an *orderly* Universe — rather than a Chaos, and that there is inherent in nature something that is real and enduring which may become known, at least partially, to man, through diligent, rational search.

Truth is not something that any person, group, nation, or religious organization knows infallibly or in its entirety. Indeed, the only possessor of truth is the Cosmos itself, but knowledge of it can be attained to some extent by any individual or group sincerely willing to search for it.

The word *freedom* in the Bond of Union refers to the opportunity that every person should have of exploring his life and experience as fully and widely as he is capable, to find whatever measure of truth is most meaningful to him. Everyone should be allowed to exercise his reason with respect to any and all ideas which may attract his curiosity. We assume that if one follows his natural interests, and uses his reason to analyze all ideas relevant to his interests (including opposing ideas), he will come progressively to know more and more of the truth. All ideas must be heard; all new theories, however improbable, must be examined for their possible worth.

All Souls' services, programs, and activities are planned to encourage this individual search, and to provide a wide range of ideas and opportunities from which each person may choose to further his own understanding of truth. As each new person joins the church, he agrees "to discard whatever beliefs [he discovers] to be false and to accept whatever [he is] convinced are true." [3] It is also important that he prevent passion or prejudice from compelling him to accept or to reject any idea.

The "spirit of Jesus" is also an elusive ideal, though perhaps in a different way than are either truth or freedom. In the almost 2000 years since Jesus' death, there have been many interpretations about the person of Jesus. Most members of All Souls tend to agree with the generally held liberal view that the myths, legends, and supernatural events associated with the birth and death of Jesus have obscured Jesus the man, making the true character and "spirit" of Jesus, and the teachings attributed to him, difficult to evaluate. Although each member of the church may have a different view about the person of Jesus, in general, the members believe that Jesus was a *human* being who, through his reason and intuition, developed a higher, more "divine" understanding of the Cosmos. It is not Jesus as miraculously conceived, or Jesus as the focus of a special theology, that concerns us, but Jesus as a spiritually enlightened human being who came very close to the center and substance of Being, which some call by the name of God.

"The worship of God" is probably the most difficult phrase in the Bond of Union to explain, for both *worship* and *God* offer a wide range of interpretations. By *God,* many Unitarians would mean the highest governing principle of the universe that one can conceive, allowing a wide latitude for individual interpretations. For some, this principle is something to which one can relate directly and personally through meditation and prayer; for others, it is impersonal and cannot be communicated with in any more personal way than can, say, a current of electricity. But people in this latter group, also, often find personal meaning and inspiration through the uplifting words, music,

[3] From *The Hymn and Service Book,* Unitarian Church of All Souls of New York City, 1957, p. 27.

and visual beauty provided at the Sunday morning service. Others in the congregation experience a satisfying silent communion with their fellow worshipers during these services. The members are in general agreement, that the word *worship* refers to whatever is meaningful, uplifting, and consistent with the universal human ideals of reverence and spiritual renewal.

As a church with roots in the tradition of liberal Protestantism, the service of worship at All Souls tends to follow the basic format of this tradition, using hymns, readings, prayers, musical interludes for private meditation, and perhaps placing the chief emphasis upon the sermon. The essential difference between a service at All Souls and one in most other Protestant churches lies in the *content* — that is, the ideas expressed — in these aspects of the program. Freed from specific dogmas, the readings, hymns, and prayers express the highest sentiments known to man — sentiments which are universal in character: the miracles of nature and of human life, the human struggles to attain peace and righteousness, pleas for compassion and human brotherhood, and other ideas in a similar vein.

The sermon is intended to be a reasoned discourse which not only informs and stimulates the intellect, but also inspires the feelings which go with a worshipful attitude. The sermon is also intended to leave individuals in the congregation with the personal impact of religion on their own lives. Although sermon topics cover a wide range of themes, the sermon does not impose on the congregation any set of ideas as the final truth which must be accepted and adhered to. The church is not, in the estimation of the congregation, a place to accept dogmatic ideas about God or human duty, but a place to point out that man's religious concern should develop around whatever he conceives to be the primary unity in this universe, and that his own life and conduct should be consistent with his understanding of this truth.

Nearly everyone, and certainly every religious person and organization, wants to serve humanity. The urge to bring about human brotherhood is not unique to All Souls. The difficulty has always been to know exactly *what constitutes* a service to man, and how that service is best to be rendered.

At All Souls we tend to believe that how one best serves his fellow men is an *individual* matter; that the way one serves his fellow human beings is an aspect of truth which one must search for and find in the same way as he searches for any other aspect of truth. We believe that each individual should have the freedom to search out with his own reason and conscience the way in which he believes he can best serve his fellow men, and then follow the dictates of his heart and conscience accordingly. In so doing, the individual may enlist the aid of others who have similar beliefs, interests, and abilities; but a person is expected to refrain from trying to impose his beliefs upon others, and to grant others the same freedom of individual choice. No one way of serving our fellow men is the "true" way, and as part of the search for truth every way must be tried and found either to be helpful or to be wanting.

Another important belief common to the members of All Souls, and implicit in the Bond of Union, is the conviction that no truly beneficial act can be done for the service of man without this act deriving from a larger world view.

A religious view which has as its primary premise the maintaining of a rational, open mind and a sense of humility that no one has the absolute truth helps to provide the elements of caution, acute observation, self-evaluation, and flexibility to change which are so necessary if true progress in human improvement is to be achieved.

It is with such aspirations that the people of All Souls gather week by week in their red-brick and sandstone building. To many modern Americans the idea of freedom in religion may appear to be simple enough, and largely taken for granted. But the struggle against tyranny in religion and the right of everyone to express his own concern for the truth as he personally sees it has been a long struggle. For the people of All Souls it began more than 150 years ago, in a more conservative community of about 120,000 inhabitants — the rapidly growing city of New York.

1. Religion in New York City Before 1819

THE NEW YORK BAY AREA was early explored by Italians, Portuguese, the French, and finally the Dutch. These latecomers made the first settlement here, at the beginning intended only as a trading post to which the Indians and other fur trappers and traders could come to barter. It thrived and in 1626 Peter Minuit arrived with additional colonists and purchased Manhattan from the Indians. Under Minuit, public buildings, farms, and a fort were laid out at designated spots on the lower end of the island. In the spring of 1628 Jonas Michaelius arrived from Holland to become the first professional and regular minister in the colony, and thus established the first religious society in New York City — the Dutch Reformed Church — which derives its name from Calvin's version of the religious reforms of Catholicism conceived during the sixteenth-century Reformation. A church building was not erected to house the Dutch Reformed Congregation until after 1633.[1]

Calvinism was not the only theology to be accepted among the New Amsterdam colonists. Because there was much religious tolerance in Holland, people with many differing views eventually found their way to New Amsterdam. Mennonites, Lutherans, and even Catholics settled among those adhering to the Dutch Reformed Church; and some Calvinists with Puritan tendencies also mingled with the early settlers of New York. But none of these practiced their faith in the open, and there were no formal religious societies or churches formed other than the Dutch Reformed for some time.

Interestingly, the second religious group to appear in New York City was Judaism. In 1654 Jews began arriving in Manhattan from

---

[1] See Edward R. Ellis, *The Epic of New York City* (New York: Coward-McCann, 1966).

Brazil and Curaçao to which they had fled earlier during the Inquisition. In New York, the religious intolerance of Peter Stuyvesant, then governor of New Amsterdam, forced these people to meet in secret at first, but by 1656 they had acquired a plot for a cemetery, evidencing their religious organization.[2] They continued to meet in secret as the Congregation Shearith Israel, the oldest existing Jewish congregation in America, which survives today on Central Park West and 70th Street. By 1695, the Jews had built their first synagogue on what was then Mill Street.

Three years after the arrival of the Jews, a shipload of Quakers who had been exiled from Boston arrived in New Amsterdam. At first they were accepted, but when they began preaching their religion in the streets, the bigoted Stuyvesant began a severe persecution of them. Not only were they not allowed to preach to others openly, but even the secret meetings they began to hold among themselves were raided by Stuyvesant's men. Many arrests were made, not only of Quakers but also of those who tried to shelter them; and not until 1671, when New Amsterdam had come under British rule, were the Quakers able to hold their religious meetings openly. They built their own meetinghouse on Liberty Street at the beginning of the eighteenth century.[3]

The British took control of New Amsterdam on August 27, 1664, renaming the city New York in honor of the Duke of York. The following Sunday, the chaplain of the English troops conducted the first Anglican services. Colonels Richard Nichols and Francis Lovelace, the first and second British governors of the colony, were tolerant in matters of religion, and the diverse people they governed were permitted to worship as they pleased. In 1671, the Lutheran segment of the population was affluent enough to build its own church, and the Huguenots, also, were worshiping according to their own rites rather than under the Dutch Reformed Church. Although the Huguenot population had grown steadily since the colony was founded, it was not until 1688 that the Huguenots had a church building of their own.[4]

Even Catholics were permitted religious freedom and, during the 1680s, were also given political franchise until a plot by the Catholic-converted King James II of England to Romanize his country changed the climate, and the Catholics came under suspicion. No

[2] *Ibid.*, p. 61.
[3] *Ibid.*, pp. 62–64.
[4] *Ibid.*, p. 80.

organized Catholic worship services were conducted regularly until a century later, when the first Roman Catholic society was formed.

In 1693, the Church of England became the religion of the city, despite the fact that only about 90 families adhered to the Anglican Church as compared to more than 1,700 families subscribing to the Dutch Reformed Church, and 1,365 Protestant families who openly disputed the authority of the Anglican Church. All citizens, regardless of religion, were required to pay taxes for the support of the English church and its ministers. On March 13, 1698, Trinity Church at Wall Street was first used for religious services. The establishment of Trinity Church ended an era of relative religious freedom, and not only Catholics but also Protestant dissenters and Jews were persecuted for several years. The persecution of Protestant dissenters ended in 1707 when the Rev. Francis Makemie, an Irishman called the Father of American Presbyterianism, was arrested for preaching without a license while on a visit to New York, and was acquitted. The trial set a precedent and encouraged the Presbyterians to erect a church on Wall Street in 1719. The Baptists, too, took their place among the proliferating number of religious sects, and set up their first church building in 1727.[5]

After the American Revolution, the Church of England was disestablished, and Anglican believers found it expedient to form the Protestant Episcopal Church. Since all religions were now on a more or less equal basis, the long-persecuted Catholics were free to attend Mass openly, and made haste to build their first house of worship, Saint Peter's, at Barclay and Church streets.[6]

By the latter part of the eighteenth century a wave of rationalistic philosophy had made its way to the shores of the New World and was affecting the intellectual circles of the day, including the clergy. In the mid-1700s, Jonathan Mayhew was preaching anti-Trinitarianism and related ideas to his parishioners in the West Church of Boston, though neither he nor his congregation was avowedly Unitarian. There were other ministers and congregations in New England whose sentiments were primarily Unitarian, but who did not call attention to themselves as such. In 1785, however, the Episcopal King's Chapel in Boston adopted the British Unitarian Theophilus Lindsey's revised Prayer Book, and omitted from its liturgy all references to the Trinity

[5] *Ibid.,* pp. 102, 111.
[6] *Ibid.,* p. 178.

and all prayers to Christ. Thus, in 1785, King's Chapel, although it did not become Unitarian in name, became in fact the first Unitarian church in America.[7]

§   §   §

The year 1794 was to prove to be a highly significant one for liberal religion in the city of New York, for, in that year, Elihu Palmer, John Butler, and Joseph Priestley, the famous English scientist and Unitarian minister, all came to the city and made their separate and vain attempts to have the Unitarian message accepted there. Elihu Palmer was a most interesting man. A Phi Beta Kappa from Dartmouth College, he became a radical in religion and lasted only six months in a Presbyterian church in Newtown, Long Island. He moved to Philadelphia and joined the Universalists, but a sermon there against the divinity of Jesus was too much for the local citizenry, and he had to quit the city in order to escape the outraged citizens. He then studied law and was admitted to the Pennsylvania Bar in 1793. His wife died shortly thereafter and he was stricken with blindness. Yet, in spite of this handicap, he soon became a free-lance Deist preacher.

Early in 1794, Palmer moved to New York City, where he founded a Deistical society where he preached every Sunday evening. This society was known successively as "The Philosophical Society," "The Theistical Society," and "The Society of the Columbian Illuminati." Sister societies in Philadelphia and Baltimore called themselves "The Philanthropists." In Newburgh, New York, the branch society was called "The Society of Druids." He also edited two newspapers in New York and Philadelphia.

The religion which Palmer preached and the political radicalism which he espoused would not have been at all popular with the men and women who founded the Unitarian church in 1819. Most of them were scarcely in their teens, and none of them seems to have been living in New York when he was doing his preaching. His movement died with him.[8]

John Butler rented a large assembly room in the beginning of the

[7] See Conrad Wright, *The Beginnings of Unitarianism in America* (Boston: Starr King Press, 1955).

[8] See *Dictionary of American Biography;* also see John Fellows, *Posthumous Pieces by Elihu Palmer* ... (London: R. Carlile, 1824).

year 1794, on Courtland Street, not far from Broadway. He began his ministry in the city by delivering what he called a "lecture." His views were liberal and, it is said, were similar to some then being advocated in the spirit of the French Revolution. As a consequence, it is reported that large crowds gathered to listen to him. The clergy of the city became alarmed and there must have been some vigorous sermons against his ideas, for Butler issued a public notice in the *Daily Advertiser* for January 24, 1794, stating that "in consequence of the liberality of the principles he had endeavored to inculcate, some improper liberties had been taken in the pulpit and upon the altar, the clergy and others were therefore informed that he would deliver another lecture on the following Sunday evening at six o'clock in the Great Room on Courtland Street. Those who had then condemned his doctrines would then have a chance of refuting them." [9]

The lecture was delivered as scheduled, and among those who heard it was a man who termed himself "A Lover of Truth." In the *Daily Advertiser* of February 1, 1794, this writer stated that "the number of persons who came to hear the evil was truly alarming." But he was disappointed because he had assumed that "some persons of abilities would have come forward and refuted so dangerous a doctrine." He wrote that "if Mr. Butler were suffered to go on, the worst consequences were to be feared." It was much to be hoped that some of the clergy would "condescend to oppose the Sole-Mending Lecturer," who intended to preach again the following Sunday.

Yet Butler's lectures grew more popular every week, and his audiences multiplied. "Before March arrived a 'Unitarian Society' was formed." The clergy of all denominations now felt called upon to interfere. They began by asking Butler to come to a private conference. Butler refused and said that the clergy should instead come to his lecture "and searching the Scriptures together, let them make public the arguments for and against his doctrine." The invitation was not accepted. Unitarianism continued to be denounced, and to a Roman Catholic priest who had been especially severe, Butler now addressed a statement. He told the priest that if he would attend one of the Sunday lectures, he would be given an opportunity to refute the doc-

[9] *Daily Advertiser,* January 24, 1794, John Bach McMaster, *A History of the People of the United States* (New York: D. Appleton & Co., 1885), Volume II, p. 238.

trines, or Mr. Butler would wait upon him for a like purpose in the Catholic Church.[10]

At this stage of the dispute, a statement came out in the *Advertiser* strongly defending the Unitarian preacher. The writer stated that Mr. Butler could not be accused of illiberality because he invited anyone who wished to come forward and dispute with him. He said that among the other great founders of Christianity, neither Calvin, Luther, Wesley, nor Whitfield had done this. "Why, then, do not the ministers embrace the opportunity so freely offered? Why not confute his doctrines? To insult him in their pulpits is but to stir up curiosity and send people to hear him." [11]

The crowds were enhanced in size by language such as this and the silence of the clergy. Butler now wrote his "Address to Trinitarians." In this article he promised to stop speaking as soon as he was shown the error of his ways. "Tell them that common justice requires that the men who accuse me of spreading false doctrines should prove it a fact, or retract the charge." Evidently this article produced its effect, for on Sunday evening, April 16, 1794, "an unknown opponent appeared, a discussion took place, and the audience went home in much the same mind as they came." [12]

The preaching of Mr. Butler produced no lasting effect, and the Unitarian Society simply disappeared. It is very difficult with the sources available to us now to say, with any certainty, the nature of the doctrine that John Butler preached. There are no known records of what he said aside from the interesting commentary in the newspapers. We learn much more about his challenges to the clergy than the nature of those challenges. Whether his was a doctrine which was essentially theological in character, or whether it was more in the political vein of French Revolutionary ideas, we, unfortunately, do not know. From the accounts, it sounds more like a political discussion than a religious one. All that can be said is that John Butler's preaching had no lasting effect in New York City, and it may only have alerted the clergy and aroused their antipathy, so that when a truly great Unitarian preacher, Dr. Joseph Priestley, arrived in New York

[10] *Daily Advertiser*, March 14, 1794; *New York Daily Gazette*, March 6, 1794; *Daily Advertiser*, March 23, 1794.

[11] *Daily Advertiser*, March 29, 1794.

[12] *Ibid.*, April 11 and 18, 1794.

*Dr. Joseph Priestley by Rembrandt Peale. Courtesy of
the New-York Historical Society, New York City*

City, within a few months they greeted him as a famous personage,
but did not open their pulpits to him.[13]

Joseph Priestley, a British chemist and theologian whose experi-
ments with "dephlogisticated air" (oxygen) helped to lay the foundations of modern chemistry, was as infamous for his radical ideas in
religion and politics as he was famous and respected for his scientific
achievements. When, as a Unitarian minister in Birmingham, England, Priestley added support of the French Revolution to his radical

[13] See also Thomas F. Devoe, in an unpublished paper submitted to the Rev.
Dr. Osgood and later printed in the Appendix of A. P. Putnam, *Unitarianism in
Brooklyn, a Sermon Preached . . . in the Church of the Savior, Brooklyn, N.Y., at
the Commemorative Services* (New York: Rome Brothers, April 25, 1869),
pp. 56 f.

theological views, hostilities in his community burst their bonds. Priestley's home was burned and his laboratory equipment destroyed in the Birmingham Riots of 1791. In April 1794, Priestley and his family sailed for America from Gravesend on the *Samson,* to escape such persecution, and on June 4, disembarked in New York City. When word of the arrival of the famous man was circulated, many distinguished citizens came to call upon Priestley, including Governor Clinton and Samuel Provoost, the Bishop of New York. He also received testimonials from the medical, democratic, and Tammany societies and other groups.[14]

Priestley was impressed with the city, which then had 33,000 inhabitants, and he held hopes of being asked to preach. But no suggestion that his ministerial services might be wanted, was made. Priestley himself visited with various members of the clergy about town, but none was interested in opening up his pulpit to Priestley's heretical Unitarian ideas; indeed, on Trinity Sunday, Dr. Abraham Beach, Provoost's senior associate at Trinity Church, seized the opportunity of preaching against Priestley.[15]

Thus, in New York as in England, Priestley was well respected as a famous scientist, but his religious ideas were coolly received. Despite this reserved climate, Priestley wrote to Theophilus Lindsey in London, begging this well-known Unitarian minister to come to America where there was more religious freedom. Priestley even offered to go back to England to fetch Lindsey, but his colleague declined the offer. At the end of June, Priestley left New York for Philadelphia, where his theological ideas were given a somewhat warmer reception. Two years later, in 1796, the Unitarian Church of Philadelphia was established, although Priestley made his residence in the small town of Northumberland, several days' journey to the west. There he lived until his death in 1804.

There is no indication that Priestley made any attempt to found a Unitarian church in New York City. The climate of the city was not as friendly as that of "The City of Brotherly Love," where he was instrumental in founding the first church in America that was called "Unitarian." A study of the persons who later founded the Unitarian Church in 1819 would indicate that they probably would have been

[14] *Dictionary of American Biography.*

[15] Anne Holt, *A Life of Joseph Priestley* (London: Oxford University Press, 1931), p. 182.

more closely drawn to Priestley than to Butler. But almost none of them was resident in New York at that time, with the possible exception of the Armitage brothers and William Glaze.

The Universalists were somewhat more successful than the early Unitarians. John Murray and other Universalist pioneers preached in the city in 1795, but did not succeed in establishing a church in that year. During the following year, however, three members of the John Street Methodist Church withdrew from that body because of their Universalist convictions, and established what they called, "The Society of the United Christian Friends in the City of New York," which began with 14 members. The membership gradually increased, and the society moved to its own church quarters on Vandewater Street. The John Murray version of Universalism was quite Calvinistic, with the distinction that it held that *every* man, rather than only the "predestined," was subject to divine Grace through Jesus Christ. Other Universalists placed Jesus in a subordinate position to God, as compared with the orthodox Trinitarians who held that Christ was co-equal with God. But, outside of these specifics, Universalists held to the traditional dogmas.[16]

In 1816 a controversy broke out in New York City which shows the intolerant temper of at least some of the clergy of the city. Loring R. Dewey published a discourse which he had given before a private society of the Theological Seminary in New York. For this offense, the young seminary student was promptly expelled, and Dr. James Mason, the principal of the Seminary, wrote him a letter calling him a "misguided youth," and claiming that his doctrines were

> so deeply erroneous, so radically subversive of the whole Gospel scheme, and so ruinous to the souls of men, that they cannot be tolerated in the Seminary under our care. It shall not here be so much as questioned ... whether attacks upon the essential parts of our Redeemer's work, are to be permitted in any shape, or upon any pretence whatever.

Dr. Mason indicated that young Dewey was to be expelled from the Seminary unless "it shall please God to give you a sounder mind, and enable you to recover yourself out of the snare of the devil." [17]

[16] Jonathan Greenleaf, *A History of the Churches of All Denominations in the City of New York* ... (New York: E. French, 1846), pp. 344–345.

[17] *The Christian Disciple*, Volume 4, p. 299.

The heresy to which young Dewey had admitted was termed the Hopkinsian heresy. It related to the doctrines of justification by faith and atonement and was much more rigorous than the typical Calvinistic view of these matters. Although this was not a Unitarian controversy, *The Christian Disciple*, a Unitarian journal, was quick to point out the intolerance of the views of Dr. Mason. The editor was much concerned that there be controversy at all, and he warned his Unitarian readers that they must not be guilty of the same error.

> The Calvinistic clergy in New York have as good a right to denounce their brethren of the New England orthodoxy, and to treat them as heretics, as the orthodox of New England have so to treat other Christians. Whichever of the two parties may be in the right . . . that party is always in the wrong which is disposed to revile, defame, or persecute.[18]

An episode such as this makes it apparent why it was to be difficult to found a Unitarian church in the religious climate of New York City. It also makes it very clear why so many transplanted New Englanders could not bear the religious climate of the city and were extremely anxious to establish a liberal church.

New York City's particular resistance to Unitarianism notwithstanding, liberal religion in general, and Unitarianism specifically, were burgeoning in the Eastern states at the turn of the century. A great many of the Congregational churches of New England were espousing anti-Trinitarianism and other ideas associated with the Unitarian movement. Yet very few of the liberal ministers and church leaders were advocating a break from the Congregational denomination. When, in 1805, Henry Ware, the avowedly anti-Calvinist minister of the First Church in Hingham, Massachusetts, was appointed Hollis Professor of Divinity at Harvard, this split was reinforced. Orthodox churchmen spoke out vociferously against Ware and the liberals, and, in 1808, Andover Theological Seminary was founded by the orthodox. Naturally, this publicity brought the conflict into the open and raised some provocative questions.

At the time of Ware's appointment, William Ellery Channing, a passionately religious young man of 24, and only recently out of Harvard himself, was the minister of the Federal Street Church in Boston.

[18] *Ibid.*, p. 247.

*The Reverend William Ellery Channing, from an Engraving by
William Hoagland, from a Painting by Chester Harding*

Like most of the other ministers of his day, Channing did not profess
to be a Unitarian, but he was deeply humanitarian in his religious
outlook, and he pled for religious tolerance. At this time, Channing
had no desire to see himself and his fellow liberals break away from
the Congregational denomination, and he pled against the growing
inclination to form a separate group. He felt that there was plenty of
room for differences within the existing denomination. Yet, as it was

to turn out, it was Channing, more than anyone else, who founded the Unitarian church in New York City.

By 1816, the Unitarian controversy had gained a great deal of publicity all over the Eastern seaboard, and in that year a group of citizens as far south as Baltimore wrote to liberal leaders in Boston asking for their help in establishing a Unitarian Church in their city. The call was answered by James Freeman of King's Chapel. Dr. Freeman preached in a ballroom in Baltimore for three consecutive Sundays, and, two years later, the First Independent Church of Baltimore, founded as "Unitarian Christian," was dedicated. Jared Sparks, newly out of Harvard, was called to be the minister of the new church. His ordination was to be held on May 5, 1819, and William Ellery Channing was invited to preach the ordaining sermon. This choice was to have profound consequences for the future of Unitarianism, not only in the country but also in New York City.

Lucy Channing Russel by Washington Allston.
Courtesy of Mrs. F. L. Gwynn

2. The Founding of All Souls

ON HIS WAY TO BALTIMORE, William Ellery Channing stopped in New York to visit his sister, Mrs. William Russel, and, on Sunday afternoon, April 25, 1819, a group of about 40 people gathered at the Russel home to hear Channing speak. The audience was composed largely of the New York friends of Lucy Channing Russel and her husband, although some of the guests were personally acquainted with Channing himself.[1]

Many years after Channing spoke, the Rev. Dr. Samuel Osgood, a minister of the Second Church, told some intimate details of the way in which Lucy Russel collected the group to hear her brother speak. William Channing Russel, named for his uncle, was sent around the neighborhood inviting the friends of the Russels to come to hear the great Channing. The little boy was only five years of age at the time. Later he recalled having particular success among the Quaker acquaintances of the Russel family.[2]

One of those present to hear Dr. Channing was Jonathan Goodhue, a leading merchant and citizen of New York. He was married to

---

[1] All Souls Minute Book, Volume I, p. 1. Orville Dewey, who had lived with the Channings for several months in Boston, knew the family weil. Channing's brothers, he felt, were well respected; Henry lived in retirement in the country, George was an auctioneer, Walter a respected physician in Boston. "Their sister Lucy, Mrs. Russel of New York . . . , was a person of great sense, of strong quiet thought and feeling; and some of her friends used to say that, with the same advantages and opportunities her brother [William] had, she could have been his equal." Mary E. Dewey (ed.), *Autobiography and Letters of Orville Dewey, D.D.* (Boston: Roberts Brothers, 1884), pp. 54–55.

[2] Samuel Osgood, "Twenty Five Years of a Congregation: A Discourse Given in the Church of the Messiah, New York, December 7, 1851, a Quarter Century from the Founding of the Congregation" (New York, 1851).

an ardent Episcopalian, but was evidently open to the ideas which he heard from Dr. Channing, for he wrote in his diary:

> Having been informed by a friend that the Rev. W. E. Channing would perform Divine Service this afternoon at the house of his brother-in-law, Wm. W. Russell [*sic*], I attended with great satisfaction. He was in delicate health, and read a Sermon from his seat, but it was an excellent one — on the advantages and disadvantages of life in a great City, full of sound reflections and calculated to excite a train of useful thoughts in the mind, and not to bewilder it with incomprehensible and useless dogmas.... This is the first "Liberal Preaching" in New York.[3]

The others who made up the private audience must have agreed with Jonathan Goodhue, for the members asked Channing to speak again on his return trip from Baltimore. Ignorant of the overnight fame his "Baltimore Sermon" would bring him, Channing agreed.

§ §§

Channing had decided to use the ordination of his protege, Jared Sparks, as an occasion to lift the whole Unitarian-Trinitarian controversy to a higher and broader scope than the relatively limited discussion among New England ministers it had occupied. All of this was aided by the able stage-managing of Jared Sparks, who had invited no less than seven New England ministers to be present in Baltimore for the occasion. Channing aimed his 1½-hour, epoch-making sermon at bringing the traditional Trinitarian orthodoxy to the bar of reason and conscience. In the first part of his sermon, which he titled, "Unitarian Christianity," Channing outlined the principles of reason which he felt ought to be adopted in any interpretations of the Bible. Having set up these criteria, he then devoted the second part of the sermon to showing how traditional doctrines, and particularly those dealing with the Trinity, did not measure up to these criteria, and were unscriptural, when the Bible is properly interpreted, with the use of reason.

[3] Jonathan Goodhue, *Diary*, entry for May 30, 1819, Goodhue Papers (unpublished document), New York Society Library. See also "Unitarianism in New York," *The Christian Examiner*, III:6 (November-December 1826), pp. 515–520. For a sketch of Goodhue, see Appendix C, pp. 256–259.

In brief, Channing said that the Bible is a book containing revelations of God, but that it is "written for men, in the language of men, and . . . its meaning is to be sought in the same manner as that of other books." Thus, if we are to understand the Bible correctly and as God intended, we must make allowances for the perplexities of human language and for the differing circumstances through human history. All of the criteria of reason must be brought to bear upon the sacred texts, just as these criteria are used with respect to any other book. Using these criteria as tools of scriptural interpretation, Channing then argued for the unity of God, and for the unity of Christ.[4]

Channing criticized the Calvinistic doctrines of depravity, election, and damnation on the grounds that this would make a morally imperfect God. A morally perfect God, Channing said, would be wholly loving and wholly forgiving to all of his creation, not to an elect few. Channing also objected to the orthodox idea of the mediation of Christ, for, he said, if Jesus had died to placate an angry God, as the Calvinists insisted, then God would not be wholly loving and not wholly forgiving. True holiness for man, then, would be love to God, love to Christ, and benevolence toward one's fellow man, in keeping with what Channing felt to be the true spirit of God.

In essence, Channing's "Baltimore Sermon" reveals his deep belief in the perfectibility of man rather than in man's "fallen state." It is this aspect of Channing's sermon which is perhaps of the greatest significance, although much of what he said about the Trinity has come to be widely held. To those who heard him that Wednesday morning in Baltimore, there was little doubt that Channing had delivered an intellectual exposition of the Unitarian position.

The sermon left shock waves all over the country that were to last for several decades. Orthodox clergymen implored their congregations to pray for the Unitarians and their sad delusions. Pamphlets defending orthodoxy were printed and widely circulated. Many newspapers in the East carried the entire sermon or excerpts of it, and a good number of people were attracted to the new religion.

Orville Dewey, later to be the minister of the Second Congregational Unitarian Church in New York City, and then a student at

4 William Ellery Channing, "Baltimore Sermon," in Conrad Wright (ed.), *Three Prophets of Religious Liberalism: Channing, Emerson, Parker* (Boston: Beacon Press, 1961), p. 49.

Andover Theological Seminary, wrote late in life in his *Autobiography* of the effect of Channing's Sermon on him at that time:

> I had been accustomed to use the words "Unity" and "Trinity" as in some vague sense compatible; but when I came to consider what my actual conceptions were, I found that the Three were as distinct as any three personalities of which I could conceive. The service which Dr. Channing's celebrated sermon . . . did me, was to make that clear to me.

At this point he left the seminary to spend a year in thought. He wrote:

> I spent that year in examining the questions that had arisen in my mind, especially in regard to the Trinity . . . especially I made the most thorough examination I was able, of all the texts in both Testaments that appeared to bear upon the subject. The result was an undoubting rejection of the doctrine of the Trinity.[5]

It is interesting to note that not all of the Channing family in Boston had approved of the attempt on the part of William Ellery to convert others to the Unitarian view. His brother Edward wrote Catharine Sedgwick in New York complaining of the fact that William was "journeying Southward upon such a wicked affair." Edward felt that truth should "be left to work its own way . . . We should profess openly what we believe . . . & then, if we are right, leave the hearer or reader to his own judgement, & a Divine blessing." [6]

On May 9, 1819, Henry D. Sedgwick wrote to Channing in Philadelphia that he had heard from Mr. Augustus Greele that the Baltimore sermon was a great success. He felt that "this is a great point gained in the advance of sober & rational Christianity." He stated that the New York group had secured the Medical Hall

> for the services next Sunday & Mr. [Isaac Green] Pearson will see that it is in order. . . . There are so many of the Eastern Clergy now in this part of the Country, that we hope to be able to have a service not only in both parts of the day, but in the [evening]. Indeed, this last

---

[5] Mary E. Dewey, *op. cit.,* pp. 45, 47.

[6] Edward Channing, Boston, to Catharine Sedgwick, New York, April 19, 1819, in Henry D. Sedgwick Papers, Massachusetts Historical Society.

is the more important in one respect — it would probably be best attended.[7]

When Channing, thereupon, stopped again in New York on his way home from Baltimore, he was a famous man. The little group who had heard him on his first visit to New York appointed Henry Sedgwick, Isaac Green Pearson, and Henry Sewall to hire the largest hall available — the Hall of the College of Physicians and Surgeons of the State of New York — for two Sundays, May 16th and 23rd. The group also arranged for public notices to appear in the newspapers on May 15th announcing that Dr. Channing would preach the next day. Channing spoke at 10:30 A.M., and at 3:30 and 7:30 P.M. on May 16th. At each session, particularly the evening meeting, there were reportedly hundreds of persons turned away for lack of space. Jonathan Goodhue attended all three services, and briefly recorded his observations that evening:

May 16, Sunday. Attended Divine Service three times today at the Hall of the Medical College in Barclay Street, to hear the preaching of Mr. Channing and the Rev. J. G. Palfray [*sic*] of Boston. The services were admirable, and the audience numerous and highly respectable, though a vile spirit of un-Christian bigotry is too generally manifest in this community.[8]

Undaunted by these "vile spirits," the original group which had heard Channing at his sister's house agreed that it should find a suitable place for holding regular services where people could hear the same kind of preaching. The very next evening, on Monday, May 17th, a few leaders from the original group met at the home of Henry D. Sewall at 74 Franklin Street. The group decided to post a public notice in the newspapers inviting all those who were interested to a meeting the next Thursday, again at Mr. Sewall's home.

Fourteen persons attended the meeting on May 20th, all of them men, and probably most of them had heard Channing on his first visit to New York. Jonathan Goodhue was not among them, because, despite his considerable and growing interest in liberal religion, Good-

[7] Henry D. Sedgwick, New York, to W. E. Channing, Philadelphia, in Henry D. Sedgwick Papers, Massachusetts Historical Society.

[8] All Souls Minute Book, Volume I, p. 2; Jonathan Goodhue, *Diary,* entry for May 16, 1819, New York Society Library.

hue continued to adhere to the stout Episcopalianism of his wife's prestigious family. In addition to Sewall, the host for the evening, Henry Sedgwick, Isaac Green Pearson, George Dummer, Frederick Sheldon, Elihu Townsend, Augustus Greele, John Shepard, Elijah Paine, Phinehas Whitney, Joseph Blunt, Thomas Witt, Joseph Lathrop, and Enoch P. March were present. These men met to consider organizing a permanent church of Unitarian persuasion for the city of New York. The All Souls Minute Book indicates the enthusiasm of the meeting and the reasons for calling it:

> So great an interest was evidenced by the services of the 16th of May, that it was determined to call a meeting to consult upon measures for securing a suitable place for public worship, where the privilege of hearing preaching of the same character might be enjoyed whenever opportunity offered.[9]

A good part of the evening was devoted to a discussion of the objectives of the meeting, but finally a committee was appointed to search for premises which would be suitable for conducting regular public worship services each Sunday, for the temporary use of the Medical College would stop on the next Sunday, May 23rd. Even at this early date, this nucleus of All Souls' founders was considering building its own church, for the committee was also asked to look into how much such a project would cost. Sewall, along with Pearson and Joseph Blunt, comprised this committee. Before the fourteen men adjourned, they agreed to hold another public meeting on the following Monday, May 24th, this time at the City Hotel.

On May 21, 1819, Henry D. Sedgwick wrote to Channing, giving him a report on what had happened since Channing's visit. Sedgwick said that everything was going well except that he was disappointed that only fourteen persons had turned out for the meeting in Henry D. Sewall's home.

> This we ascribe to the extreme reluctance which anybody here feels to becoming conspicuous on such an occasion. A great deal of interest has certainly been excited & we have no doubt that a church of the largest dimensions would be thronged with hearers.... But the first step is difficult. Most of those who have given us the strongest encour-

[9] All Souls Minute Book, Volume I, p. 3; *ibid.,* p. 2.

agements are timid from fear of public opinion, & of expenses, or are
deterred by the sentiments of their family connections & particular
associates, from taking any decisive step. Still however we are confident that many persons would subscribe for the erection of a church
who could not be induced to attend a meeting for that avowed purpose. . . . Upon the whole we do not feel discouraged — the courage
& zeal of individuals are indeed less than we had hoped but the public
feeling is better than we expected. With prudence, perseverance, &
the blessing of Heaven, we shall succeed.[10]

*The City Hotel. Courtesy of the New-York Historical Society,
New York City*

§   §   §

The ordination of the Rev. Mr. Sparks in Baltimore had also been
attended by the Rev. John G. Palfrey, who had delivered the right
hand of fellowship to the Rev. Sparks. Palfrey, then only twenty-three
years old and brand-new to the Unitarian ministry, had accompanied
Channing to New York and was engaged to stay on and preach to
the New York gathering on May 23rd, the Sunday following Chan-

---

[10] Henry D. Sedgwick, New York, to W. E. Channing, Boston, May 21, 1819,
in Henry D. Sedgwick Papers, Massachusetts Historical Society.

ning's preaching marathon on May 16th. A year earlier, Palfrey had been ordained as the minister of the Brattle Street Church in Boston. Later, Palfrey was to take over the editorship of *The Christian Disciple,* the leading Unitarian organ of that day, changing its name to the *Christian Examiner* (1824). Still later (1835), Palfrey was to become the editor and proprietor of *The North American Review,* before political inclinations led him to distinguish himself as a member of the U.S. House of Representatives for two years (1847–1849).

On Monday, May 24th, nineteen persons gathered at the City Hotel to make further arrangements for continuing the services. Six of these men had not been present on the preceding Thursday at Mr. Sewall's house: Henry Wheaton, Robert White, Daniel Low, Benjamin Blossom, Royal Peters, and Dexter Chapin. The nucleus of founders was growing.[11]

These men took their places among the others gathered at the City Hotel. The committee which had been appointed the previous week to find suitable premises for holding regular services made its report. There had been objections by some of the city's physicians to holding more services in the Medical College. The men assembled, voted to hire "the rooms of Mr. Anderson" — a second-floor apartment in a building at Broadway and Reade streets — for $500 annually, and authorized the same committee to hire a chorister and a sexton, and "generally to do what is requisite for the accommodation of a congregation." [12]

Another committee, the correspondence committee, was then appointed to handle the publicity, and Mr. Pearson now found himself on two committees. With Pearson on the correspondence committee were Henry Sedgwick and Henry Wheaton. Isaac Green Pearson was also appointed treasurer. The group of founders decided that a subscription to the society would be taken up to defray most of the current expenses, and that a collection would be taken each Sunday morning, as well. Henry Sewall was chosen to be clerk of the society and to be on a committee to select psalms and hymns for the Sunday services, which turned out to be a very important assignment.

The following Sunday, May 30th, the new congregation gathered at the rooms of Mr. Anderson to hear Francis William Pitt Greenwood. A year younger than Palfrey, Greenwood had graduated from

[11] All Souls Minute Book, Volume I, p. 4.
[12] *Ibid.,* p. 3.

Harvard College in 1814, when he was just seventeen. For the next three years, he had continued his theological studies at Cambridge under the direction of Dr. Henry Ware and, in October 1818, had been ordained minister of the New South Church in Boston.

Jonathan Goodhue attended the services on the 30th of May and the entry in his private diary indicates the feelings of a man of substance and sincerity in the city at the time. Goodhue described the auditorium as being on the second story on "the Western corner of Broadway and Duane Streets, opposite Washington Walk." He gave a donation and offered more but added,

> I am compelled by regard to the feelings of my family (who are operated upon by the villainous, diabolical spirit of the bigots to look unfavorably and with alarm at our doctrines) to desist from any active share in the proceedings. I am very thankful that I have had foresight and consistency enough uniformly to refuse every evidence of enrollment with Trinitarian denominations even when from the absence of controversy, I felt no opposition, as indeed I have now no feeling of hostility beyond that of resistance to aggression. In fact, as I firmly believe *all who sincerely strive to do the Will of Heaven are acceptable,* I should be utterly inconsistent if I condemned any man for his honest opinion, and having been amongst Catholics, Mahometans and Pagans, I have had the practical opportunity of testing the charity of my own sentiments.

He then described his own religious history. When he first came to New York (1807) he had worshiped with the Presbyterians. But since his marriage, he had gone to the Episcopal church, and he said that he had been treated with kindness.[13]

The next week, June 6, 1819, Henry Ware, Jr., of the Second Church in Boston, and son of Professor Henry Ware of Harvard, took over the makeshift pulpit at the new "chapel" on Broadway and Reade streets. Henry Ware, Jr., then 25, had graduated from Harvard College in 1812 and had been ordained as the minister of the Second Church in Boston on January 1, 1817. In December of 1818, just six months before preaching for the New York society, Ware had been to Baltimore to preach for the newly established church where Channing had so markedly distinguished himself and the cause of Unitari-

[13] Jonathan Goodhue, *Diary,* entry for May 30, 1819, New York Society Library.

Henry Ware, Jr., Engraved by J. Sartain
from the Portrait by James Frothingham

anism a few weeks earlier. On his way to Baltimore, Ware, like Channing, had stopped in New York to speak before a group, but no organized society had grown out of his efforts.

Ware preached for three or four successive Sundays and was
somewhat disappointed at the size of the congregation which came to
hear him. Only about 200 people, Ware reported to his brother-in-
law, the Rev. Joseph Allen of Northborough, Massachusetts, were
there on that first Sabbath, during which he officiated at three services.
But Ware's spirits rose during the next weeks when attendance increased, and on his last Sunday, he reported, "the Chapel was quite
full. It is calculated to have held 300 and over." [14]

Nevertheless, Ware found himself quite depressed during his sojourn in New York. The city at that time numbered almost 120,000

[14] John Ware, *Memoir of the Life of Henry Ware, Jr.* (Boston: James
Munroe and Company, 1846), p. 116.

inhabitants, and Ware found himself a stranger and unknown in the city as compared to his situation in Boston and elsewhere where he had gained a reputation. Unitarianism was also a subject which engendered much hostility among New Yorkers, a hostility which Ware had not experienced in his native Boston. He almost shrank from the overwhelming odds which seemed to be placed against his acceptance in the city. Early in June, he communicated these sentiments to Dr. Channing in Boston, for on June 16th, Channing answered:

> Your letter discourages the hope of the speedy erection of an independent church in New York; and I perceive you expect little from ministrations in an obscure chapel. On this last point I cannot agree with you. If our friends have zeal enough to withstand neglect; if they love Christianity as much in an unostentatious building, (by the way, a much better one than the upper room in which Paul preached,) as in a splendid church; if they have *made up their minds* to worship God according to their best understanding of his word, I have no fear of the result. If they have scripture, and its Author, on their side, Providence will send them friends. My only fear is . . . that the struggle may be an exhausting one.[15]

This note of encouragement from Channing must have contributed sizably to Ware's later good spirits, for in July, Ware wrote his brother-in-law, Rev. Joseph Allen:

> . . . The number of proprietors is about 30, and more than half of them have families. Their interest is of a very enlightened sort, calm and yet fervent; they understand the merits of the case, and are perfectly decided without any partisanship, and really liberal without bigotry or latitudinarianism. I think them in an admirable state, and some of them very serious, religious men. There can be no doubt of their final, though very gradual success.[16]

The chapel at Broadway and Reade streets was shut for the summer and was not reopened until the following October 30th. In the meantime, some of the founders met to draft a letter of their motives and prospects to George Bond, William Lawrence, and Amos Lawrence

[15] *Ibid.*, p. 118.
[16] *Ibid.*, p. 116.

in Boston, in which a plea for funds to erect a church building was made.

As there was not a single place of worship here where a Unitarian Christian could join in the service without some degree of mental reservation and in many Churches without being obliged to listen to doctrines wholly inconsistent with what he deems the simplicity of uncorrupted revelations, a considerable number of persons met together, formed a Society and prepared a temporary apartment where they might perform their devotions at least with decent simplicity, if not with external splendour. But many difficulties have occurred to prevent regular services, and we have reason to fear that the society will not increase or even become permanent upon its present footing. ... Many persons who sincerely accord with us will not break off their connection with the religious societies to which they now belong until they can be perfectly certain of securing a permanent place of worship and ministry....

Our present Society, though respectable in numbers, intelligence, and zeal, does not include men of great wealth; and we apprehend that without the aid of the munificent patrons of piety and learning by whom Boston and its vicinity have been so honourably distinguished, the present effort to establish a Church in this City upon the basis of primitive and uncorrupted Christianity must altogether fail. We do not indeed anticipate that the flame which had been kindled by the eloquence of those pious men who have disinterestedly imparted to us the fruits of their Christian knowledge will expire in the breasts of the little flock which have been collected. But we do fear that the lights will not be sufficiently powerful to dispel the thick mists of bigotry which have so long hung over this City, which have enveloped the simplicity of the gospel in a cloud of mystery, separated Christianity from charity and alienated the minds of many liberal and intelligent persons from revealed religion. Such is the immense and increasing population of this community, and so great is the disgust which the prevalence of bigotry has occasioned in the public mind, that we are firmly persuaded if a spacious church were erected, it would be instantly filled with a respectable and numerous congregation....

The present moment is favourable in unexampled degree to the formation of contracts for buildings; that the edifice and land situated in the best street in the city for the purpose, will not exceed in the cost of $28,000; that the pews, therefore, will average less than any other in the City, and we are confident will all be sold in one or two years; and the sale of *two-thirds* only will produce enough to pay off all the private loans, exclusive of the mortgage on the land for the purchase money, which may remain for several years if necessary.[17]

The letter was read at a meeting held on October 9th, at which a building committee was appointed and authorized to contract for the purchase or hire of land and for the actual building of a church on that land, as well as to obtain loans for the project. Messrs. Wheaton, Sewall, and Pearson were appointed to this committee. Next, the society turned its attention to the matter of legal incorporation and, before adjourning, decided to hold a special meeting for this purpose.

The meeting of incorporation was held on November 15th, after having been publicly announced for several weeks in advance. Nine trustees were elected, among whom were James Byers, Elihu Townsend, Frederick Sheldon, George Dummer, and John Shepard. All but Byers appear on the rosters of the society's earliest meetings in the previous spring. Isaac Green Pearson was already treasurer and Henry Sewall, clerk, so it is not surprising that they do not appear among the trustees.

A new name for the society was also chosen at the meeting on November 15th. The committee appointed earlier to think up a suitable permanent name recommended simply, "The Independent Church." The congregation did not like this name, and "The First Independent Congregational Church" was proposed. But this name was found unsuitable also. The difficulty stemmed from the fact that no precedent had been set in New York State — or in New England, for that matter — for establishing a church that was Unitarian in theology but congregational in form of church government.

Most of the liberal religious societies now professing Unitarianism in New England had been incorporated as congregational both in theology and in government, and their theological break with their original denomination in no way affected their legal incorporation. The New York group was to be Unitarian from the start. "The Independent Church" specified neither the Unitarian theology nor the congregational form of government and, under the state law, the state legislature would need some sort of category under which to file the incorporation. To call the society "The First Independent Congregational Church" was inadequate, for there was at that time already an

[17] Transcribed in All Souls Minute Book, Volume I, pp. 7–9.

"Independent Congregational Church" on Pearl Street. The new Unitarian group finally decided upon "The First Congregational Church in the City of New York," and to this day this remains the legal name of what we now know as "The Unitarian Church of All Souls."

The name has some amusing paradoxes associated with it which reveal the confused religious history of the city. For one thing, it was *not* the first "First Congregational Church of New York." Before the establishment of the Independent Congregational Church, the Rev. John Townly had founded, in 1804, a group which called itself "The First Congregational Church of New York." In 1809, that congregation had built its own church on Elizabeth Street, but then had disintegrated because of too heavy a financial burden. Thus, the Independent Congregational Church was actually the *second* Congregationalist group, in theology as well as in political character, to come to the city.

To add to the confusion, several other churches of Congregationalist persuasion were being organized. Even in the same year that the Unitarian Society was forming, the "Providence Chapel" was established, a Congregationalist church founded by the Rev. Joseph Harrison. Thus, the Unitarian group was actually the fourth or fifth "congregational" church to be founded, yet the church was not to be Congregational in its denominational identity. In fact, at one point, All Souls was the only church in the borough of Manhattan with the word *Congregational* in its official name, despite its not belonging to that denomination.

No time was lost in drawing up the certificate required by law for the incorporation of religious societies, complete with each of the trustees' names. So November 15, 1819, six months almost to the day after Channing's preaching the previous May 16, marks the official founding of All Souls. It was recorded by the Office of the Register in and for the City and County of New York in "Liber No. 1 of Religious Incorporated," page 91, on the twentieth day of November 1819.

After he returned home from the very fruitful meeting on the 15th of November, Henry D. Sedgwick sat down and wrote a long letter to the spiritual mentor of the church, Dr. William Ellery Channing in Boston. "We have had our meeting and organized our Society," he wrote. Sedgwick mentioned the discussion at the meeting about the name and hoped that Channing would not be unhappy with the name "Congregational" rather than "Independent," which Sedgwick knew that Channing favored. "We have every ground to hope that in the Providence of God we have given ourselves a great blessing." He told Channing that they would need a "stated preacher" before they could complete a church building, and asked the Boston divine to put his mind to this matter. He concluded, "It is late, and my eyes will not suffer me to peruse what I have written." Even the indomitable Henry Sedgwick was tired on that eventful evening which marked the legal beginning of the Unitarian Church of All Souls.[18]

Tablet to William Ellery Channing, Erected by the Congregation of All Souls in 1972. Photograph by Rita E. Jamason

William Ellery Channing himself was much pleased with the results of his several visits to New York. He wrote to his sister-in-law, Mrs. Susan Higginson Channing:

[18] Henry D. Sedgwick, New York, to W. E. Channing, Boston, November 15, 1819, in Henry D. Sedgwick Papers, Massachusetts Historical Society.

I had much to encourage me in my mission to the little church, which was the object of my journey. Their number is not large, but their zeal very sincere & strong, & I never ministered to people who seemed to set such a value in my services, or to persevere.[19]

[19] William Ellery Channing, Boston, to Mrs. Susan Higginson Channing, Lancaster, November 23, 1819, Pierpont Morgan Library, New York.

3. *Strangers from Inland and Outland*

CATHARINE SEDGWICK has given us an intimate description of the personality of the early congregation. She wrote to her friend, Eliza Lee Cabot:

> It requires no little zeal and skill to make the discordant elements of which our church is composed, mingle. Excepting one or two little knots in the church they are strangers here from inland and outland, English radicals & daughters of Erin, Germans and Hollanders, philosophic gentiles and unbelieving Jews. In short, the promise is accomplished to us, the "north hath given up and the south hath not kept back." In this our ass'n [association] . . . there is at least one of every sort. There are also those who have been seen "righteous in this generation," a peculiar people zealous of good works. It seemed becoming that those who passed by on the other side when all the popular charities of the world were going on, should have something of their own trying to do good. Beside the zealous writing and distribution of enlightened essays, which is but a perpetual scattering of seed, without any ingathering of fruits, a free school for some of the ten thousand children of this city that are without any instruction was determined on.[1]

The most obvious fact about the founders is that they were all men. In these emancipated days it may be difficult to realize that for the first century of its existence, all official acts of the society were participated in only by the men. The women attended the services, and when it came to the point of joining the "church" rather than the

[1] Catharine M. Sedgwick to Eliza Lee Cabot, February 16, 1823, in Catharine M. Sedgwick–Eliza Cabot Follen Papers, Massachusetts Historical Society. For a sketch of Catharine Sedgwick, see Appendix C, pp. 262–263.

Clipper Ships at South Street Wharf, New York City. Courtesy of the I. N. Phelps Collection of American Historical Prints, New York Public Library

"society," they were more responsive than the men in signing their names to the Bond of Union prepared in January 1821 by Henry Ware, Jr. The men were not being arbitrary; they were only following the laws of the state when they alone did the voting at the meetings of the society.

All of the founders whom we shall thus consider were men, but their women were right beside them, and, as in any church, the women did much of the day-to-day work of the organization, ministering to the sick and needy and engaging in the charitable works of the church.

On the last page of the first All Souls Minute Book there is a list of the names of these founders in two columns with numbers beside them: 34 such names. There must have been some significance to the numbers beside the names. Probably they indicate the actual order in which they signed their names as members of the society. This list gives us a basis upon which to evaluate the makeup of the men who founded the church.

About some of these men we can discover almost nothing except that they joined the society. Of Frederick Sheldon we know that he was a merchant in the China trade, was a trustee in 1819, served one year, and then disappeared from the church. John Shepard was elected a trustee in 1819 and soon left the church. David Armstrong was elected a trustee and served only one year. About Royal Peters, James Lamb, George Hood, Henry Watkinson, and Enoch March we know almost nothing, and a modest amount of genealogical research on each man has not proved very fruitful.

The most amazing fact about this list is that it contains only a single man who was born in New York City, James Byers. All except Byers were "immigrants" or "foreigners." Most of them came from New England, particularly from Massachusetts. One was a New Englander born in Virginia. Two came from England.

Not only were these men immigrants, but they were recent ones. Most of them arrived in the second decade of the nineteenth century, or literally just a few years before the founding of the church. In addition, they were mostly young men, in their twenties, their thirties, and their forties.

In political philosophy they were undoubtedly not of a single mind. Robert and Henry Dwight Sedgwick came from a Federalist background as did probably most of the others, but they moved to new more liberal views in politics. William Cullen Bryant, who joined the church in 1825, became the chief political spokesman of the group largely because of his editorship of the *New York Evening Post*. Most of the founders undoubtedly joined the Jacksonian party.

Edward K. Spann, in a study of the political thinking of men such as those who founded All Souls, says of their political idealism:

Each considered himself to be working within an already established liberal democratic tradition that centered on two fundamental principles; first, equality of opportunity . . . as freedom for the individual from the restraints and discriminations so characteristic of aristocratic Europe; and second, the democratic dogma that *the People* — not merely a temporary majority but Americans generally should rule. The members of the group shared the hope of persuading the People to rid themselves of those European beliefs and practices which were antagonistic to democratic principles and, thus, to perfect their society. In sum each of these men hoped to participate in the purification of an established social system whose very strength in tradition (European in origin) was also its weakness.[2]

Their professions are equally interesting. Some were merchants dealing in various types of merchandise, such as glass, china, paper, and dry goods. Two of the men, James Byers, a founder, and R. G. Van Polanen, who became active early but was not a founder, are listed by William Ware in his "Pew Book" of about 1825 as simply "Gentlemen." Obviously, they were merchants who had made a fortune and retired. Lawyers were very much in evidence, then as now, among the members.[3]

In this list, only two men, William Glaze and William Honay, really worked with their hands. Glaze was a glass cutter and had obviously brought his trade with him from England. But he was a skilled cutter of "cut glass." William Honay was a carpenter and builder. The discovery of the "Pew Book" of William Ware in the New-York Historical Society has helped greatly in learning more about the professions of these men.

They were not only "immigrants" but a rather high caliber of immigrants. In many cases, they were some of the most ambitious men in New England, and they emigrated to New York because they were perceptive about the future of the United States. They were college men: from Harvard, Dartmouth, Brown, and Williams. They became a very important professional and business group in New York City, and many of them made fortunes.[4]

It would be possible to treat these men exactly as they appear by number in the Minute Book, but, since there appears to be no reason

[2] Edward K. Spann, *Ideals and Politics: New York Intellectuals and Liberal Democracy, 1820–1880* (Albany: State University of New York Press, 1972). Professor Spann has made an in-depth analysis of the political philosophy of a group centering around William Cullen Bryant. He treats the political idealism not only of Bryant but of the three Sedgwicks: Henry, Robert, and Catharine, and Parke Godwin, Bryant's son-in-law. The founders of the church were evidently not only strangers in origin, but they also represented more liberal political views than those usually held by the native New Yorkers.

[3] The William Ware Pew Book is in the New-York Historical Library Manuscript Collection. It is undated, but it was begun before 1825 because John C. Sigourney is listed in it, and he died in 1825.

[4] The table on pages 69–71 is an attempt to make all of this analysis more graphic and to show the founders in comparison with one another as to date and place of birth, date of coming to New York City, and profession.

for the order except possibly the order of joining the society, they will be treated in two general classifications: the professional men and artisans, and the merchants and shippers.

Among the important professional men there were five lawyers:

Henry Dwight Sedgwick was a member of a most remarkable family of which two other members (his brother Robert and his sister Catharine) appear as important in the church. Henry Dwight Sedgwick rightfully belongs in a place of prominence, for in the early days he was one of the moving spirits among the founders. Born in Stockbridge, Massachusetts, in 1785, he was graduated from Williams College, Class of 1804, and practiced law first in Stockbridge and then as a partner with his brother Robert in New York. He married Jane Minot of Boston in 1817, and they had five children.

Sedgwick most likely attended the first meeting at the home of the Russels, although we have no list of those present. One of the signers of the letter to Dr. David Hosack of the College of Physicians for the use of their hall for services upon Channing's return from Baltimore, he was the chairman of many of the early meetings, was elected a trustee in 1820, and reelected in 1826. He lived at 34 Cedar Street, and in his day was called a "counsellor." It was he who introduced William Cullen Bryant to the city, and he suffered a loss of health when he defended the Greeks in the case of the "Greek frigates," an early flagrant case of fraud.

Joseph Blunt also came from a very distinguished New England family. William Blunt, the progenitor of the clan had settled in Andover, Massachusetts, in 1634. Joseph's father, Edmund March Blunt, was a well-known publisher of oceanic charts, who moved to New York City about 1805.

Joseph Blunt was born in Newburyport, Massachusetts, in 1792 and did not follow the profession of his father and brother. After the study of law he settled in New York City and practiced at 269 Pearl Street. Both he and other members of his family were active in the establishment of the church. Joseph Blunt attended the early meetings which led to the founding of the church, and he was appointed with Isaac Green Pearson to find a hall for the services of worship. He was very active in the New-York Historical Society. Later in life he was a prominent Whig, an ardent protectionist, and one of the early organizers of the Republican Party. He was appointed as Commissioner to China by Millard Fillmore, a fellow Unitarian, but declined.

Shortly before Blunt's death, Abraham Lincoln appointed him a United States District Attorney for New York City.

There are many anecdotes about him because he was evidently not only a bachelor but an eccentric one. Someone once said that he was aptly named "Blunt" for that showed the true side of his character.[5]

Elijah Paine II was the son of Elijah Paine, a native of Brooklyn, Connecticut, who fought in the American Revolution. This elder Elijah also took an active part in politics, was a Vermont State Senator, a United States Senator (1795–1801), and a judge of the United States District Court.

The younger Elijah Paine followed in his distinguished father's footsteps. Elijah the Second was born in Williamstown, Vermont, in 1796. He was graduated from Harvard College in 1814, and a look at his classmates indicates that he was early brought under Unitarian influences, for among his classmates were Francis William Pitt Greenwood, Ebenezer Gay, and James Walker. After his graduation he studied law at Litchfield, Connecticut. He became interested in the compilation of law reports for the use of lawyers in preparing precedents and briefs. It was almost inevitable, therefore, that when he came to New York City early in his career he should become a law partner of Henry Wheaton, a famous compiler of law reports. At the office at 41 Pine Street he assisted Mr. Wheaton in the preparation of "The Supreme Court of the U.S. Reports" from 1816–1827, and in 1830 with John Duer he compiled the two volumes of *Practice in Civil Actions*.

He was one of the most active men in the establishment of the Unitarian Church in New York. At Harvard he had been a student with Henry Ware as well as an associate of many of his classmates who were later to become Unitarian ministers. He was appointed with Henry D. Sewall to a committee to compile a new hymnbook, but we do not know how active he was on this committee or whether Henry Sewall did the entire job himself — which appears likely.

In 1850 he was appointed a justice of The Supreme Court of New York City, from the bench of which he issued a famous decision in

[5] See Charles Edwards, *Pleasantries About Courts and Lawyers in the State of New York* (New York: Richardson and Co., 1867), pp. 206–207. See also *Dictionary of American Biography*.

Elijah Paine II, by A.G.D. Tuthill.
Courtesy of the Frick Art Reference Library
and Mrs. Elizabeth Sturgis Paine

"The Lemmon Slave Case," one of the earliest decisions about the question as to whether a slave was "property."

Henry Wheaton is the well-known historian, expounder, and interpreter of international law. His New England ancestors had emigrated from Wales to Massachusetts in the early 1600s. Henry was born in Providence, Rhode Island, on November 27, 1785, the son of Seth and Abigail Wheaton. He attended Rhode Island University, later to become Brown University, and was graduated in 1802 at the early age of thirteen. For three years he read law in a Providence law office. In the spring of 1805 he went to France where he studied civil law at Poitiers, and translated the Napoleonic Code into English at this time. He returned to Providence to practice law, and married his cousin, Catherine Wheaton, in 1811.[6]

In 1812 Henry Wheaton moved to New York City to become the editor of *The National Advocate*, the local organ of Thomas Jeffer-

[6] *Dictionary of American Biography.*

51

*Henry Wheaton by John Wesley Jarvis (?). Courtesy of
Harvard University Law School Collection*

son's Democratic Party. During the War of 1812 he was appointed a
division judge advocate in the United States Army, and in May of
1815 he was appointed a justice of the Marine Court of New York
City. In 1816 he was also appointed a court reporter for the United
States Supreme Court, a post he held until 1827. His name appears
on the many volumes of reports of the actions of the United States
Supreme Court which he edited, and which are to be found on the
shelves of most law offices so that his name is well known to lawyers
and jurists. He was a member of the New York State Constitutional
Convention in 1821, and in 1823 was elected to the New York State
Assembly. In November of 1825 he was an unsuccessful candidate for
the United States Senate from New York State. In 1827 Wheaton
began what amounted to a second career in the diplomatic corps,
which took him out of the country and thus out of the life of the
church.

For a man who had such an active career which even in the early
days of the church often took him away from the city, he played an
important part in its life during this early period. He served on many
of the committees. As a judge he was a perfectly natural choice to

preside at early church meetings. He was elected a trustee in 1821 and served until 1825. He was a most distinguished citizen, and it was unfortunate for the First Church that his later career took him out of the country.

Luther Clark is listed as a lawyer in William Ware's Pew Book. Actually we know very little about him except that he was a member of the Dartmouth class of 1815. He did not graduate with his class for he was expelled from the college for "treating" other students to drinks. He was in the college from 1811 to 1813, was expelled, and then returned to the college and received his degree in 1818. Even with this hectic start he did well, for he was elected as an honorary member of Phi Beta Kappa with the class of 1821. He served on various committees of the church, and the records indicate that the trustees agreed to return a $50 pew payment to him when he left the city for a brief time in November 1822. The pew was then put up for auction, but he soon returned to the city and reclaimed it. However, he died a few years later on February 11, 1826, a young man who had not really reached the peak of his legal career.[7]

The professional men also included two artisans:

William Glaze was listed in William Ware's Pew Book as a "glass cutter," but further research shows that he was a man of some stature and not a common glass cutter at all. However, he did work in glass, and the name Glaze shows that he probably came from an English family whose background was in the working of glass. Henry Ware, Jr., in his letter in 1839 to Henry W. Bellows, the new minister of the First Church, suggested a visit to the Glazes. "Over at Powles Hook you will find Mr. Glaze, an English family — but long here — staunch Unitarians and perfectly devoted to the Church." [8]

Powles Hook was an island across the Hudson River from Manhattan, the closest of the New Jersey islands to Manhattan. In 1838 it was incorporated into an entity known from then on as Jersey City. While it was a town William Glaze served as president of the Board of Selectmen in 1833 and again in 1836–1837. His personal

---

[7] Various letters about this college escapade are in the Dartmouth Archives; All Souls Minute Book, Volume I, p. 57; All Souls Funeral Records, Book I, p. 8.

[8] *New York Evening Post*, May 24, 1859; Henry Ware, Jr., to Henry W. Bellows, January 9, 1839, in Box 2, Henry W. Bellows Papers, Massachusetts Historical Society.

status must have been high. He was not a workman as William Ware's designation would indicate, although he may have started his career as such. He was a politician, and he dabbled in real estate.

He was associated with George Dummer's firm, the Jersey Glass Co., with a factory in Jersey City which made flint glass for chemical, scientific, and domestic purposes. The firm had been established as early as 1824. William Glaze first incised glass on a wheel for George Dummer in New York around 1824 where Dummer maintained a china, glass, and crockery outlet which evidently had a cutting department associated with it. The cutting department was part of the business in order to compete more readily with the English agents selling glass in this country. He then went with George Dummer when he established the Jersey Glass Co. in Jersey City. His will mentioned a "silver cup presented to me by the Glass Makers on my leaving the Glass Works, and it is my desire that this silver cup shall continue to be possessed by one of my descendents." He lived to the age of 81, dying in 1859.[9]

William Honay was a native of Maryland, probably from Queen Anne County on the Eastern shore. He came to New York about 1811 and owned a carpenter shop at 5 Chapel Street. His occupation in the city directories changed from carpenter to lumberyard owner in 1829. Eventually he was also engaged in the storage business and near the end of his life was an inspector at the United States Customs House. He was married to Aletta Honay and had at least one child, a daughter named Mary Eliza who was married to Charles Jones. When he died in 1850 he was survived only by his widow and their daughter.[10]

He appears to have been connected with the church not particularly for reasons of conviction but as a builder. At about the same time the First Church was under construction, he is listed as living at 155 Chambers Street, just a block from the site of the first church building. He may very well have been involved in the building of the First Church, although this is a surmise, for there are no known records extant. He does not appear in William Ware's Pew Book, so his

[9] Will probated July 9, 1859, in Hudson County, New Jersey.

[10] U.S. First Census, 1790, Queen Anne County, Maryland; William Honay's will, Liber 100, p. 353, Wills, New York County Surrogate's Court; and petition of Aletta Honay to execute the will of William Honay, August 12, 1850, probate file, September 1850, Surrogate's Court.

connection with the church may have been of short duration, perhaps only long enough to build the church.

By far, the greatest number of the "founding fathers" of the church were not professional men, but traders, merchants, and shippers engaged in the growing commerce that was to make New York the greatest and richest port in the world. Seventeen of the founders are included in these occupations. Many of them were quite important in the life of the church.

Isaac Green Pearson was the son of a ship's captain of the same name who served in the Revolutionary War. The church founder was born at Newburyport, Massachusetts, in 1791, the fourth child and second son of the captain and his wife. From Newburyport he moved to Boston as a young man and worked as an apprentice in the commercial firm run by J. Nathan Bond. He married the boss's daughter on March 16, 1813. She had been previously widowed and this was her second marriage.

Pearson and his family moved to New York City sometime about 1815, where he formed a company known as Pearson & Bond, located at 67 South Street, merchants dealing in glass and china, one of the many such businesses that prospered as trade was opened up with the Orient. He also engaged in much real estate activity and became a very wealthy man, the society buying the lots from him for the church building in 1819 for $9,000. In addition to the wealth produced by his own endeavors, the Bond family of Boston were wealthy, and his wife inherited much from her father. In 1816 the family resided at 1 Beaver Street at the corner of Broad Street.[11]

Like Henry Sewall, Pearson was appointed to almost every committee in the early church: to find a suitable hall, to supply the pulpit, and to find a minister. He was elected the first treasurer of the church in 1819 and served until 1822. He served a term as trustee from 1822 until 1825, and for a while served as both secretary and clerk from 1823 to 1824. It was Isaac Green Pearson who suggested writing a letter to George Bond, who was, of course, a Boston relative, for funds to build the new church.

George Dummer was born in New Haven, Connecticut, in 1782. The Dummer family was prominent in that state, and it is reported

---

[11] All Souls Minute Book, Volume I, p. 15.

that an early Dummer had persuaded Elihu Yale to contribute funds
to a new college being founded in New Haven. George married Elizabeth Osborne of New York City. He had settled in the city by 1819,
for he is listed in the City Directory for that year as being in the china
and glass business at 112 Broadway. His family were neighbors and
good friends of the Elihu Townsends, for, in a letter to her husband at
sea in 1820, Mrs. Townsend wrote that "they are all well at our
friend Dummers except the baby who still continues feeble. . . . Mrs.
Dummer desired me to remember her to you." The baby may very
well have been George Dummer, Jr., who is listed in the All Souls
records as having died in June 1822.[12]

A glass works across the river from Manhattan at Powles Hook,
New Jersey, was set up in 1824 by Dummer and two others. In
1825 Dummer organized the Jersey Porcelain and Earthenware Company next to his glass works. He is thought to have learned the business
at the Hamilton Glass Works in Albany. He had been a glass dealer
in New York from at least 1821, probably earlier. He was a dealer
who "sought a steady and more profitable supply of stock for his
shelves . . . as a defense against competition of auctioneers and English
agents, he established his own glass cutting department in conjunction
with his store." This proved profitable enough for him to get two
partners and to venture into the glass manufacturing business in Jersey City. He also had the expert help of William Glaze, a fellow church
member. The factory grew, and by 1826 had 32 steam-driven cutting
wheels. About 1830 the factory came to be known as P. C. Dummer
and Co., and then later, as the Jersey Glass Works when Jersey City
became a named entity. A specific star pattern came to be associated
with the firm's cutting style. Dummer glass is highly prized today.[13]

Mrs. Dummer died in 1829 and George Dummer shortly thereafter went to live in Jersey City where he became the mayor for a few
years. He died in 1863.

Elihu Townsend is very important in the history of All Souls not
only because he was one of the men involved in the founding but also

---

[12] Eliza Townsend to Elihu Townsend, March 23, 1820, in Box 1, Henry W.
Bellows Papers, Massachusetts Historical Society; All Souls Baptismal Records.

[13] George S. and Helen McKearin, *Two Hundred Years of American Blown
Glass* (Garden City, 1950), p. 83; Margaret E. White, *The Decorative Arts of
Early New Jersey,* Volume 25 of the *New Jersey Historical Series* (Princeton:
Van Nostrand, 1964), pp. 23–26.

George Dummer by Samuel L. Waldo and William Jewett.
Courtesy of the Newark Museum

because he became the father-in-law of Henry W. Bellows. It was his daughter, Eliza, who captured the young Bellows' fancy and who was married to him in 1839.

Elihu Townsend was born in New Haven on December 6, 1786, the eldest son of Ebenezer Townsend and Thankful Sophia Mather of New Haven. He married Elizabeth Nevins in the spring of 1812, and they moved to New York shortly after the wedding. Mrs. Townsend's brother, Russell Hubbard Nevins, was a prominent broker and banker in New York; and young Elihu went into partnership with Nevins, forming the firm of Townsend & Nevins. Because some letters of the Townsend family were later collected in the Henry Whitney Bellows Papers in the Massachusetts Historical Society, we are able to gain some insights into the family life of the Townsends.

One of these letters is particularly interesting in that young Elihu

Mrs. George Dummer by Samuel L. Waldo and William Jewett.
Courtesy of the Newark Museum

was preparing to fight the British who were menacing New York City in the War of 1812. His young wife and her brother were moving to Connecticut apparently to avoid an impending battle for New York. Townsend implored his wife not to worry about his safety, and reminded her to be patriotic, as he was. He promised not to volunteer in any hazardous enterprise. He indicated that he meant to join a company of militia so that if any attack was made on New York City he could do his part. Preparations were going on for the defense of the city, but Townsend presumed that the enemy would never come.[14]

Elihu Townsend took a most active part in the founding of the new church. Yet sometime in this period of 1819 or 1820 he "shipped before the mast" with Captain Curtis Holmes, also a founder of the

[14] Elihu Townsend to Eliza Townsend, his wife, September 7, 1814, in Box 1, Henry W. Bellows Papers, Massachusetts Historical Society.

church. His wife wrote to him on March 23, 1820, that "Captain Holmes likes you very much and thinks you will come out right at last." She also quoted Holmes as saying, "You are so diligent a sailor." [15]

At the time of the publication of the *City Directory* of 1820, he was listed as being a partner of Nevins & Townsend, brokers at 40 Wall Street, and the family lived at 341 Pine Street. He attended the organizational meetings, and in 1819 was elected to the first board of trustees, and was elected again in 1823. Several years later, however, he was one of those instrumental in the founding of the Second Church, was a delegate of the Second Church to the ordination of Henry Bellows at the First Church on January 2, 1839. It was not too many months later that Bellows began to court his daughter. That same year he became Bellows' father-in-law, and then quite naturally he returned to the First Church and left the Second Church.

Thomas Witt was a descendant of John Witt, a settler at Lynn, Massachusetts, by the year 1640. He came to New York City shortly after his marriage in the early part of the first decade of the eighteen hundreds and set up a shoe store at 272 Pearl Street. He was at the organization meeting in Henry Sewall's home, received one vote for trustee in 1820, and was on Henry Sewall's committee to select the Psalms for the hymnbook, although we cannot know how active he was on that committee. Some of his children also appear in the birth and death records of the early church. It was perfectly natural that coming from Lynn, which was a shoe manufacturing town, Thomas Witt should run a shoe store in Manhattan.

Augustus P. Greele was a member of a family whose lineage went back to Massachusetts in the early sixteen-thirties. Augustus Greele was born on December 27, 1787, at Wilton, New Hampshire. He taught school near his home, but in 1808 he began to study law with Daniel Abbott in Nashua. He changed his mind about his career and entered Dartmouth College, graduating in 1813. That same year, he moved to Manhattanville, New York, and opened a school which was patronized by the sons of distinguished families.[16]

In 1819 he again changed careers, moved into New York City, and became a paper merchant. He operated the first commission

[15] Eliza Townsend to Elihu Townsend, March 23, 1820, in Box 1, Henry W. Bellows Papers, Massachusetts Historical Society.

[16] *Greeley Genealogy,* pp. 146–148, 303–304. See also George T. Chapman, *Sketches of the Alumni of Dartmouth College* (Cambridge, 1867), p. 166.

paper warehouse in the city. The following year he bought out his partner, and in 1827 he took his brother-in-law Daniel Elliott into the business. He prospered so much that he was able to retire in 1838. When the church was founded, he was still a bachelor, but he rectified that condition in 1820 when he married Caroline Cornelia Lovett. They had no children.

He was present at the early organizational meetings, was elected a trustee in 1825 to fill an unexpired term, and then reelected to a full term in 1826. He was related by marriage to Henry Sewall, for his older brother, Samuel Greele, married Lydia Maria Sewall, Henry's sister. (They were active in the Federal Street Church of Dr. Channing, and Samuel was a deacon there.)

Henry Devereux Sewall along with Henry D. Sedgwick was one of the moving spirits in the organization of the congregation. It was Sewall and Sedgwick who were the spokesmen for the new religion, who engaged in the controversies, and it was Henry Sewall who edited the new hymnbook.

Henry Devereux Sewall came from a distinguished line of Boston Sewalls. His father, Samuel Sewall (1757–1814), had been a member of Congress from Massachusetts from 1797 to 1800, and from 1800 until his death was the Chief Justice of the Supreme Judicial Court of Massachusetts. He had married Abigail Devereux, and Henry was perhaps their second child.

In 1816 Henry Sewall married Mary C. Norton, and they had six sons and three daughters, four of whom are listed in the baptismal records of the church. One son, Henry F. Sewall, was later active at All Souls and was a trustee in 1885–1886. Sewall was a merchant, and was listed as such in the 1817 *City Directory,* with an address at 44 Broad Street.

It was evident that he played an important part in the early church, for no one served on more committees. He was one of the signers of the letter to Dr. David Hosack of the College of Physicians and Surgeons for the use of their rooms for divine services. Sewall hosted the first organizational meeting at his home on May 17, 1819, at 74 Franklin Street. At that meeting he was appointed along with Pearson and Byers to find a place of public worship for the new society. The second meeting was also held at his home on May 20, 1819. He attended the City Hotel meeting and helped to procure "the rooms

Benjamin Blossom by J. H. Lazarus.
Courtesy of the Frick Art Reference
Library and Mrs. Katherine W. Sawford

of Mr. Anderson" so that the new society could hold public services of worship. He was appointed with Sedgwick and Robert White to the hymnbook committee. He was elected the first clerk of the society, and it is undoubtedly in his hand that the early minutes are written, for he served as clerk from 1819 until November of 1824. He also served as treasurer for four years (1824–1828), a trustee from 1822 until 1824, and was a member of the first building committee.[17]

Unfortunately for the city's first Unitarian church, shortly after the founding of the Second Church, in which he was instrumental, Henry Sewall was elected president of the new church. He submitted

[17] All Souls Minute Book, Volume I, p. 2.

Mrs. Benjamin Blossom by J. H. Lazarus.
Courtesy of the Frick Art Reference
Library and Mrs. Katherine W. Sawford

his resignation on April 29, 1829, when, because of family inheritance, he moved to Watertown, New York, where he lived for the remainder of his life.

William Washington Russel was the husband of William Ellery Channing's sister Lucy. Although he was prominent for many years in the church, it has been extremely difficult to trace many of the facts about his life. He was born in Richmond, Virginia, probably of New England stock. He was married by Channing to Lucy in Boston, May 5, 1813, and lived at 8 Broome Street.[18]

Mr. Russel was a merchant who, over the years, prospered in

18 *Ibid.,* p. 1.

business as did many others of his fellow founders. Aside from acting as the host at the first meeting he was also very active in the affairs of the church. He was elected a trustee of the society in 1821–1824, and was reelected in 1830–1834 and 1836–1840. He twice served as president of the board, from 1830 to 1833 and from 1836 to 1837. He later moved to Staten Island, where he was one of the pioneers in founding the Staten Island Unitarian Church.

Benjamin Blossom's early ancestor was Thomas Blossom, who fled from England to Holland during the persecution of the Pilgrims. With his family, he arrived in 1629 in Plymouth, Massachusetts, where he was made a deacon of the church. His daughter Elizabeth married Edward Fitz-Randolph. Deacon Blossom also had two surviving sons, Thomas and Peter, and Benjamin Blossom is the direct descendant of Peter.[19]

Unfortunately, we know very little about Benjamin Blossom and his relationship to the New York church. He was born in 1790 at Fairhaven, Massachusetts, and William Ware, in his Pew Book, lists him as a merchant. He had a business at 35 Burlington Slip, according to the *City Directory*. He was present at the City Hotel meeting, and joined the society along with many others on May 24, 1819. But in the late 1820s, he moved across the East River and settled in Brooklyn, where he was one of the founders of the Brooklyn Unitarian Church in 1833, although he retained his pew at the First Church for some years.

Benjamin Armitage has several distinctions in the history of All Souls. So far as is known, his is the only family among the founders with persons still active in the church.[20] Along with William Glaze, Benjamin Armitage was probably the only other English Unitarian in the congregation. The Armitage family was originally from a town called Armitage Bridge, dating back to medieval times. The family trace their descent from Godfrey Armitage, a nonconformist who lived at Manchester. A descendant, Benjamin, came to America about 1794 to represent the family's textile business in New York. Since the date

---

[19] Elizabeth Blossom is a direct ancestor of the author of this book, on the maternal side.

[20] Mrs. Edward R. Gay and Mrs. Edgar J. Brower represent the ninth generation of Armitages, although the name itself has long ago disappeared from the rolls.

coincides with the persecution of the English Unitarians under the leadership of Joseph Priestley, there may be some coincidence in his coming to New York at that time.

Benjamin is listed in the New York *City Directory* of 1819 as simply a merchant whose business was at 54 Pine Street. William Ware listed him as occupying Pew No. 86. In 1819 he was elected a trustee for a two-year term on the first board of trustees. He was the treasurer of the church for the years 1822–1824, and was the president of the board from 1826 to 1828. He must have been a man of the type of Henry Sedgwick, for he was appointed along with Sedgwick and Van Polanen to prepare a statement for presentation to the society of the "view and principles of this Society to prevent misconceptions and to correct erroneous impressions." This was the period when the new society was under attack, and perhaps some of the material which has been credited to Sedgwick may have been partially the product of the thinking of Benjamin Armitage.[21]

Oroondates Mauran was one of the most interesting of the founders. He was the eighth child of Joseph Carlo Mauran who came from Villefranche, France. At the age of 12, Joseph was impressed as a sailor in the British navy, but he escaped ship when it lay off anchor at New London, Connecticut. The young lad was adopted informally by David Mason of Westerly, Rhode Island. Joseph went to Barrington, Rhode Island, in 1768 to work for Joshua Bicknell, and married Bicknell's daughter Olive in April of 1772. They settled in a house on her father's land, next to the Congregational Meeting House; and Joseph Mauran adopted New England Congregationalism over his native Catholicism. Here they raised a large brood of children.[22]

On December 14, 1814, their son, Oroondates Mauran, born in 1791, married Martha Eddy, the daughter of Judge Samuel Eddy, a member of Congress from Rhode Island. Mauran's name first appears in the *City Directory* of 1817. He came to New York City and, like many of the other founders, set himself up in business. He is listed as living at 43 Hudson Street, and his firm was located at 8 Fulton Street. He prospered exceedingly in all of his business enterprises, where he engaged in the southern trade and also made money by running a steam ferry to Havana. He owned the Staten Island Ferry in

[21] All Souls Minute Book, Volume I, p. 20.

[22] John C. Stockbridge, *Memorial of the Mauran Family* (Providence: Snow and Farnham, 1893).

*Benjamin Armitage, Painter Unknown. Courtesy of Mrs. E. R. Gay
and Mrs. Edgar J. Brower*

partnership with Cornelius Vanderbilt, and he also owned some of the
earliest tugboats in New York harbor.[23]

From the start, he was active in the church, being elected to the

[23] Moses Yale Beach, "The Wealth and Biography of the Wealthy Citizens
of the City of New York," sixth edition (New York Sun office, 1845), p. 22.

Mrs. Benjamin Armitage, Painter Unknown. Courtesy of Mrs. E. R. Gay and Mrs. Edgar J. Brower

first board of trustees for a two-year term. He was reelected in 1828, and served on the early bylaws committee and on the committee that bought the lots for the new building from Mr. Pearson.

Curtis Holmes is listed by William Ware in his Pew Book as a sea captain. It was he who supervised the training of Elihu Townsend in

66

shipping before the mast. Holmes was married to Anna Burling, who was born in New York in 1791. In spite of the long sea journeys, Curtis Holmes was elected a trustee in 1825, but resigned before the annual meeting in 1827, presumably to make another sea voyage. He was asked to be the church treasurer in 1841 but refused the task, and was elected a trustee for a one-year term in 1843.

James Byers was the only man among the founders who was a native of New York City. He was born in 1771, the son of James Byers and Hannah Bicker Byers. He must have moved to New England early in his life for in 1800, when he was a resident of Springfield, Massachusetts, he was married to Sophia Dwight, the daughter of Jonathan Dwight, Sr., and Margaret Ashley Dwight. But the first Mrs. Byers died on February 23, 1803, at the age of 27, whereupon James Byers married a Boston widow, Mrs. Sarah Duncan. Sarah Brown Duncan Byers died at the age of 45 at the home of the Byers at 3 Bowling Green on July 2, 1828, and was buried from the church. Byers eventually left New York and moved back to Springfield, Massachusetts, where he died on February 22, 1854, leaving no children.[24]

William Ware listed James Byers as a "Gentleman," but he had had a distinguished career prior to becoming active in the church. He was an army contractor during the War of 1812, and for most of his life was involved in some sort of merchandising, for he had a business address at 29 Burling Slip, very close to his fellow member, Benjamin Blossom. He must have been a very distinguished gentleman, for he was appointed to many committees and chaired the first meetings of the board of trustees. He was elected by the board as president in 1820–1821, very crucial years in the history of the fledgling church.

Daniel Stanton is listed by William Ware as being a merchant who occupied Pew No. 52. In 1820 he was appointed to a committee to examine the treasurer's accounts, and in 1821 was placed on a committee to arrange Mr. Ware's ordination as the first minister. In 1825 he was elected a trustee, and he was again elected in 1838 to replace Mr. Brooks and served almost three years.

These are the stories of some of the more important of the thirty-four men whose names appear on the last page of the first minute book of the church and are listed as founders. This small group of men who

[24] Benjamin W. Dwight, *The History of the Descendents of John Dwight of Dedham, Mass.* (New York, 1874), p. 894; *New York Evening Post*, July 2, 1828; and All Souls Funeral Records.

*Daniel Stanton by Charles L. Elliott. Courtesy of
the New-York Historical Society, New York City*

were instrumental in the founding of the church was essentially alien
to New York. They were not members of old New York families, and
most of them had not married into New York families but had brought
their wives with them to the city. But New York City in 1819 was well
into the process of becoming the most important trade center of the
American Republic. The growth began about 1800 and was accelerated
in 1825 with the opening of the Erie Canal, which made New York
City the port for the agricultural products of what was then "the
West." New Englanders were attracted by these growth prospects, and
they migrated south during the first and second decades of the nineteenth century.

As New York became a commercial center that soon would surpass
Boston and other New England port cities, men who had built up
prosperous businesses in trading and mercantile trades in such cities
as Boston, Salem, and New Bedford came to start businesses in New

68

TABLE I

Analysis of the Founders and Early Members of All Souls by Date of Birth, Place of Birth, Arrival in New York, Profession, and Date of Death

Name	Number in Membership Book	Birth Date	Birth Place	Arrival in New York	Age in 1819	Profession	Death Date
Sedgwick, Henry Dwight	1	1785	Stockbridge, Mass.		34	Lawyer	1831
Pearson, Isaac Green	2	1791	Newburyport, Mass.	1815	28	Glass and china merchant	1874
Dummer, George	3	1782	New Haven, Conn.	c. 1819	37	Merchant and manufacturer of glass	1863
Townsend, Elihu	4	1786	New Haven, Conn.	1812	33	Broker	1853
Sheldon, Frederick	5	1785	Litchfield, Conn.	1813	34	Merchant	1859
Blunt, Joseph	6	1792.	Newburyport, Mass.		27	Attorney	1860
Paine, Elijah	7	1796	Williamstown, Vermont	c. 1817	23	Lawyer and judge	1863
Shepard, John	8					Merchant	

Name	Number in Membership Book	Birth Date	Birth Place	Arrival in New York	Age in 1819	Profession	Death Date
Witt, Thomas	9	1776	Lynn, Mass.		43	Shoe store owner	
Lathrop, Joseph, Jr.	10	1791	Wilbraham, Mass.	1815	28	Dry goods merchant	
Whitney, Phinehas S.	11	1785	Shirley, Mass.		34	Merchant	1855
March, Enoch P.	12		Newbury, Mass.			Merchant	
Greele, Augustus P.	13	1787	Wilton, N.H.	1813	32	Paper merchant	1843
Sewall, Henry Devereux	14	1786	Marblehead, Mass.	1817 or 1818	33	Merchant	1846
Wheaton, Henry	15	1785	Providence, R.I.	1812	34	Lawyer	1848
Russel, William Washington	16	1786	Richmond, Va.	1812	33	Merchant	1863
Low, David	17	1777	Salem, Mass.	1818	41	Merchant	
Chapin, Dexter	18	1793	Malden, Mass.		26	Dry goods broker	1842
Peters, Royal	19	1783	Uxbridge, Mass.		36		1827
Blossom, Benjamin	20	1790	Fairhaven, Mass.		29	Merchant	1877
Armitage, Benjamin	21	1770	England	c. 1793	c. 49	Merchant	1850

Name	Number in Membership Book	Birth Date	Birth Place	Arrival in New York	Age in 1819	Profession	Death Date
Mauran, Oroondates	22	1791	Barrington, R.I.	1817	28	Merchant and shipper	1846
Armstrong, David	23					Merchant	
Kinder, Arthur	24						
Glaze, William	25	1777	England	1793	42	Glass cutter Glass expert	1859
Clark, Luther	26	c. 1797	Claremont, N.H.		c. 22	Lawyer	1826
Lamb, James	27					Sexton of Second Church	
Holmes, Curtis	28	1779	Massachusetts		40	Sea captain	1857
Honay, William	29	c. 1775	Maryland	1811	c. 44	Carpenter and builder	1850
Hood, George	30			c. 1819		Hosiery and lace merchant	
Byers, James	31	1771	New York City	prior to 1812	36	Contractor— merchant	1854
Fisk, Allen	32	1789	Amherst, Mass.	c. 1814	30	Lawyer— teacher	1875
Stanton, Daniel	33					Merchant	
Watkinson, Henry	34					Broker	

York or to represent the old New England firms in the city. There was also in New York a plethora of ship captains who, tired of the rugged business of the long and grueling sea voyages, and with fortunes made from shares in the business, began to settle in New York City and to set up mercantile firms, counting houses, and banks.

The inauguration of the great shipping lines out of New York to American ports, to Europe, and to the West Indies began just a few years before the church was founded. In late October of 1817, for example, four little ships in a row appeared in an advertisement in a New York newspaper. This grouping was significant, for the public was being informed that beginning in January 1818, "The Black Ball Line" was announcing that a fleet of ships would make sailings on a schedule. Other shipping lines with stated schedules were formed by energetic young men, most of them from New England. Enterprising merchants were quick to take advantage of the security of a regular shipping schedule rather than the random sailings to which they had previously been accustomed. Two early members (not founders) were Henry Eckford, the shipbuilder, and Moses H. Grinnell, the famous shipping merchant.

If one goes through the list of the founders of the church, one observes how many of them were old New England names and how many of these persons traced their ancestry back to the Pilgrims and the Puritans. A further study of the ancestry of the founders shows that most of them came to New York as young men; in fact, they were largely still young men when they founded the church. Imbued with the liberal religious ideas of New England Congregationalism and Unitarianism, they found in New York no church that was a satisfactory spiritual and intellectual haven for themselves and their families. Most of the churches were theologically too conservative for those raised in the austere New England meetinghouse. Finding themselves religious aliens and strangers in the city, it was perfectly natural that they should found a church more responsive to their needs. In fact, until the city's growth brought this group of men to New York neither Elihu Palmer, John Butler, nor Joseph Priestley found in the city a strong enough nucleus around which a liberal church could be built.[25]

[25] Charles Richard Denton, "American Unitarians, 1830–1865: A Study of Religious Opinion on War, Slavery, and the Union" (unpublished Ph.D. dissertation, Michigan State University, 1969), pp. 32–33. This study of Unitarian

While it is true that the founders of the First Church were not specifically drawn from the wealthy of the old New York aristocracy, they were largely representatives of old New England families, and they came to New York City within the decade before the church was founded. Although they were not then rich, most of them were either professional men, shopkeepers, or traders on their way to wealth and fame. Our study has not disclosed a single working man unless William Glaze, who was a glass cutter of a highly skilled type and later became a foreman for George Dummer's glass works, could be called a working man. They were intelligent men and women, several of whom were college graduates. All in all, a very solid group of citizens upon which to base a new institution.

---

class structure prior to the Civil War makes the point that "Unitarianism in New York City did not at first attract as many of the wealthy and fashionable as it did later." But the author confuses the members of the church with those who were served by the ministers-at-large which we shall discuss later. These ministers were called specifically to serve in a poor area in the city. Denton makes the point in his study that Unitarians were not as much upper-class people as former studies had supposed.

4. *The First Building*

THREE PROBLEMS now faced the newly incorporated church: the erection of a church building, the temporary filling of the pulpit, and the selection of a permanent pastor for the fledgling congregation. To these tasks the new board of trustees now turned its attention.

The first trustees' meeting was held the very evening the certificate of incorporation was filed; the first order of business was to reestablish a building committee — the same as had been appointed on October 9th, with the addition of James Byers, who was also chairing the meeting that evening. The trustees also formally reestablished Pearson and Sewall as treasurer and clerk, respectively, but did not select a permanent chairman at this time. The board then settled down to the business of planning to build a church. Funds were running a little behind expectations despite a few additional subscriptions that had been taken in. Nevertheless, the trustees decided to buy the two lots on Chambers Street which Mr. Pearson, as a member of the building committee, had located for $9,000. Five days later, at the second trustees' meeting, Mr. Pearson — this time as treasurer — was instructed to step up the subscription campaign. Not less than one half of the cost of the property was to be collected in this way. Mr. Mauran and Mr. Sewall were then appointed a committee to obtain examples of bylaws, and another committee — composed of Sedgwick, Wheaton, and the very busy Mr. Pearson — was appointed "for supply of the pulpit."

In the meantime, the society had apparently decided to open its Sunday services for the fall season of 1819 with its star performer, for Channing himself preached on October 30th. Again he drew crowds, morning and evening. Channing stayed in New York for the next two weeks or so, probably preaching on the following two Sun-

Broadway and the City Hall, 1819. Near the Future Site of the First Congregational Church. The J. Clarence Davies Collection, the Museum of the City of New York

days. On the evening of November 14th, the society met to adopt a resolution of thanks to Dr. Channing, and appointed Wheaton, Pearson, and Sewall to "wait upon Mr. Channing and to present him with this resolution and our best wishes for his safe return to his family and friends and for his future health and prosperity." [1]

A committee comprising Henry Wheaton, Isaac Green Pearson, and Henry D. Sedgwick proceeded to fill the pulpit from Sunday to Sunday until a permanent minister might be selected. Andrews Norton of Harvard responded for both himself and Edward Everett by stating that neither of them could "visit New York during the present college term." Norton said that he would endeavor to be there the "first Sunday after Christmas, and that immediately upon my leaving, it is Mr. Everett's intention to follow and to continue the supply of your pulpit. I may perhaps supply for three Sabbaths." [2]

A few weeks later William Ellery Channing wrote to Henry Sedgwick in New York begging the church community to pay particular attention to Andrews Norton: "I hope it will be in the power of you

[1] All Souls Minute Book, Volume I, p. 12.

[2] Andrews Norton, Cambridge, to Messrs. Wheaton, Sedgwick, and Pearson, November 22, 1819, in Henry D. Sedgwick Papers, Massachusetts Historical Society.

& our other friends to give him more of your time than most of us would need. He is not only a stranger to New York, but has never travelled, & has none of a traveller's experience. His habits have been those of a student." [3]

Isaac Green Pearson, visiting in Boston, wrote to Sedgwick in New York on the next day, December 22, 1819, to say that Mr. Norton was to be succeeded by Mr. Everett and then by Mr. Francis H. W. Ware. Pearson hoped that such arrangements might be extended for several months so that there would be no interruption of the Sunday services. But the important part of the letter is the expression of the hope that some of the New Yorkers entertained that William Ellery Channing might be persuaded to become the minister of the church in New York. Pearson wrote to Sedgwick, "I mention to you in confidence (for I think it ought not to be talked about at present) that many here think it not impossible that Mr. Channing would remove to New York and some even of the clergy think it would be his duty to go. But I should not refer to this subject till I see you." [4]

On January 16, 1820, the congregation met to formulate its official thanks to Professor Norton for his services. But the society already had its hopes set on calling Channing for its permanent minister. Early in 1820, Sedgwick, Wheaton, and Pearson wrote to Dr. Channing:

> We are convinced that your aid is indispensably necessary to the rapid and permanent success of the cause of uncorrupted Christianity in this quarter of the Union. . . . The Church which you have so essentially contributed to . . . would be immediately built up, and we confidently anticipate that other societies would be formed, united in the same faith and hope.[5]

It is small wonder that the founders hoped above all for Channing to be their permanent minister, for not only had he repeatedly drawn large crowds to the small chapel on every occasion on which he had spoken; he had also lent strong encouragement and support to the New York enterprise. Indeed, we may infer that Channing himself

[3] W. E. Channing to Henry D. Sedgwick, December 21, 1819, in Henry D. Sedgwick Papers, Massachusetts Historical Society.

[4] Isaac Green Pearson, Boston, to Henry D. Sedgwick, New York, December 22, 1819, in Henry D. Sedgwick Papers, Massachusetts Historical Society.

[5] William Henry Channing, *The Memoirs of William Ellery Channing* (Boston: William Crosby and H. P. Nichols, 1848), Vol. II, p. 166.

was somewhat tempted to accept the position, for in a letter to a friend he confided, "Were I a young man, and unfettered by any engagements, I should prefer the situation . . . to any within my hopes." But to the New York Committee, he replied:

I cannot for a moment hesitate as to the answer which I should give to your application. I regard the situation to which you invite me as honorable and important. But Providence has appointed me another lot. Public, domestic, and private considerations, which I need not enlarge upon, leave me no liberty of forsaking the post which I now occupy. Its duties and responsibilities are, indeed, above my strength, and I believe that no selfish regards attach me to it. But I think that I distinctly read in a variety of circumstances the will of God that I should continue here; and unless these change in a very unexpected manner, I shall remain whilst I have the strength to labor.[6]

After Professor Norton, the Reverend Professor Edward Everett, then 25, took over the pulpit at the chapel at Broadway and Reade streets, from January 23rd to February 13th, 1820. In 1814, Everett had been the Unitarian Minister of the Brattle Street Church in Boston. Under the auspices of Harvard, Everett had then gone abroad to study in 1815, and he had only recently returned when he preached for the infant church in New York. The Rev. Convers Francis preached the following two Sundays, February 20th and 27th, 1820. Francis, too, was a young man and only recently ordained by the Harvard Divinity School. For the past several months, he had been the minister of the church in Watertown, Massachusetts.

The first three Sundays in March were supplied by James Flint, the 41-year-old pastor of the Congregational Society of East Bridgewater, Massachusetts; thereafter, until April 16th, by John Gorham Palfrey, who had preached in May the year before and who had been the very first minister to preach to the new group of Unitarians after Channing's three-service venture the previous May.[7]

Henry Ware, Jr., picked up where Palfrey left off and stayed through May 7, 1820, officiating also at the momentous occasion of

[6] *Ibid.*, pp. 166–167.

[7] Later, Everett was to become, in turn, a congressman, the governor of Massachusetts, the president of Harvard, United States secretary of state, and a U.S. senator.

laying the cornerstone for the First Congregational Church on April 29, 1820.

Thus, less than six months after the legal date of its incorporation, and a year almost to the day since William Ellery Channing had addressed the friends of his sister, the first Unitarian group in New York was officially beginning the construction of its house of worship. Building plans had been approved by the society as early as November 4th the previous Fall, and the lots on Chambers Street had been purchased shortly after November 17th. Evidently the letter to George Bond and others in Boston had borne fruit, for later references in the minute book allude to Mr. Bond's generosity; and, in the minutes of a meeting of January 24, 1820, it was noted that "a lady belonging to Boston" had donated $100. If these are at all representative, the new society may have gathered a measure of support from that city. Apparently also, the founding subscribers themselves must have donated or loaned more than the amounts of their subscriptions to the society. These contributions did not supply the society with all the funds it needed to implement its plans, but, notwithstanding, the society launched its building program with a great deal of optimism.

An inscription on parchment bearing this message was put into the cornerstone of the new edifice: "Dedicated to the worship of the only God, through the only mediator, founded on the great principle of the Reformation, the sufficiency of the Scripture, the right of private judgment and liberty of conscience." Another message, the text from John 17:3: "This is life eternal, to know thee the only true God, and Jesus Christ whom thou hast sent," was inscribed on a plate and buried underneath the cornerstone. Ware delivered a fine "sidewalk" address at the ceremony. The bystanders heard him stress that "it was not in the spirit of rebellion or hostility, but in allegiance to conscience, to truth, and to God" that the First Congregational Church of the City of New York was erecting this Unitarian house of worship.[8]

On Monday, May 15, 1821, the society gathered to choose a permanent pastor, but adjourned after much discussion revealed that it was too early to make the choice. Clearly, if Henry Ware, Jr., then only 26, had been among the possible candidates, the congregation had had plenty of opportunity to hear him and to get to know him, as

[8] All Souls Minute Book, Volume I, pp. 23, 22.

he had been a chief ministerial help to the new society from the beginning. It is thus obvious that Ware was not the minister under consideration. Two weeks later, on May 30th, the society again gathered for the express purpose of choosing a pastor, but again adjourned because, "the business not having been so matured," no decision could be reached. For the next two months or so, no further action was taken on this matter, but on July 23rd, the congregation met again and formally resolved, unanimously, "that this Society, impressed with a deep sense of the piety, learning, and talents of the Rev. John Brazer, do cordially invite him to take upon himself the pastoral charge of this Church and Society." Probably Brazer had preached on May 14th, the week after the conclusion of the engagement of Henry Ware, Jr., and during the ensuing weeks.[9]

John Brazer was at that time a youth of only 23 years, and out of Harvard for seven years. Having come from an impoverished background, he had been forced for financial reasons to work for a while before entering college; but his thirst for knowledge was such that he had brilliantly succeeded at Harvard, and he was given the post of professor of Latin in 1817. Thereafter, Brazer had avidly pursued the paths of scholarship in almost every conceivable subject until he realized that he could not spend all of his years in "the secluded shades of academic life," and turned to seeking his own pulpit.[10]

By now persuaded that the young man was all that the aspiring, high-principled society desired in its very first pastor, the members voted Brazer's salary to be $2,000 a year, and appointed Henry Wheaton, Elihu Townsend, and Isaac Green Pearson to be a committee to convey the invitation to Mr. Brazer. One infers that the budding Unitarian Church had entertained lofty expectations of any man it might select as its permanent pastor, and for some quite understandable reasons. After all, had the society not been encouraged by some of the most distinguished liberal religious scholars in the country? No less a man than the famous and popular William Ellery Channing had helped to initiate the society, and the son of the illustrious Henry

[9] *Ibid.*, p. 25.

[10] William B. Sprague, *Annals of the American Pulpit: Commemorative Notes of Distinguished American Clergymen of the Various Denominations,* Volume VIII: Unitarian Congregational (New York: Robert Carter and Brothers, 1865), p. 507.

Ware, Sr., of Harvard had taken up where Channing left off. Many of those who had filled the pulpit since the little group had hired the rooms of Mr. Anderson were also distinguished Harvard scholars, Andrews Norton and Edward Everett among them. Further, many of the new congregation's members traveled in the same social circles as these eminent men.

Another reason the New York Unitarians had for being particularly discriminating in their selection of a pastor is that the success of their new church heavily depended upon the kind of influence the chosen minister could wield in the religiously orthodox city. A William Ellery Channing or a Henry Ware, Jr., could reasonably be expected to ensure the infant church a respectable place among the other churches in New York, but a young, and as yet untried and unproven, man perhaps could not. It is hardly surprising, then, that the society deliberated for so many weeks before finally deciding that young John Brazer was worthy of the call.

But with all the attention and cautious reserve the members put upon the assessments of Brazer's fitness, it may have been largely assumed that such a young man in search of a pulpit would gladly accept their offer. After the summer months passed, the main item of business at the September 26th meeting was the report of the committee appointed to call Brazer. The members of the society were grimly and surprisingly told that Brazer had declined! The congregation was bitterly disappointed, but it was resolved that a letter of appreciation of Brazer's motives, and of the "continued affectionate and respectful regards" of the congregation he had disappointed, be sent to him. No further discussion on the matter of a pastor took place. Instead, the society briskly turned to a wholly different matter, that of the library which had been planned for one of the rooms in the still unfinished church.[11]

Why had Brazer declined? By the time he was ready to accept a pulpit of his own, his reputation as a brilliant scholar and articulate speaker was already well known in Unitarian circles. He had suffered no lack of invitations to preach, and at the time he was candidating for the New York society, he was also well known to the North Church in Salem. When a call to accept that pulpit came in the middle of 1820,

[11] All Souls Minute Book, Volume I, p. 26.

he accepted. It may be hard today to understand why such a promising young man chose Salem over the city of New York, but it must be remembered that Salem was not only close to Boston, the center of liberal religion, but also the Salem church was thriving and the New York church only a hope and a promise in the midst of a deeply entrenched orthodoxy.

The "rooms of Mr. Anderson" and the chapel which the new society had set up in those quarters had been permanently abandoned when services were suspended for the summer. Those premises had faithfully served their purposes for the congregation during its year of formation, and the society had not planned for the interim before the new church building was completed. Thus, it is probable that no services were held during the autumn months of 1820. After their disappointing meeting on September 26th, the founders convened with surprising frequency. The "annual" meeting, the first since the founding on November 15th the preceding year, was held on November 6th, in ample time to prepare the financial accounts and to elect three new trustees to the board for the coming year.

The society assembled at the Washington Hotel with many of the cumbersome details of organization already accomplished. The nine trustees chosen the previous year were now headed by James Byers, who had been elected president of the board early in 1820. The congregation had also ratified a system of bylaws in which it was stated that the trustees should be grouped into three classes of three men each. Every year three men would go off the board, making room for three new trustees. Once the momentum of the years got underway, this system would allow every trustee to serve for three years and no more. This remains essentially how it is done today, more than a century and a half later. But, as the board had been in existence for only one year, three men were now slated to step down before a normal term had expired. Frederick Sheldon, John Shepard, and David Armstrong had drawn lots to form this group; and Benjamin Armitage, Daniel Low, and Oroondates Mauran had similarly been grouped to give up their office the next year after serving for only two years.

Of the 57 votes recorded, 19 went to Roger G. Van Polanen, who appears in the minute book for the first time with this election. The same number of votes went to Henry Sedgwick; now this seeming "pillar" of the society since its founding was to become a trustee.

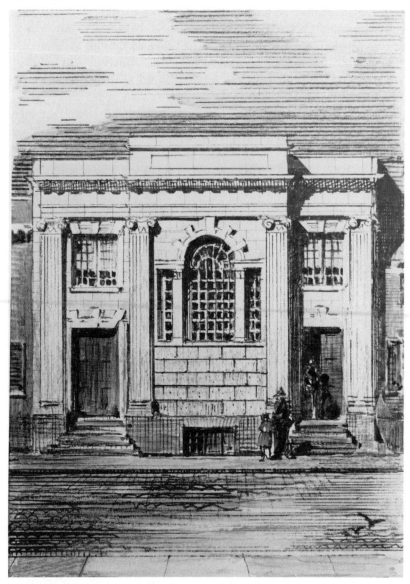

*The First Church Building, 1821. From the Collection of the
Unitarian Church of All Souls*

Another 17 votes went to I. T. Whittelsey who was on the psalms and hymns committee. These three men took their places on the board. Two other members of the society received one vote each.[12]

A financial report of the first year's income and expenditures was also read, the most significant aspect of which is that outlays — for paying the chorister and Mr. Baldwin, the sexton; for lighting the chapel at Broadway and Reade, and for outfitting it with such items as prayer and hymnbooks; and for paying the rent for those premises — were in excess by nearly $400 of the moneys raised through subscriptions, Sunday collections, and other income. But the society was undismayed; it merely transferred this deficit to the separately maintained account designated as building expenses for the new church.

The trustees for 1820–1821 — meeting in one another's homes — confined their meetings primarily to the details of the dedication of the new church building which was rapidly nearing completion, and to the arrangement and assessment of the pews. Little could be decided finally without the approval of the entire membership of the society, but the board agreed upon the layout of the pews and fixed their assessed value at 11 percent of the appraised value. Originally, the ceremony for the dedication of the building had been set for the first week in January 1821, but arrangements for the occasion had not been completed in time, and so it was rescheduled for Saturday, January 20. Two days before the dedication, the society gathered in its brand-new quarters to adopt the board's recommendations regarding the pews, which were to be put up for sale officially on January 22nd. The purchase price of the 161 pews ranged from $500 for the front rows to $60 for those in the rear, and was expected to bring in 11 percent of this amount annually in assessments.

At last the long-awaited moment was at hand. At 11 A.M., Saturday, January 20th, the eager members of the congregation gathered at Chambers Street to dedicate their first real home. The building itself was small but elegant, an impressive structure for so newly established a congregation. As Goodrich described it in 1828:

> The first [Unitarian Church] in Chambers Street between Broadway and Church Street, is a very ornamental edifice, the front of which is faced with white marble, with pillars in *bas relief,* and surmounted with a pediment. The interior is very elegant, the pews being finished

[12] For a brief account of Van Polanen, see his sketch in Appendix C, p. 263.

83

with mahogany ornaments, carpeted and cushioned; the pulpit is raised on ornamental pillars, with an area and railing in front, before which the pews rise gradually to the rear, and facing to the front of the house; there is also a gallery and an organ. The whole is beautifully lighted from a spacious circular skylight that rises from the centre of the roof. The size of the house is 68 by 50 feet.[13]

Another and somewhat more detailed description of the church is found in the reminiscences of Mary Hustace Hubbard, written late in her life, around 1900. In the front center of the building, said Mrs. Hubbard, was "a large window composed of small panes of greenish ground glass." On either side of this window were the entrance doors, and just inside the doors, in the vestibule, were stairs leading to the galleries. One entered the church thus facing the organ in the rear gallery "with the clock in front," although this clock had not been installed at the time of the dedication.

The clock of which Mrs. Hubbard spoke was given in 1822 by George Bond of Boston, friend and benefactor of the society since its founding. Although the original works have been lost to time, the numerals carved out of wood and covered with gold leaf on the clock at the rear of the present church at 80th Street and Lexington Avenue are the original numerals that were on George Bond's gift. The pulpit stood against the large window at the front of the church apparently placed between the two entrance doors. Mrs. Hubbard described the interior of the church as "painted white, and the pews bordered with polished mahogany. The carpet and cushions were red." [14]

The galleries held 17 pews, with 44 pews on the main floor, and the church was capable of holding comfortably from 500 to 600 people. When singing the last hymn, the congregation turned toward the rear gallery to face the organ, a practice common in many New England churches. In 1821, "The Ladies of the Society" presented a magnificent communion set which is still in use. It consists of six large cups, two large tankards, and two plates, all suitably inscribed and fashioned by William Thomson, a New York silversmith who worked from 1810 to 1840.

[13] A. T. Goodrich, *Picture of New York and Stranger's Guide* (New York, 1828), p. 226.

[14] Mary Hustace Hubbard, unpublished manuscript (New York: The Unitarian Church of All Souls, c. 1900).

The Original Communion Service of 1821 by the Silversmith William Thomson. Photograph by Rita E. Jamason

The Original Clock Face. Photograph by Rita E. Jamason

An unknown correspondent "S.A.," writing in the *Christian Register* in December 1821, added a detail about the interior of the church. "Beneath the church are a vestry, in which is a parish library; a lecture room, fitted up with seats and a desk; and a large room, suitable for a Sunday school." [15]

The Rev. Edward Everett, who had preached in the temporary chapel at Broadway and Reade streets the year before, officiated at the dedication service which started with the 100th Psalm. The hymns selected for the occasion were from Henry Sewall's new hymnbook, recently published, and bore such messages as: "Greatest of beings! Source of Good: We bow before thy throne, ... Wilt thou visit men below? ... Wilt thou vouchsafe thy presence here, ... While with united hands we rear an altar to thy praise?" [16]

Everett's sermon was equally appropriate, beginning as it did with an obscure text from II Chronicles 2:4: "Behold, I build an house to the name of the Lord my God, to dedicate it to him." In ringing rhetoric Everett dedicated the building:

> To no earthly power, to no human name; but to God who reigns on high. It is henceforth not ours but his: we resign, devote, and consecrate it to him.
>
> [It was to be, he said,] the great asylum — the place of refuge — the one spot left on earth (blessed be God that one is left) where business and pleasure cannot come; where the outward service of the world, at least, cannot enter.... It is here that you are to perform some of the most interesting acts, and enter into the most solemn engagements; that you are to take upon you ... the holy vows of the gospel.

The preacher warned that the erection of this house of worship did not necessarily mark an easy path forward:

> You are dedicating a place of worship to the support of views of revealed truth, different, in some important points, from those of the respectable community in which you live; not extensively understood by your brethren and neighbors.... Under these circumstances, it is impossible that you should not be the objects of the prejudices, of the

---

[15] *Christian Register,* December 28, 1821, p. 79.
[16] All Souls Minute Book, Volume I, p. 36.

*The Reverend Edward Everett, Engraved by J. C. Buttre after
a Photograph by Brady. Courtesy of the New-York Historical
Society, New York City*

unfavorable opinions, of the opposition, with which whatever is
thought new is apt to be regarded.[17]

Everett then went on to illustrate how it was necessary to face this
opposition. First, the new congregation must, by its "personal character for probity and worth" prove its mettle. Nothing would make people believe that Unitarianism is a true doctrine so effectively as demon-
strating that it makes its believers good men. Second, Everett insisted,
there must be serious, rational inquiry: "No serious inquirer, who has
wrestled himself with doubt, and has formed his own faith on deliberate and careful investigation, will unkindly question the honesty

[17] Edward Everett, *A Sermon Preached at the Dedication of the First Congregational Church in New York* (Boston: Cummings and Hilliard, 1821).

of your inquiries, because they have led you to a different result." Finally, Everett admonished his listeners not to be overzealous in this support of their new faith. There would be enough support from the community among those who were not openly against the new society. But the congregation should not ask that others leave their churches and pastors to join the new faith. "It is enough that they bear you Christian charity."

Concluding, Everett adjured them that:

If this church is founded on private feeling or worldly zeal, or has been erected from any motive of human interest, then not the Lord but you have built it, and you have most assuredly labored in vain. But if it is erected on the faith and hope of the Gospel; if it is consecrated in your hearts to the glory of God, and the purity of Jesus . . . then you are founded on a rock, that shall not be moved.[18]

On January 30, 1821, Henry Ware, Jr., came to the society's aid once again, this time primarily to help it to establish a covenant, and also to assist in making an official distinction between the members of the "Society," and the members of the "Church." It was customary in those days to make such a distinction.

The definition of a "Church" member was usually one who had been baptized, and who subscribed to and signed a covenant. These conditions enabled the "Church" member to take communion, and in many churches only these particular "Church" members were entitled to choose a pastor and to decide other important religious matters, while the more secular matters could be decided by a vote of all the members of the society.

When the founding fathers of the First Congregational Church had formulated its bylaws the previous year, they had followed this custom and had clearly delineated what constituted a member of the "Society" as distinct from a "Church" member. But they had made the distinction more nominal than real. Anyone who owned or rented a pew could be a voting member of the society, but only those who had attended "Divine Worship" for a full year could take part in the choice of a pastor, the election of trustees, and other similar issues. Given this distinction, a "Church" (as compared to a "Society") had not yet

[18] *Ibid.*, pp. 22–23.

been established, and the society asked Henry Ware, Jr., to help them.

On the 30th day of January, 1821, after due notice had been given from the pulpit, a group of persons gathered in the lecture-room of the church building on Chambers Street "with a view to the formation of a regular Christian Church." Mr. Ware stated "the nature of that form of Church government denominated Congregational — that it was independent, accountable to none without itself but the great Head of the Church universal. Its officers were a Pastor or Bishop, and Deacons whose duties were clearly defined in the New Testament." Mr. Ware went on to say that "the Constitution of this Church was a matter of usage, not of written law; that each Church might provide its own rules in by-laws." [19]

A discussion followed about the nature of the covenant to be adopted, "it being understood that the meeting were decidedly in favor of such a compact as would not shut out even the Trinitarian or Calvinist, if they should desire at any time to join in it." The covenant was then adopted, and 24 persons immediately signed it. Two of this number had not been baptized so this rite was performed by Henry Ware, "this initiatory rite into the Church General being considered necessary previous to admission to communion in any particular Church."

The constitution that was then adopted had nine articles in which it was agreed "that no other form of admission into this Church shall be required but subscription to its Covenant; it remaining however in the power of the Pastor and Members to reject the subscription of the profligate and irreligious." Anyone who belonged to any Christian church should "have free access" to the communion service.

They agreed to meet annually as a "Church," but other meetings could be called by the pastor after due notice. Every member was entitled to vote (the women could vote in the "Church" if not in the "Society" meetings). The pastor was to preside at all meetings, to have

[19] All of this and the subsequent material about this meeting are contained in a small bound blank book which contains a record of the discussion of the meeting and a copy of the constitution. When the book is reversed and opened at the other end it contains the wording of the covenant and the signatures of those who subscribed to it. The book is labeled "Records of the First Congregational Church in the City of New York." See Appendix A for a list of the original signers.

a vote, and was requested to keep a record of the proceedings. They agreed that there would be two deacons chosen for life "whose duty it shall be to receive the offerings of the communicants at the Lord's Table to be appropriated to the necessary disbursements of the Church." They were to administer any surplus money to the poor; first, to the poor of the church, and second, to the poor of the society. If the pastor was absent the eldest deacon was to preside. "Every child shall be considered as entitled to the rite of Baptism whether the parents be a member of the Church or not." The ordinance of the Lord's Supper was to be served on the first Sunday of every other month.

The church adopted this constitution, and then made a choice by ballot of the two deacons specified in the constitution. They elected Benjamin Armitage and Henry D. Sewall to be deacons "who both declined, but being requested to attend to its duties for the present and, to give an answer when they should have considered the matter more maturely." Unfortunately the only records of the "Church" end with this meeting, so we do not know what the "mature" consideration of Messrs. Armitage and Sewall might have been.

The covenant which Henry Ware, Jr., helped the society to formulate is a far cry from the simple but profound words espoused by All Souls today; but it represented very liberal theological thought in 1821.

In the presence of God and in the name of Jesus Christ: We, whose names are underwritten do, by this act, profess our faith in Jesus Christ and our subjection to the laws of his Kingdom. We receive the Scriptures of the Old and New Testament as our rule of faith and guide of life; and in a humble and grateful reliance on the mercy offered for the pardon of our sins, and for assistance in our duties, we take upon ourselves the engagements of the Christian profession. By this transaction, we profess our earnest desire to obtain the salvation made known to us in the Gospel, and our serious purpose to comply with the terms on which it is offered. We promise to manifest our fidelity to our Lord and Master by observing the ordinances which He has appointed, by submission to the laws of Christian Order and by all the offices of Christian fellowship; beseeching the God and Father of our Lord Jesus Christ that, being faithful unto each other and to the great Head of the Church, we may enjoy the consolations of our Religion, and receive its rewards hereafter, through riches of Divine favor manifested by Jesus Christ.

Thus, solemnly covenanted and properly housed, the members of the young congregation were ready to take upon themselves "the engagements of the Christian profession."

5. The Sewall Hymnal

Words from a new hymnal were used at the service of dedication of the new church building. When they started, the congregation had lacked a suitable hymnbook. But now a new one had been prepared by that indefatigable layman Henry Devereux Sewall for their use.

To understand the true significance of Sewall's hymnbook, one must know something of the history of the church hymnbook in the United States. Throughout the seventeenth century and down to the middle of the eighteenth century, nearly all of the New England churches of the Congregational order used the *Bay Psalm Book*. This was gradually superseded by either the *New Version of the Psalms* or one of the editions of *Watts and Select*, which was essentially a selection of hymns by Isaac Watts with a supplement of hymns selected from other writers.

With the rising liberalism of the last part of the eighteenth century, there began to appear hymnbooks prepared for individual congregations. Generally, these were not adopted by other congregations. In 1782 the West Church in Boston published *A Collection of Hymns, More Particularly Designed for the Use of the West Society in Boston.* In 1788 the East Church in Salem published *A Collection of Hymns for Publick Worship*. These two books were of only local significance. In 1795 Jeremy Belknap brought out a hymnbook which he called *Sacred Poetry*, a futile attempt to bring out a book that would be useful for both the liberal and the conservative wings of Congregationalism.

During the course of the nineteenth century the Unitarians produced a total of 34 different hymnbooks, a far larger number than any other denomination in America. One would think that Unitarians really liked to sing! But the true reason for this proliferation was that no one hymnbook seemed to satisfy every parish.[1]

Just as the eighteenth century ended, in 1799, the Rev. James Freeman of King's Chapel brought out a hymnbook, *A Collection of Psalms and Hymns for Public Worship,* which was the first of the hymnbooks prepared for use in King's Chapel. Ralph Waldo Emerson's father, William Emerson, the minister of the First Church in Boston, brought out a hymnal in 1808, *A Collection of Psalms and Hymns.* This elegantly bound book was unusual in that prefixed to each hymn was the name of a hymn tune, although the book contained no music. Another hymnal for liberals in America was titled: *A Selection of Sacred Poetry Consisting of Psalms and Hymns from Watts Doddridge, Merrick, Scott, Cowper, Barbauld, Steele, and Others,* published in Philadelphia in 1812, and edited by Ralph Eddowes and James Taylor. This hymnal was used primarily in the Unitarian Church in Philadelphia. Henry Sewall's *A Collection of Psalms and Hymns, for Social and Private Worship,* dated 1820, was thus the seventh hymnal to be published in America in the liberal tradition, and one of the first conceived to be for more general use than by a single church.

It is important to note that the congregation of the First Church did not want a specifically Unitarian hymnbook of a sectarian nature. Instead, what they most desired was a hymnbook that was as universal as possible, avoiding sectarian controversy. It also appears that Henry Devereux Sewall had begun his collection of hymns and psalms on his own initiative. On July 23, 1820, a committee of the board of trustees of the church was chosen "to examine A Collection of Psalms and Hymns understood to be in preparation, and to report whether the same can be recommended to the adoption of this Society." A week later the trustees met again, and, "the committee appointed to examine A Collection of Psalms and Hymns recommended its being adopted by this Society, and it was unanimously accepted." [2]

In this almost impersonal way thus was inaugurated one of the first hymnbooks suitable for Unitarian congregations in America. Characteristically Henry D. Sewall is not mentioned in the church

[1] See Henry Wilder Foote, "Descriptive Catalogue of American Unitarian Hymn-Books," in Unitarian Historical Society *Proceedings,* Volume VI, pp. 31–49 (Boston: American Unitarian Association, 1938).

[2] All Souls Minute Book, Volume I, pp. 25, 27.

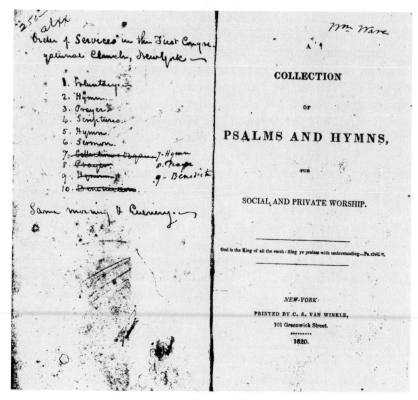

The Title Page of the Sewall Hymnal

minutes (he was the clerk who wrote the minutes), nor is his name affixed to the hymnbook which subsequently appeared in early 1821, titled *A Collection of Psalms and Hymns*.[3]

Behind the compilation of the hymnbook is one of the fascinating stories of American Unitarian literature. Henry Sewall took most of his hymns from the traditional hymnbooks of the time and, in the manner of most publishers of hymns, felt that he had the right to change the traditional words if they violated his concepts of universal ideas or were too specifically theological in any sectarian sense. He chose many hymns from English writers, chiefly Isaac Watts, Doddridge, and Mrs. Steele, and from other collections.

[3] Henry D. Sewall, *A Collection of Psalms and Hymns* (New York: printed by C. S. Van Winkle, 101 Greenwich Street, 1820).

94

The most significant part of the preparation of the hymnbook is that Henry Sewall also asked some of his friends and acquaintances to contribute hymns for the work in progress. In the hymnbook there are fifteen such hymns marked with an asterisk. The Church of All Souls fortunately owns the copy of this early hymnbook that was owned and .used by William Ware, the first minister. Underneath each of these hymns with an asterisk there is some indication as to who wrote it, or some abbreviation. Most of these indications are undecipherable. But five of the hymns were written by a very young poet named William Cullen Bryant, later to become a member of the church, a famous poet, and a newspaper editor in New York City. These five are the earliest of the published poems of Bryant with the exception of "Thanatopsis" (published in Boston, where the publisher, not thinking that it could possibly have been written by a 17-year-old, printed it under Bryant's father's name). The five hymns of Bryant in this first All Souls hymnbook do not contain the name of Bryant after them. But William Ware wrote the name five times in his own personal copy of the hymnbook, and the correspondence between Henry Sewall and Bryant about the hymns is extant.

Bryant, living in western Massachusetts at Great Barrington, became acquainted with the Sedgwick family in Stockbridge. Bryant first met Charles Sedgwick, who was a member of the Bar in Berkshire County; Bryant was at that time practicing as a lawyer. But the most influential member of the family on Bryant in these early days was Catharine Sedgwick, the youngest of three sisters who, very shortly after meeting the poet, was to become one of America's most famous novelists. Bryant became a frequent visitor to the Sedgwick home at Stockbridge, beginning in May 1820. The invitation to the Sedgwick home first came from Catharine, whose purpose was to convince Bryant to write some hymns for the volume being collected by Henry Sewall. Bryant called in the afternoon when his court work was over and agreed to contribute to the collection. Catharine felt that she had accomplished a coup in getting Bryant to write the hymns, but she also felt quite pleased that the occasion had enabled her to meet such a charming man as the young poet.[4]

At this time, Bryant was not a Unitarian. He was a pewholder in

[4] Charles H. Brown, *Bryant* (New York: Scribner's, 1971), p. 92.

the Congregational Church in Great Barrington. Charles H. Brown, his recent biographer, says that "he had been brought up in the Calvinist faith, but its grip on him had loosened over the years." Dr. Bryant, his father, had visited Boston often and had brought the new doctrines of Unitarianism home with him. Bryant himself, in his studies of the classics, had found many ideas that interested him, especially stoicism. He also inclined to Deism, which was popular among free thinkers of that period. "He was not much in sympathy with dogmatic religion. . . . He might perhaps have allied himself to the new religion if there had been a Unitarian society in the village." [5]

On August 29, 1820, Henry Sewall wrote to Bryant at Great Barrington and personally acknowledged the "five beautiful hymns I have received from you through my friend Miss Sedgwick. I consider them as constituting a very valuable portion of my original hymns. That I am quite sincere in this, you will more readily admit, when you perceive that one object I have in addressing you is to beg for more." [6]

Sewall wrote that he could not get the book to press until the middle of October. He proposed several areas in which he felt the hymn collection was deficient, and asked Bryant if he would not be willing to fill these areas: 1. The paternal character of God, 2. the moral bearing of our Savior's miracles, 3. duties of parents, 4. duties of children, and 5. fortitude. Sewall also suggested a fact of which every writer and minister is cognizant — that sometimes it is more difficult to pick a subject than to do the writing. He hoped that his suggestion of these five subjects might inspire some further poems from Bryant. In this he was unsuccessful.

Sewall mentioned in his letter that he had taken some liberties with the hymns that Bryant had already sent. Sewall was later to regret that he had made these alterations, for Bryant did not answer his letter for several months. Bryant evidently replied to Sewall's letter in November, for writing to Bryant again on January 2, 1821, Sewall breathed a sigh of relief, "I had begun to feel no little anxiety with regard to the alterations I had made in some of your hymns. I attributed your silence at last to the displeasure you felt at the liberty I

---

[5] *Ibid.,* p. 93. See also Bryant's account in his "Reminiscences of Miss Sedgwick," quoted in Mary E. Dewey, *The Life and Letters of Catharine M. Sedgwick* (New York: Harper and Brothers, 1871), p. 438.

[6] Henry D. Sewall to W. C. Bryant, August 29, 1820, in Bryant–Godwin Collection, Manuscript Division, New York Public Library.

Henry Devereux Sewall by William Dunlop. Courtesy of the
Frick Art Reference Library and Charles J. Sewall

had taken, and I set about making the only amends in my power, by
restoring all which were not printed, to your copy." [7]

What Henry Sewall did to Bryant's hymns is an interesting puzzle
which can be worked out quite accurately from the changes in the

[7] Henry D. Sewall to W. C. Bryant, January 2, 1821, in Bryant–Godwin
Collection, Manuscript Division, New York Public Library.

first and the second editions of the hymnbook. Sewall wrote Bryant that he was changing back to their original version the poems that had not yet been set into type and printed. But when one examines the two editions it is apparent that the first three of Bryant's hymns (numbered 29, 73, and 129) are exactly alike in both editions. Therefore, for these poems, Sewall either did not want to make any corrections or changed them back. It is the last two of the hymns in the latter part of the hymnbook that he altered.

In Number 157, he made changes in three sets of lines. Bryant had written:

> The light of smiles shall beam again
> From lids that now o'erflow with tears.

Sewall had altered these lines to:

> The light of smiles shall fill again
> And lids that overflow with tears.

Bryant had written:

> And ye, who o'er a friend's low bier
> Now shed the bitter drops like rain.

Sewall had altered these lines to:

> And thou, who o'er thy friend's low bier
> Sheddest the bitter drops like rain.

Bryant had written:

> Nor hopeless sorrow break the heart
> That spurned of men, fears not to die.

Sewall had altered these lines to:

> Though with a pierced and broken heart
> And spurned of men, he goes to die.

In Number 373, which also was altered, Bryant wrote:

God made his grave, to men unknown,
Where Moab's rocks a vale enclose;
And laid the ancient seer alone
To slumber there in long repose.

Sewall had altered these four lines to:

God made his grave to men unknown,
Where Moab's rocks a vale infold,
And laid the aged seer alone
To slumber till the world grows old.

None of these alterations can be considered earth-shaking, but the procedure must have irritated Bryant at the time. It seems likely that the last part of the hymnal was set in type and printed before the first part; otherwise Sewall, when he felt that he had offended Bryant, would have changed the words in hymns 157 and 373 back to their original words — which he did do in the second edition four years later.

Mr. Sewall's letter of August 29, 1820, also listed some other changes which he proposed to make. But since he changed these back again in the three hymns that are identical in both editions, they do not really concern us.

Thus, the hymnal which Henry Sewall hoped to publish in 1820 (the date on the title page) did not get into print until early in 1821. By May of 1821, Sewall wrote to Bryant again, for somehow the hymnbook which he had sent in care of Thomas Sedgwick in Albany had miscarried, and Bryant had not received the two copies he had been promised. This letter also contains a very interesting bit of information: sometime between the January letter and the May letter, there had been a fire in the publishing house and 800 copies of the hymnbook had been destroyed. It was evidently originally published on both good and inferior paper, and Sewall lamented the fact that it was unfortunately the copies on good paper that had been destroyed. The William Ware copy of the hymnbook that the church possesses is on the inferior paper. Ware arrived in New York in December of 1821, and all of the copies then left were of the inferior stock of cheap rag bond.[8]

---

[8] Henry D. Sewall to W. C. Bryant, May 12, 1821, in Bryant–Godwin Papers, Manuscript Division, New York Public Library.

*William Cullen Bryant by Samuel F. B. Morse. Courtesy of the
Frick Art Reference Library and the National Academy of Arts*

The first notice of the publication of the new hymnal was in the
Christian Disciple by the editor Henry Ware, Jr. The January-February issue of 1821 took notice of the publication, and then postponed a
long review until a later issue. Ware, however, praised the hymnbook
and recommended its adoption. In the September-October issue of
1821, Ware wrote a long review not only of Sewall's hymnal but also
of a new hymnal out of Andover. Of Sewall's, Ware said he did not
"know of a hymnbook which we think better adapted to serve the ends
of worship. . . . It embraces a large circle of subjects, and thus seems
to furnish something appropriate to all the feelings and topics which

belong to religious service." Ware said that it was a hymnbook of a "calm, rational piety." His highest commendation was that "There is not a vestige of sectarianism in it. It deals out no disputed dogmas. It recognizes none of the religious differences that divide the Christian church." Ware felt that not even Unitarian doctrines were contained therein. "It would seem as if our public devotions at least should have no savour of party in them, but be such as all can join in, though it is not possible in this way to satisfy all. It is certainly the only principle which Unitarians can, with any consistency, adopt." [9]

In this review, Henry Sewall is clearly named as the compiler. Ware suggested that Sewall got his hymns largely from Watts, Doddridge, and Mrs. Steele. Henry Ware then mentioned that the original poems are 15 in number, "Some of them possess great merit. In several, as the 29th, 73rd, 129th, 157th and 373rd [the Bryant hymns], we think we trace plainly the same hand, and that an uncommonly poetical one." Ware thought that some of this poetry was too fine for the sanctuary. But he did not reveal Bryant as the author. Next, he discussed the fact that Mr. Sewall altered over 100 of the 504 hymns.

Sewall's fondest dreams were realized (perhaps partially by the destruction of the fire) and the hymnbook was published in a second edition in 1824 with fuller indices and with Bryant's poems restored to their original version.[10]

The hymnal is a small book in spite of the 504 hymns it contains. There is no music, as was the custom of hymnbooks of that period, only words. There are 13 different metres of poetry, and any good organist or song leader could select hymn tunes with which the congregation was familiar, and put the words to this music. We know from William Ware's hymnbook, which contains the order of service used both morning and evening, that three hymns were sung during the service: one to begin the service after the organ voluntary, one immediately before the sermon, and one following the sermon.

The publication of the second edition of the hymnbook gave rise to some controversy, not particularly from the orthodox who simply ignored it but, strangely, among the Universalists. After the publication of the second edition, this controversy appeared in the *Christian Tele-*

[9] Henry Ware, Jr., *The Christian Disciple,* September-October 1821, pp. 360–364.
[10] Two copies of the second edition of the hymnal are in the New York Public Library. All Souls Church owns William Ware's copy of the first edition.

scope and in the *Christian Inquirer,* both Universalist publications. Abner Kneeland, an outspoken Universalist minister, later jailed in Boston for sixty days for allegedly blaspheming God in some of his writings, spoke out for the hymnbook. He added some additional hymns and recommended it to his society. The more orthodox David Pickering preferred a different hymnal for the Universalists. The controversy sputtered in the journals for some months: some of the Universalists claimed to find doctrines of eternal punishment in the words of the hymnal; others professed to find doctrines of a judgment day, purgatory, and endless misery for sinners in the words.[11]

Henry Wilder Foote, who devoted a good deal of his life to Unitarian hymnody, said, "Henry D. Sewall's *Collection of Psalms and Hymns,* 1820, commonly called 'The New York Collection,' was *one of the best* early hymnbooks." A second edition was published in 1824, but editions in those days were limited to a thousand or so copies. There were no further printings. Sewall had hoped that his hymnal might be suitable for all Unitarian churches and might be adopted by many of them. In this he was to be disappointed, for so far as we know, only the churches in Charleston, South Carolina, and Baltimore, Maryland, officially adopted the Sewall hymnal in addition to its use at the New York church. Sewall himself moved to Watertown, New York, in 1827 and drifted away from the Unitarian faith. We must assume that the useful life of his hymnal was short-lived even in the New York church. There is no indication in the church minutes exactly how long the hymnal was used.[12]

[11] *The Christian Telescope,* April 8, 22, May 20, 1826; *The Christian Inquirer,* April 15, May 6, 1826.

[12] Henry Wilder Foote to the author, January 8, 1958.

*William Ware's Sketch of the First Church, from His "Pew Book"
(c. 1825). Courtesy of the New-York Historical
Society, New York City*

6. A Period of Controversies

ALMOST IMMEDIATELY AFTER THE CHURCH WAS FOUNDED it became the target of certain ministers of New York City who saw in the establishment of the new church the beginnings of a Christian heresy that should not be tolerated.

The first of these attacks was to be answered on the part of the Unitarians of New York City by one of the ablest ministers of the day, Henry Ware, Jr., of the Second Church in Boston. Having delivered the morning sermon for the church on April 30, 1820, he attended services at the Reformed Presbyterian Church that evening. Perhaps because only the day before the new Unitarian society had loudly proclaimed its presence by laying the cornerstone for its new edifice, the Rev. Mr. Alexander McLeod included in his sermon that evening some disparaging remarks about Unitarians.

Aroused, Ware went to hear McLeod again the next Sunday evening, only to hear stronger and more pointed remarks directed against the new society. For his second sermon on May 7th, McLeod had taken the passage of Scripture which had been inscribed on a plate and placed under the cornerstone of the new church: "This is life eternal, to know thee the only true God, and Jesus Christ whom thou hast sent." This time, McLeod alluded directly to the new group and to the ceremony held the previous week.[1]

Both irked and inspired, Ware retired to his quarters that evening and set himself directly to the task of composing a reply. This was published on May 11th in the form of a pamphlet containing two letters addressed to McLeod, just four days after McLeod had de-

[1] John 17:3.

livered his second sermon. Ware sent a copy of the pamphlet to Mc-
Leod with a respectful covering note.

McLeod replied by sending Ware a copy of his *Sermons on True
Godliness* and observing — accurately enough — "Your religious principles are as different from mine, as are those of Zoroaster from
the faith of Abraham." But on March 14th, McLeod preached a
third and sharper sermon in which some of the most distinguished
professors of Unitarianism were singled out as targets. And there the
first controversy ended.[2]

But there was no Henry Ware, Jr., present when the Unitarians
were attacked a second time within a few months. This time the laymen of the church were able to carry on the controversy themselves,
with great ability, and showed themselves to be familiar with theological subtleties. The attacks backfired, for three of the most prominent
and eminent members of the church were inspired to join the new
society because of the absurdity of the attacks: Jonathan Goodhue
and Robert and Catharine Sedgwick.

The controversy began in one of New York's newspapers, the
Commercial Advertiser, of July 8, 1820, when the newspaper published — "as a curious historical document" — a paper on Unitarianism and Mahometanism. The article had been given them by the
Rev. Henry James Feltus, a prominent Episcopalian minister and
rector of New York's St. Stephen's Church.[3]

When one reads the document that was printed in the *Commercial Advertiser,* one gains more of an impression of what the editor
meant when he called the document "curious." It contained an accusation that, during the reign of Charles II, the Unitarians of England had opened negotiations with the Mahometans through the
medium of the English Ambassador of the Emperor of Morocco. Dr.
Joseph Priestley, said Mr. Feltus, at that time treated this accusation
with contempt and as an invention to bring the Unitarians into dis-
repute. However, said Mr. Feltus, "The evidence of this extraordinary
fact is still preserved in the Archepiscopal Library at Lambeth in
Folio 673 among the *Codices Manuscripts Tenisonioni.*"

[2] John Ware, *Memoir of the Life of Henry Ware, Jr.* (Boston, 1846), p. 120.
[3] *Commercial Advertiser,* July 8, 1820. For Feltus' biography see the Rev.
George Haws Feltus, *The Feltus Family Book* (Elmhurst, N.Y.: privately printed,
1917), pp. 11–12.

On July 17, 1820, the second round of the controversy began. The *Commercial Advertiser* tried to wriggle out of publishing any reply by the Unitarians on the grounds that the early publication had merely been that of "an interesting historical document" and that it had not been meant to wound Unitarians. It objected to the reply to Mr. Feltus which had been written by a group of Unitarians, because it was anonymous. Then, the paper promised to publish the reply in full if it were signed as was the original article, by one person.

An editorial in the *Advertiser* summarized the arguments of the reply which had been received. It rested on two points: (1) "That there is nothing bordering upon conclusive evidence, that the document said to have been communicated by the Socinians of London, ... is genuine," and (2) "That even if such a document were presented to the Ambassador from Morocco, it ought not, at the present day, to be brought up as a charge against the Unitarians, because it was a visionary project of some few Socinians." [4]

Henry Sewall immediately resubmitted the Unitarian reply. He deplored that it was necessary to bring his name into the controversy, "a man of business ... may feel a strong reluctance at being brought before the public as a controversialist, and it was on this account that the author's name was not before given you." The article was printed in full. Sewall wrote that "Unitarians do not fear free discussion: They have no reason to do so, for experience has not taught them that it is unfavorable to the prevalence of what they deem the pure and simple truths of uncorrupted Christianity."

Sewall then proceeded to discuss at length what the editor of the *Advertiser* had already mentioned as his two arguments, some real question as to the genuineness of the document, and even if it were genuine why should the work of a few Socinian zealots be used against New York Unitarians in 1820? Henry Sewall concluded by expressing the hope "that criminations of this sort will not be favored by Christians of any party. They cannot elucidate the truth. The questions between us are indeed important — they are to be settled by the *Word of God,* and by that alone." Appropriately, as if to detach himself from Henry Feltus's accusation of being a Moslem, he signed the article, having already given his name in the attached letter, as "An Unitarian Christian." [5]

[4] *Commercial Advertiser,* July 17, 1820.
[5] *Ibid.,* July 18, 1820. For Henry D. Sedgwick's part in writing this reply

This argument in the *Commercial Advertiser* was not the end of the matter. Henry Sewall wrote another article which, since the pages of the *Advertiser* had been denied the controversy, was published in pamphlet form. The Rector of St. Stephen's Church replied with another pamphlet.[6]

A careful reading of Henry Sewall's pamphlet shows that this time it must be entirely his own work. It carries the controversy further than the newspaper articles. After some minor cavils, Sewall went into details about the attempt of this Socinian group in England to negotiate an alliance with the disciples of Mahomet in the year 1682. He questioned the authenticity of the letter which purported to prove this. Sewall implied that the letter was really an effort by the Socinians to convert the Moslems, and not a proposal of an alliance. It was a misguided individual attempt and did not represent the opinion of the great body of Unitarians a century and a third later.

Even assuming that the letter was genuine, said Sewall, and assuming that all of the English Unitarians were in sympathy with the attempt to convert the Ambassador, "they believed . . . that the Mahometans approached nearer on one point to the true faith, in holding the proper unity of God, than many Christians. Every Unitarian must believe the same; and it is quite unnecessary to search the manuscripts of the Lambeth Library to prove the fact." [7]

At this point, the missionary spirit of the early Unitarians in New York is made manifest, for attached to the attack on Henry Feltus is a four-page description of what Unitarians really believe. Since their opinions and beliefs had been attacked and misrepresented this pamphlet gave this energetic layman a chance to explain what Unitarians really believe. The reader is referred in a footnote to the Channing address at Jared Sparks' ordination. But Sewall's own statement is such a concise and excellent document that it might well serve as a summary of the Baltimore sermon.

In his reply, Feltus came to grips with Henry Sewall's argument that such principles ought not to be applied to the Unitarians of the present

---

see Henry D. Sewall to Henry D. Sedgwick in Boston, July 18, 1820, in Henry D. Sedgwick Papers, Massachusetts Historical Society.

[6] Henry D. Sewall, *Reply to the Rev. Henry J. Feltus, Rector of St. Stephen's, on the Alliance of Unitarianism and Mahometanism: With the Unitarians' Appeal* (New York: C. W. Van Winkle, 101 Greenwich Street, 1820).

[7] *Ibid.*, p. 16.

time. He disagreed with Sewall that this was a document aimed to convert the Mohammedans. He claimed that the "Unitarian creed, as a system is in perpetual variation." He quoted Dr. Priestley concerning his religious pilgrimage, claiming that Priestley himself said that he was first a strict Calvinist, a High Arian, a Low Arian, a Socinian, and finally a Low Socinian. He quoted Priestley as saying in 1787 that he "does not know when his creed will be fixed." Feltus added that "This last sentiment may, perhaps, be applied without breach of charity to the Unitarians as a body." Yet he maintained that the more permanent convictions of the Unitarians could make the Unitarians and the Mohammedans "Your nearest fellow worshippers." This reply concluded the second controversy.[8]

A pamphlet printed in New York in the year 1821, probably shortly after the Feltus controversy, is called *An Impartial Investigation of the Nature and Tendency of the Unitarian Doctrines,* by a "Friend of Truth." The authorship of this 20-page pamphlet is unknown. The pamphlet was written in an attempt to be rational and not rhetorical about the new doctrine. Its opening sentence was also its conclusion: "The Unitarian or Socinian system of religion is one of the most dangerous any individual can embrace; especially if he makes any pretensions whatever to the Christian Religion." [9]

The unknown author felt that the very words that "have proceeded out of their mouths shall condemn them." He summarized the things about the Savior that the Unitarians denied: (1) that he had no existence before his incarnation; (2) that he is not Creator; (3) that he is not God the Father; (4) that he is not the Almighty, the all-wise Jehovah; (5) that he is not the proper object of religious worship; (6) that he had no preeminence over his brethren; (7) that the atonement which he made was not the cause of God's being reconciled to man; (8) that the punishment of the damned is not eternal; and (9) that there is no such thing as a Trinity in unity in the Godhead. To each of these nine statements which the author

---

[8] Rev. Henry J. Feltus, *Historical Documents and Critical Remarks on Unitarianism and Mahometanism in Reply to Henry D. Sewall* (New York: William A. Mercein, 93 Gold Street, 1820), pp. 21–22.

[9] A Friend of Truth, *An Impartial Investigation of the Nature and Tendency of the Unitarian Doctrines* (New York, 1821).

claimed Unitarians believed, he gave a positive answer, quoted Scripture, and averred the truth of the typical orthodox doctrines.

His Trinitarian doctrines however, are a little confused in their historical context, at least as regards the orthodox doctrine of the Trinity as espoused at Nicea and other church councils, which leads one to believe that the author was a layman or a poorly educated minister. For example, no good Trinitarian would aver that Jesus was the "all-wise Jehovah." Jesus in orthodoxy is of the same nature as the all-wise Jehovah, but a different Person. Jesus similarly is not the Father. He is of the same substance, in the orthodox opinion, but a different Person. All in all, the pamphlet was a sensible and rational answer to the Unitarians and not the rantings of the ministers that made the headlines in the early controversies. Exactly how this pamphlet related to the new church is not known.

The ink had scarcely dried on these earlier pamphlets when an attack against the Unitarians came from another quarter, this time from the Presbyterians. The Rev. Gardiner Spring, the minister of the Brick Presbyterian Church, was asked to give a sermon to the New England Society of New York City in celebration of the two hundredth anniversary of the landing of the Pilgrims. On the 22nd of December 1820, he delivered his sermon before the New England Society. About two-thirds of the way through the sermon, Dr. Spring began to express strong anti-Unitarian sentiments. In their publications the Unitarians had been scorning the Presbyterians and others for their emphasis upon revivalism and the public conversion experience. The Unitarians were suspicious of these purported visitations of the Holy Spirit which they claimed had no place in a sober and intellectual religion.

Spring believed firmly in the methods of revivalism which then were dominating some American churches, was a thorough Calvinist, and he and his church belonged to the conservative branch of the Presbyterians. At the time of his attack upon the Unitarians, he was a young man, just 36 years of age. He was to spend the rest of his life at the Brick Church, building a new edifice at Fifth Avenue and Thirty-seventh Street in 1858.

In his sermon, Spring bemoaned the fact that this new Unitarian faith was a very different one "for which our fathers bid adieu their native land." He continued, "There is something in the apostacy of these latter times to be bitterly bewailed. . . . But we dare not suppress the fact and to us it is a source of the heaviest grief that many of the sons of the Pilgrims have forsaken the Lord, have provoked the Holy One of Israel to anger, are gone away backward."

He foresaw only doom and disaster in this degeneracy of the sons: "Little do the advocates of liberal religion and morality anticipate the influence of their views on future generations, or suspect that they are devoting their offspring to a system of faith and practice that will plant thorns on their dying pillow, and embitter their reflections throughout eternity." [10]

This was not to be the end of the discussion. When Sedgwick and others who had attended the meeting of the New England Society heard the charges, two members of the church called upon the Rev. Dr. Spring the day after the celebration and requested a copy of his remarks. They told him that their feelings had been hurt; they could not disguise this fact, and they presumed that he would not refuse a copy of what he had said so that they could be accurate in their refutation.

Dr. Spring said that he would take their request under "serious consideration," and appointed an interview with the same gentlemen the following Monday. When the two gentlemen waited upon Dr. Spring at the appointed time they were handed a note: "Gentlemen, The object of your call on Saturday evening, was of so extraordinary a character, and I am sorry to say, was presented with so little civility, and so much menace, as to impose upon me the painful obligation of declining to comply with your request." That same evening the two men returned a note to Dr. Spring saying that they meant no uncivility, and again asked for a copy of Dr. Spring's remarks.[11]

They received no reply (although the whole was later printed at Dr. Spring's initiative), so Sedgwick outlined in his pamphlet what the minister had said at the New England Society. Actually, it was a

---

[10] Rev. Gardiner Spring, *A Tribute to New England: Sermon Delivered Before the New England Society of the City and State of New York, December 21, 1820* (New York: L. and F. Lockwood, 1821), pp. 40 and 44.

[11] Henry D. Sedgwick, *On the Charges Made Against the Religion and Morals of the People of Boston and Its Vicinity by the Rev. Gardiner Spring, D.D. A Sermon Preached Before the New England Society of New York, December 22, 1820* (New York: printed by C. S. Van Winkle, 101 Greenwich Street, 1820).

fair summary of what Dr. Spring later printed as his remarks. But, said Sedgwick, in spite of the fact that they were not anxious for religious controversy, and they tried to be more than "mere sectarians," they felt that a reply was necessary.

What then followed was a direct counterattack upon the reasons for Dr. Spring's attack upon the New Englanders. Sedgwick maintained that the New Englanders did not set up a new religion which was not founded upon the Bible, as Dr. Spring claimed. The exact opposite was instead the truth. He challenged the idea that New England should be cut off from the rest of the country for its "pestilent heresy." Sedgwick defended the character of his fellow New Englanders and stated that one would "find the whole weight and influence of these members exerted in support of order, good government, 'piety, religion, and morality.' "

He was optimistic about the future. "But patience and time will work the remedy for these wrongs. The progress of opinion and religious toleration, has wrested civil power from religious bigotry, and the same progress will assuredly put a termination to such excesses as we now have occasion to lament."

The pamphlet had its influence, at least among Unitarians. William Minot, Henry D. Sedgwick's brother-in-law, wrote from Boston, "I read the . . . copy of your pamphlet. . . . The few copies which have reached Boston have been pretty extensively circulated & met with unqualified approbation. . . . It can well be of much service to the cause of liberal religion in your city." [12]

Henry Ware, Jr., made his reply to the new attack. Under an article titled, "Notice of some attacks upon liberal Christians at New York," Dr. Ware recalled to his readers that in the issue for September-October of the previous year he had reviewed the pamphlet of Mr. Feltus "the purpose of which was to show the near alliance between Unitarianism and Mahometanism. . . . To speak plainly . . . there was nothing remarkable about his pamphlet, but its silliness." [13]

Ware then remarked that since the pamphlet of Mr. Feltus there had appeared this Anniversary sermon by the Rev. Dr. Spring:

[12] William Minot to Henry D. Sedgwick, January 15, 1821, in Henry D. Sedgwick Papers, Massachusetts Historical Society.

[13] Henry Ware, Jr., Editor, *Christian Disciple* for January-February 1821, pp. 68–69.

It contains nothing which would give it claims to a moment's attention, except several pages of virulent abuse of New England. The rest
of the discourse is distinguished only by its barrenness and triteness of
thought, its want of propriety in the use of language, a general clum-
siness of expression, and one or two blunders in matters of history. . . .
It is the production of a very ordinary and undisciplined mind; and
if it be true that its writer holds a very considerable rank among the
preachers of New York, we have only to regret that the standard of
preaching is not higher in that city.

Ware then referred to the pamphlet "by a member of the Unitarian
Society at New York." He suggested that it was for sale in the book-
stores. "While there are men among the Unitarians of New York," he
concluded, "who think and write like the author of this pamphlet;
and we know of more than one of their number of whom any city
might be proud; we think they have little to apprehend from any fair
opposition which they are likely to encounter."

Within a year the congregation was subjected to another attack,
again from a Presbyterian, Dr. John Mason, minister of the Scotch
Presbyterian Church on Murray Street. Having resigned his New
York pulpit to accept the presidency of Dickinson College in Carlisle,
Pennsylvania, he preached his final sermon on December 2, 1821. In
this he strongly attacked the Unitarians.[14]

Dr. Mason warned his parish in selecting his successor not to
choose a vain or a showy man, or a man of dubious principle. But
even more to be dreaded than such a preacher would be one who was
a traitor to their souls. Dr. Mason left no doubt as to whom he meant:

> Above all things, it is to be devoutly hoped, that you will never invite
> to the "care of your souls" a man who cares nothing about them. I
> mean more particularly, for I would not be misunderstood, a man
> who belongs to that rank of traitors who miscal [sic] themselves "ra-
> tional Christians." Against these men I have ever warned you, as the
> enemies of our Lord Jesus Christ, and all that is valuable in his re-
> ligion, and peculiar in his salvation.

[14] John Mason, "The Evangelistic Ministry Exemplified in the Apostle Paul:
A Sermon Preached in Murray-Street Church, December 2, 1821, on the occasion
of his resigning his charge of his congregation," with an appendix, published by
request (New York: published at the Literary Rooms, Corner of Broad and
Pine streets, Abraham Paul, 1822).

Catharine Sedgwick, who had already left the church of Dr. Mason, was present when he gave his "Resignation" sermon. She wrote to a friend:

I heard Dr. Mason's farewell sermon to his people on Sunday last. It was, on all accounts, a lamentable performance, and, as I thought, indicated considerable debility of mind, as well as almost incurable disease of heart. As usual, he gave the "rational Christians" an anathema. He said "they had fellowship with the devil; no. he would not slander the devil, they were worse," etc. Will you not say, as a pious Catholic once did after a furious attack of the doctor's upon the true Church, — "We must pray for Dr. Mason"? [15]

On January 9, 1822, Catharine wrote to her brother Charles:

Dr. M's intemperate abuse had been published and though it seems to me no more worthy of notice than the ravings of a madman. . . . An appeal from the denunciations of Dr. M to all those who fear God and not man is announced. It is attributed to Mr. Sewall. I believe few persons approve of Dr. M's abuse. But it is a dishonor that this community will not easily efface, that any have been found among them to request its publication. [16]

Sewall's pamphlet, as usual, was highly effective. The laymen of the church could obviously take care of this sort of religious controversy. After summarizing the attacks of Dr. Mason in his pamphlet, Sewall moved into his argument. "A direct attack is made upon the religion of Jesus Christ. That religion is not one of systems, of creeds, and of speculative opinions. It had little to do with opinions. It teaches us to walk humbly before God, and to deal justly and kindly with our fellow men." Sewall then went on to ask what the purpose of the denunciation might have been. He concluded, "Its effect is . . . to prevent free and unbiased inquiry into the truth." [17]

[15] Catharine M. Sedgwick to Mrs. Frank Channing, December 5, 1821, quoted in Mary E. Dewey, *The Life and Letters of Catharine M. Sedgwick* (New York: Harper and Brothers, 1871), p. 146.

[16] Catharine Sedgwick to Charles Sedgwick, January 9, 1822, in Henry D. Sedgwick Papers, Massachusetts Historical Society.

[17] Henry D. Sewall, *An Appeal from the Denunciations of the Rev. Dr. Mason Against Rational Christians: Addressed to All Who Acknowledge the Religion of Jesus Christ, and Fear God Rather Than Man,* by a Unitarian of

Sewall pointed out that Mason's arguments confuted themselves. If, as Mason said, "Rational Christians or Unitarians are worse than the Devil," then this meant that Mason's position actually was that "the Devil is better than Unitarians, because he is a hypocrite, and they are sincere, because he attempts to make men believe what he does not believe, while they only seek to disseminate their own opinions."

The last portion of the pamphlet is a defense of the usual charge that the Unitarians degrade the person of Jesus because they make him less than the Father. But Sewall declared, "He came as the Ambassador of the Most High. We therefore honour the Son, as we honour the Father. We recognize his credentials and submit implicitly to his authority. We receive his words as the words of God himself. We look for immortality only because he brought it to light." But he maintained that Unitarians do not worship the Christ. It was a convincing polemic, and it gave many who were on the fence or for family reasons had not acknowledged Unitarianism the courage to do so.

Although the sermon and the answer did not appear until December of 1821, the November-December issue of *The Christian Inquirer* contained a full report by Henry Ware, Jr., the editor, of the controversy in New York City. The importance that the Boston Unitarians attached to the controversy is apparent from this article and the space devoted to it. Ware was merciless on both the author and the content of the sermon, and he made the point, which may or may not have been true, that Dr. Mason was resigning under pressure because his congregation was tired of just such vituperous attacks as were contained in the "Sermon of Resignation."

Evidently this attack in December of 1821 was not the first that Dr. Mason had made against the Unitarians, for there is a letter from William Ellery Channing which is clearly dated as March 9, 1821, nine months earlier, in which Channing answered a letter of Henry Dwight Sedgwick about a prior attack by Dr. Mason. Henry had sent to Dr. Channing some extracts from a Mason sermon and Channing was at his most eloquent and finest Christian self when he advised Mr. Sedgwick as to how to deal with such abuse.[18]

New York, published by the New York Unitarian Book Society, Van Pelt and Spear, printers, 1822.

[18] W. E. Channing to Henry D. Sedgwick, March 9, 1821, in Henry D. Sedgwick Papers, Massachusetts Historical Society.

Channing was incensed that such ideas should be uttered in a pulpit, "A place with which we have associated ideas of sanctity, and from which the spirit of Christianity should speak audibly and tenderly." He did not feel "that the church should be turned into a theatre for the exhibition of such ferocious bigotry. This to me is horrible."

What he advised Mr. Sedgwick to do was to let Dr. Mason and his ilk utter all of these obscenities that they desired because they would do no good and would only make it evident that they were bigoted and crude. He felt that the Unitarians in New York should not try to vindicate themselves, "The effect of this preaching would be to excite in upright and ingenuous minds a desire to inquire into the grounds of the unparalleled style of invective." He concluded in typical Channing preaching style: "Let the rage of your persecution be a new motive to watchfulness over your own character and lives." Aside from the defense of their opinions in the pamphlet of Henry Sewall and the article by Henry Ware, Jr., this was exactly what the Unitarians did.

7. A Pastor for the Pulpit

A RATHER CLEAR IMPRESSION as to how things were going at the new church can be gained from a letter by Henry D. Sedgwick to William Ellery Channing in Boston on March 5, 1821, which goes into some detail as to conditions. Evidently William Ware had been candidating for the pulpit, for Sedgwick commented that

> We are very much delighted and edified by Mr. W. Ware. He is in every respect, save only the feebleness of his voice, what we want, and with this exception we should prefer him to any other man.... His voice is strong and fine but wholly undisciplined. He merely reads his sermons & that in a muffled and scarcely distinct manner. One would almost suppose that he read from a manuscript poorly written & with which he was imperfectly acquainted.... Cannot something be done to combat this?[1]

Sedgwick told his friend Channing that the church was tolerably well attended mornings, but that the evening congregation was very small, a problem that was to continue to plague the church. However, the thing that concerned Henry Sedgwick was the continued fulminations of the local clergy against the new congregation.

The church was facing other problems besides partisan attacks and the thorny problem of the choice of a pastor. Their problems appear to have been largely financial; at least, these are the problems which were discussed at the meetings of the trustees. The trustees did not meet until May 7, 1821, and then the only order of business was the finances which were in a rather depressing state. In fact, so de-

[1] Henry D. Sedgwick to W. E. Channing, March 5, 1821, in Henry D. Sedgwick Papers, Massachusetts Historical Society.

pressing that the trustees decided to put off discussing them until June 4th, at which time they decided upon the inevitable.

It had emerged at the annual meeting the preceding November that the operating expenses of the society since its formation were $400 behind what had been collected. Moreover, the congregation was heavily in debt. In addition to the mortgage, the church owed some $7,000 to various creditors who were now pressing for their money. A loan was absolutely necessary to pay these debts; and Townsend, Sewall, and Pearson were appointed to be the committee to arrange such a loan.

The financial reckoning for the trustees came on October 24, 1821, when the committee reported that they had been unable to procure a practical loan on the already heavily mortgaged church. Merely to meet emergencies, Pearson and Sewall had taken out temporary *personal* loans. They proposed that the other trustees lend their names to a longer-term note which would reduce the mortgage owed to the United Insurance Company, repay the amount borrowed by Pearson and Sewall, and cover other demands against the society. Two of the trustees did not agree to this, but the remainder decided to go ahead anyway, relieving the two dissenters of any financial responsibility in the matter.

The society was not in much better financial shape by the time of the annual meeting on November 5, 1821. The moneys received for pews sold or rented (only 57 out of the 161 available) plus gifts to the building committee did not measure up to what was needed by the building committee or by the society to cover current expenses. In addition, there were still some unsettled accounts with past creditors. The members of the society had no satisfactory answers to this serious problem, except to leave the matter in the hands of the struggling trustees. The board was authorized "to make such alterations in the original appraisement of the pews as they may deem expedient" to increase the revenues accruing to the church.[2]

Fortunately, the board was able, in the next week, to get the United Insurance Company to extend the mortgage from $9,000 to $16,000 at the same rate of interest, 6 percent. This gave the church an additional $7,000 to pay creditors and to cover operating expenses, but it by no means put the First Congregational Church into a solvent

[2] All Souls Minute Book, Volume I, pp. 40–41.

The Reverend William Ware by Nathaniel Frothingham. Courtesy of the Unitarian Church of All Souls

financial state. Indeed, the church was to struggle along, unable to make ends meet, for several years to come.

The precarious financial circumstances of the church put the society in a particularly embarrassing position, for at last it had found a candidate for the pulpit who seemed willing to accept it. The candidate had, in all probability, been preaching every Sunday since the church building was reopened in the fall, and may well have filled the pulpit all or a good part of the previous spring after Henry Ware, Jr., left and until the church was closed at the end of July. The lack of a settled minister had imposed all sorts of burdens upon the society and its trustees, and no doubt was seriously retarding the growth of church membership and attendant revenues. And so, finances notwithstanding and having chosen its new trustees, the society proceeded at its annual meeting in 1821 to the choice of a pastor.

The candidate was none other than William Ware, the 24-year-old brother of Henry Ware, Jr., and the son of the famous and illustrious Dr. Henry Ware, Sr., of Harvard. Considering the rather close relationship the society had formed with the younger Henry Ware and with the Harvard Divinity School at Cambridge, it seems reasonable to assume that the New York congregation had had ample opportunity before this, not only to draw upon young William's services from time to time, but also to call him as the permanent minister. Yet nowhere is his name mentioned in the minutes until the meeting of November 12th, when the decision to call him was made official.

Whether out of financial necessity or from some degree of skeptical reserve about young Ware's capabilities, the congregation offered Ware an annual salary of $1,500 — $500 less than had been offered to Brazer the year before — stipulating that this amount would be raised to $2,000 the following year, providing that, in addition to the 57 pews already sold or rented, no less than a third of the remaining pews be taken up by that time. A committee was appointed to carry the invitation to Ware, and on Sunday, November 25th, William Ware's acceptance was read to the congregation at the morning services:

Christian Friends,

    I have received through your Committee a copy of the resolutions by which I have been invited to remain among you as your pastor. To your Committee I replied that as far as I could make up a determination before consulting with my friends at the Eastward, I was willing and ready to take upon myself the trust. I am now able to say that with their full approbation and consent, I accept your invitation. It is with no small degree of solicitude that I consent to assume the responsibility incident to such a situation, for I am not ignorant of the nature and difficulty of the duties it involves, but relying most confidently on your kindness and counsel, and looking for guidance from Him from whom all good desires proceed, I do it cheerfully; and earnestly pray its issues may be for good both to you and me. Be pleased to accept my thanks for the very liberal support you have offered me.

The only request I feel the least disposition to make, is, that I may be allowed some weeks in the first years of my ministry, as a relaxation from the severe duties to which I must be devoted. I will not do it, however, not doubting but you will readily meet my wishes in this respect as occasion may require and so far as they shall be reasonable — more than this I do not require.

With best wishes for your happiness and prosperity, I am

Your friend and servant

William Ware.[3]

The next day, the standing committee met and composed a letter to be sent to all Unitarian churches then established, inviting them to send their ministers and delegates to William Ware's ordination, scheduled for December 18th.

On that day the congregation gathered in the church edifice to ordain and install their new pastor. Thirty-one churches, from Boston to Charleston, South Carolina, had received the invitation, and nine had accepted. At 10 A.M. on the day of the ordination, fourteen men representing these churches gathered in the vestry room of the New York church.

It was an impressive, if small, gathering. Dr. Aaron Bancroft of the Second Parish in the town of Worcester, Massachusetts — one of the earliest pioneers of the "liberal heresy" (before Unitarianism had become an accepted term) and now one of the most eminent exponents of the new faith — was present with a delegate from his society. The venerable Dr. Henry Ware, William's father, and the Rev. Henry Ware, Jr., William's brother, had arrived for the occasion;

[3] A copy of William Ware's acceptance letter is transcribed in the All Souls Minute Book, Volume I, pp. 44–45.

and Dr. Thaddeus Harris, pastor of the church in Dorchester, Massachusetts, since 1793, was another distinguished visitor. James Taylor from Philadelphia also came. Although the Philadelphia church was among the oldest Unitarian churches in the country, having arisen chiefly out of Joseph Priestley's writings and lectures in 1794, it had at this time no professionally trained and ordained clergyman for its pastor. The previous year Mr. Taylor, a layman who had been with the church since its founding, had taken over the leadership of the church and led its worship. John Pierpont, who had been installed in the Hollis Street Church in Boston two years earlier, came with two delegates from his congregation. Dr. Channing was unable to attend, but sent three delegates from his church in Federal Street. Likewise, the Rev. Mr. John Gorham Palfrey of the Brattle Street Church sent as his representative none other than George Bond, the faithful friend and benefactor of the New York society since its founding. And Charles H. Appleton, a distinguished citizen of Baltimore, represented the new Unitarian church in that city.

The council convened to approve, officially, young Ware's qualifications. After opening with a prayer, both the letter of call to William Ware and Ware's answer were read. Then, the certificate of Dr. Kirkland of the University Church in Cambridge was read, stating that William Ware was a member of that church and that he was recommended to the service of the First Congregational Church in New York City. The certificate of S. Willard, Scribe of the Theological Faculty of Harvard, attested that Mr. Ware had completed his theological studies and the certificate of the Rev. Charles Lowell stated that Ware had been approved as a preacher of the Gospel by the Boston Association of Congregational Ministers.

The ordination service itself opened with an introductory anthem, followed by a prayer led by Mr. Taylor of Philadelphia. The ordaining prayer was given by Dr. Harris, and the concluding prayer by Rev. Pierpont, who had also written a hymn for the occasion. Dr. Bancroft charged young Ware with his official responsibilities, and William's brother delivered the Right Hand of Fellowship. The ordaining sermon was preached by the senior Henry Ware, who used a text from Acts 28:22, "But we desire to know of thee, what thou thinkest; for, as concerning this sect, we know that it is everywhere spoken against."

It was an appropriate text, for the elder Ware warned his son that

Portrait of Henry Ware, Sr., Copied by George Fuller from an Original Painting by Frothingham (?). By Permission of Fogg Art Museum, Harvard University

the road ahead for his religious point of view was not going to be an easy one in New York City. The first portion of the sermon supported the right to hold opinions differing from the majority in matters of religion, and traced the recurrent contest between dogma and the

122

freedom to search for truth from the earliest Christian period through the present times.

In the second portion of the sermon, Ware informed his son and the congregation of their sacred duty not to let their opinions be imperfectly understood. It was their duty to explain the grounds of their faith adequately. But in doing this, Dr. Ware warned, they should proceed in a manner which did "not bring reproach upon the cause. ... It is our duty to be gentle and courteous," he said, "to exemplify the principles and spirit upon which we profess to act." Dr. Ware made this point a strong one, saying that "we must not, in our zeal to defend and support the articles of our belief, forget that the great end of religion is personal holiness." [4]

In the third portion of his sermon, the elder Ware addressed himself directly, and almost prophetically, to his son, expounding upon the solemn and weighty burdens of the office he was undertaking. He pointedly urged young William "not to feed on a gloomy imagination," but to exert his motives "to greater zeal, and activity, and diligence, that you may ... fill worthily the place which providence has allotted you."

Finally, to the society, Dr. Ware expressed his felicitations upon the successful completion and fruition of its enterprise thus far, and praised the members for their courageous and unostentatious efforts to sustain their beliefs in the midst of a hostile environment "without touching the rights, or disturbing the prejudices of others, as sincere and as conscientious as yourselves."

A correspondent in the *Christian Register,* anonymously called "S.A.," added some details about the festivities afterwards. "After the services, the ordaining council, with the male members of the society, partook of a dinner provided for them at the Mansion-House Hotel, on Broadway; during which time two hymns were sung, and many sentiments expressed suitable to the occasion." [5]

§ § §

The new pastor of the First Congregational Society was born in

---

[4] Henry Ware, *A Sermon Delivered at the Ordination of the Rev. William Ware to the Pastoral Charge of the First Congregational Church in New York,* second edition (New York: Library and Tract Society, First Congregational Church, 1821), p. 16.

[5] *Christian Register,* December 28, 1821.

Hingham, Massachusetts, on August 3, 1797, the youngest of three sons born to Henry Ware and Mary Clark Ware. His father was the minister of the First Church in Hingham and noted for his liberal religious views. Although more and more New England congregations were coming to embrace anti-Trinitarian ideas when William and his oldest brother, Henry, Jr., were born, Unitarianism in this country did not officially exist. But when, in 1805, their father was appointed to fill the post of Hollis Professor of Divinity at Harvard, which had recently been vacated by the death of Dr. David Tappen, the split between the liberal-minded clergy and orthodox Christian ministers was dramatized.[6]

In writing about the Ware family, it is customary to speak only of the paternal side of the family. But William Ware also had a distinguished ancestry on his mother's side. Mary Clark's grandfather was the Rev. Jonas Clark, a Congregational clergyman who for fifty years was pastor of the First Parish Church in Lexington, Massachusetts. Almost everything of importance that happened in Lexington during the Revolutionary period bore the stamp of the personality of Jonas Clark. He was a close friend and advisor of Samuel Adams and John Hancock. After the battle of Lexington, his house was thrown open to care for the wounded and dying. Mrs. Ware and her three sisters married ministers; Lydia married the Rev. Benjamin Greene of Berwick, Maine; Martha married the Rev. William Harris, later connected with Columbia University; and Lucy married the Rev. Thaddeus Fisk, D.D., of West Cambridge. It was a very distinguished family, and William and Henry, Jr., had ministerial influences on both sides of the family.[7]

When William Ware later moved to New York, the fact that the young Unitarian preacher not only had New England connections with Harvard and the Unitarians but also had connections in New York with the Rev. William Harris, a prominent Episcopalian and the president of Columbia College, certainly did not hurt his acceptance by the community.

The Ware family moved to Cambridge in June 1805, when Wil-

[6] See *Dictionary of American Biography.*

[7] See John Clark, *Records of the Descendents of Hugh Clark of Watertown, Mass., 1640–1866* (Boston: privately printed, 1866). See also *Dictionary of American Biography.*

liam was only seven years old. When they had been settled in their new quarters barely a month, William's mother died. William's brother Henry, too, was in precarious health during his early childhood. Thus, William was acquainted with hardship, uncertainty, and grief during the formative years of his life.

The senior Henry Ware was a man of amiable charm and well loved for his compassionate disposition as well as for his impressive intellect. Andrew Preston Peabody wrote that "His family discipline must have been, almost beyond precedent for his time, gentle and mild."

Perhaps because he had the tender and devoutly religious care of his mother for a longer period of his childhood, young Henry seems to have suffered no ill effects from these circumstances; very early in his childhood he reflected a marked inclination to follow in his father's footsteps. By contrast, William was born when his mother's physical energies were already well on the decline; and he suffered her loss at an emotionally much more vulnerable period in his life. All of the six children who survived Mrs. Ware tended to lean the more heavily upon the remaining parent, but Professor Ware's duties at the college were such as to diminish the amount of attention he might otherwise have paid his offspring.

When William was ten, his father married for the second time, but the woman died eight days later. Dr. Ware married a third time a short while later, probably late in 1807 or the early part of 1808, and sired ten more children, nineteen in all.

William spent the early part of his college-preparatory years under the tutelage of his cousin, Ashur Ware, in Cambridge, probably living at home with his father, stepmother, and his brother Henry, who was at that time attending Harvard College. Later, William went to live with his brother-in-law, the Rev. Joseph Allen, in Northborough, Massachusetts, who continued to prepare William for college. Mr. Allen described William at that time as "slow in coming to maturity" and as "uncommonly diffident and self-distrustful, greatly underrating his powers, and never doing himself justice in his public performances." [8]

William entered Harvard in 1812, the same year his brother Henry

[8] Joseph Allen, quoted in William B. Sprague, *Annals of the American Pulpit* . . . , Volume VIII (New York, 1865), p. 513.

graduated. Following much the pattern and tone of the letters his father had written to him, Henry, Jr., wrote to William in October of that year:

> I wish to speak seriously with you, for you are entering on four years, that may be happy or miserable, that will bring you good or evil, as you choose. And, as I have lately passed over the ground . . . and know its dangerous places . . . I am particularly anxious that you should start out right. . . . The path of your duty is plain. . . . Let your resolution not flag, but walk straight forward, and justify the hopes of your father and friends.[9]

The tone of this and other of Henry's letters to William, compared with specimens of Henry's letters to the middle brother, John (who became a physician), leads us to conclude that Henry and John were close, rather like friends, and that William was very much on the outskirts of close family relationships. William seems to have been forever the object of gently intended but sternly admonishing remarks from his eldest brother as well as from his father, both of whom he may have been seeking to emulate, and both of whose approval he was no doubt seeking to gain.

Upon graduation from Harvard in 1816, William went to Hingham to assist in a school there directed by the Rev. Henry Colman and to pursue his theological studies with the clergyman. After a year with Mr. Colman, William returned to Cambridge to continue his professional studies, working part of the time in the town school, and later, as assistant to Andrews Norton, then the librarian of Harvard. William preached for the first time in 1820, in Northborough, Massachusetts, where his sister's husband, Joseph Allen, was the resident minister. From then on, Ware continued to preach in various places, chiefly in Brooklyn, Connecticut; Burlington, Vermont; and then in New York at the First Congregational Church. About the same time that the New York society was deciding to call him, Ware received a call from the Burlington church, but, on the advice and actually the pushing, of his brother and friends, he accepted the New York church.

In the Henry Ware Papers in the Massachusetts Historical Society, there is a letter from William Ware to his future wife, Mary

---

[9] Henry Ware, Jr., quoted in John Ware, *Memoir of the Life of Henry Ware, Jr.* (Boston, 1846), p. 42.

Waterhouse, dated February 20, 1821, written while he was preaching for several weeks in New York City. Ware was impressed with the city and felt that he had "received more new impressions, & had more new notions engendered in the past week than in all my life put together." He found novelty on every side, "strangely shaped buildings & strangely dressed men & women, new fashions, new manners, new politics, . . . I have explored some of the knottiest & filthiest parts of the City." He found the church filled at the evening service. But he also found that controversy waxed hot as Dr. Mason, "both prays and preaches us down." William expected to stay in New York for four Sundays, but certainly no longer. "Why in the name of common sense should I be compelled to stay here against my own inclination?" Had he been induced to stay by his father and his brother? [10]

It seems strange that a young man who had this reaction to the city would accept a call from a new church in New York to presumably spend his lifetime there. But William Ware was now, for better or for worse, the minister of the First Congregational Church in the city of New York.

[10] William Ware, New York, to Mary Waterhouse c/o Henry Ware, Boston, February 20, 1821, in Henry Ware Papers, Massachusetts Historical Society.

8. The Early Years of Ware's Ministry

NOW THAT THE FIRST CONGREGATIONAL CHURCH had both its own building and its own minister, things seemed to go more smoothly for the society. The accounts for the year 1821 had balanced out to no more than about $550 in the red, and this deficit was easily charged against the contingency fund. Several benefactors, both in New York and in Boston, relinquished interest or other moneys due them. Peter Brooks of Boston, who lent the society money for its building fund, yielded the $44.25 in interest owing to him, and Luther Clark, a member who was moving out of the city, gave up his pew without requiring that the church refund the money due him.[1]

At this same time, George Bond of Boston sent the congregation an elegant clock which was installed in the sanctuary. According to Rafael Torres, sexton of All Souls for the past 45 years, the clock had a long gold chain by which it was wound and which hung down some two feet below the clock itself. Bond's gift lasted for over a century and, even today, as noted previously, the present clock in the sanctuary bears the original cedar-and-gold-leaf numerals. Early in 1822, the society also received a vase of Egyptian black marble as a gift from Elbert Anderson of New York. This handsome present was used as a baptismal font. By early 1822, sales and rentals of pews had increased, and the trustees voted to increase Ware's salary an unexpected $250 to $1,750 for the first year.

These material good fortunes notwithstanding, the early years of Ware's ministry were fraught with difficulties. From the start of his ministry, Ware had found himself isolated from his fellow clergymen,

---

[1] Clark returned a year later, however, and requested that the money he'd relinquished be used to pay for his new pew!

and, as predicted by his father at his ordination, he was constantly on the defensive for his church and its religious convictions. This theological climate represented a marked departure from that which William had known in New England. The New England Unitarians tended to comprise a large but close clan, bound not only in their theological outlook, but also in their marriages and social interrelationships which prevailed among New England ministerial families. By contrast, in New York there were no opportunities even to exchange pulpits, and William's social life was limited to those friends he could make among his congregation. Week after week, Ware ascended his own pulpit to preach not one, but two, Sunday services.

Nothing was known about the regular order of services of the early church until the church recently purchased William Ware's copy of Henry Sewall's hymnbook. This book has notations in it written as early as 1821, so it appears safe to assume that the order of services penned in the front of the book by William Ware's own hand is, in fact, the order used in the early days of the church. The service as indicated is almost austere in its simplicity, beginning with an organ voluntary, then a hymn from Sewall's Collection, and then the prayer which tended to be very long and in many cases extemporaneous. A reading from the Scriptures, usually a passage from the Old and the New Testaments, followed.

Early Unitarians believed that the Bible was the Word of God. That is the reason the pulpit was in the center of the sanctuary, and here the minister read from the Word of God, and preached about that Word. Then followed another hymn. After this came the sermon. We can understand why William Ware felt that this was so important. The brevity of the rest of the service indicates that the sermon was given a primary emphasis. It was really the sermon which the congregation came to hear. At first, following the sermon there was a collection and some organ music. But William Ware crossed out this part of the service in his hymnbook, probably because it was given up. In its place came another hymn followed by a concluding prayer and the benediction. We have no idea of the length of the service except that the sermon may have taken from forty-five minutes to an hour and a quarter.

There is a little note at the bottom of the page in William Ware's hymnbook which reads, "Same morning and evening." One of the reasons that the evening services may have lagged was the sheer fact that the service was as long as the morning service, and such length may very well have discouraged those who attended the long service in the morning from returning in the evening.

William leaned heavily on his brother for advice. Sometime in February 1822, he wrote to Henry saying that he thought his preaching might be improving, and asked his brother to direct him to some books and other source materials which might help him with a course of sermons he was planning. The series was to be of a controversial nature, and William was particularly unsure of himself in preaching controversial sermons.

Henry answered:

> Your plan for a course of sermons I think excellent; but I really cannot at once direct [you] to books which may help you. . . . The best aid you will derive from reading over and over . . . the books of the New Testament.
>
> As to Controversial Preaching, to be sure, it is less pleasant, and, for the main purpose, less profitable; but, in your situation, absolutely necessary. . . . Only never forget to be scrupulously good natured and squeamishly fair. The most detestable thing on earth is bad passion and unfairness in the pulpit.[2]

William's reply to this letter is implied in his brother's next letter:

> . . . As to a settled order of controversial discourses, . . . you must be guided entirely by views of expediency in your situation. . . . As to your plan, I fear you will find some serious difficulties. First, it is impossible that it should be *fully* executed; for such an introduction of texts . . . could not be brought forward except in a long series of sermons, which would stand a chance of being dry, from the inevitable accumulations of Scripture quotations. Secondly, you would be obliged to examine every text which is accounted strong on the other side.
>
> This leads to another remark; you like your plan because it forbids repetition. I dislike it for that very reason. Repetition is very necessary. . . .[3]

When the hot summer arrived, the trustees decided on July 1, 1822, that since "the insulated situation of the First Congregational

---

[2] Henry Ware, Jr., quoted in John Ware, *Memoir of the Life of Henry Ware, Jr.* (Boston, 1846), p. 142.

[3] *Ibid.*, pp. 144–145.

Church affording no opportunity of relief to the pastor by exchanges," the afternoon services might be discontinued for the remainder of the summer. But late in the summer of 1822, an unexpected piece of ill luck befell the city and the church. An epidemic of yellow fever hit New York, causing "the depopulation of a great part of the City." The society finally was forced to close the church altogether until November 3rd. If any members of the congregation were overcome by the epidemic, it is not recorded, but certainly the plague severely curtailed revenues anticipated from Sunday collections and other sources. A less disastrous consequence of the epidemic was the delay in holding the annual meeting, which took place on November 18, 1822, instead of the customary first Monday in the month.[4]

James Byers, Elihu Townsend, and George Dummer, who had held office for three years, had now come to the end of their term, and were replaced with Pearson, Sewall, and Thomas J. Cary. Pearson and Sewall had faithfully performed the offices of treasurer and clerk of the society through all these years. Now, Pearson had absolutely refused to carry on for another term as treasurer. Thus, Benjamin Armitage, who had gone off the board the previous year, was appointed to that post, while Henry Sewall continued as secretary as well as in his new office of trustee. Roger Van Polanen was elected as president of the board at the first trustees meeting, while Pearson and William Russel formed the remainder of the standing committee. These, then, were the chief officers of the church when Ware started his second year in the parish.[5]

A letter dated December 2, 1822, from Henry brought words of praise and encouragement to his brother:

> I rejoice at the spirit in which you seem to begin your winter's work.
> I have never yet doubted you, and doubt you less and less daily.

But now William's eyes were giving him trouble, and he was still struggling with his style of preaching. He had to write two different sermons each week, one for the morning service and another for the evening. He would begin writing both early in the week, laboring over them constantly until Sunday, in order that he might thoroughly familiarize himself with each of them. He had Henry's endorsement for this mode

[4] All Souls Minute Book, Volume I, pp. 50, 57.
[5] For an account of Thomas Cary, see Appendix C, pp. 253–254.

*Elihu Townsend by Elkanah Tisdale. From the
Collections of the New Haven Historical Society*

of practice, but as Henry was able to write his sermons only the Saturday before he delivered them, and then spoke them brilliantly, this
endorsement was probably of little comfort to William.[6]

Many of the testimonials which come to us from those who knew
William claim that he should never have gone into the ministry; that
his natural talents and inclinations lay elsewhere. Orville Dewey, who
was to become the minister of the second Unitarian Church to be
established in New York City, said outright in 1863 that "William
Ware was born for another profession than that in which he passed
his life. He should have been an artist, a painter or an author." Similarly, his brother-in-law, the Rev. Joseph Allen, said that William "had
a great love for the fine arts, especially for Music and painting. . . .
He was himself skilled in these delightful arts. Had he, in early life,

---

[6] Henry Ware, Jr., quoted in John Ware, *op. cit.*, p. 146.

Philip Jeremiah Schuyler by Gilbert Stuart.
Courtesy of the New-York Historical Society,
New York City

chosen the vocation of an artist, and devoted himself to it, he might have attained to no ordinary excellence." When William was not arduously laboring over his sermons for the week, or carrying out with exacting self-discipline his other parish duties, he would make some quick sketches which amply proved his talents. "The study walls of his house in New York were covered over with crayon sketches." [7]

As for William's preaching, the Rev. Mr. Allen wrote of his young brother-in-law: "He had more genius, as I think his writings show, than his brother, but fell far below him as a pulpit orator and a parish minister." Dr. Andrew Preston Peabody claimed that, though he'd heard William preach only once, the sermon was delivered with little energy and animation. Henry Ware, Jr., was forever alluding to the dry and dull way in which his brother would deliver his sermons. Wil-

[7] Orville Dewey, quoted in William B. Sprague, *Annals of the American Pulpit . . .*, Volume VIII (Boston, 1865), p. 517.

Mrs. Philip Jeremiah Schuyler by Gilbert Stuart.
Courtesy of the New-York Historical Society,
New York City

liam himself was far from deceiving himself about his abilities as a preacher. Apparently, William recognized the mistake he'd made in choosing his profession, for he confided to Mr. Dewey that, very early in his ministry, he had planned to retire from it as soon as it seemed feasible. But it was Henry who insisted that William remain in his post.[8]

Evidently, the sentiment that William Ware was a poor preacher was not unanimous in the New York church. On January 10, 1823, Catharine Sedgwick wrote to her friend Mrs. Pomeroy in Albany that

> William Ware we think improves constantly. His sermons have a more serious or what is called evangelical character. Religious expression is I think the work of time, and you cannot expect a very young man to be skillful in teaching, as one who is more mature, who knows from personal observation and actual experience the wants of

[8] Joseph Allen, quoted in Sprague, *op. cit.*, p. 513.

human nature and the power of religion. Mr. Ware's character is an excellent one, and I doubt not will abide severe scrutiny. He is so modest and unpretending, his talent is respectable, and his application so steady that he must command every one's respect.[9]

By the beginning of 1823, the affairs of the society had pretty much stabilized. The able Philip J. Schuyler was to be president of the board of trustees for the next three years. The building fund was balanced and the building committee had disbanded, as now only regular payments on the mortgage remained to be made. And with a regular minister and a building basically outfitted for use, the uncertain and sporadic costs of supplying the pulpit and maintaining the premises had also stabilized, with the result that, if the society continued its regular rate of expenditures, it could expect to end up with a $1,000 deficit every year.[10]

As one solution, owners and renters of pews were asked to contribute double the amount they paid for the next several years. Eighteen members did so voluntarily, but even this extra voluntary assessment did not reduce the basic deficit very much. Ware's salary, in accordance with the original agreement was now $2,000 per year. At the annual meeting in 1823, several other members agreed to double their assessments, and Benjamin Armitage gave up his commission on the collection of taxes for the year, which amounted to $69. But these efforts made little dent in the problem, and when William Ware offered to relinquish one-fourth of his salary, that is, to go back to the $1,500 he had originally been given, the trustees gratefully accepted it.[11]

In addition to accepting Ware's offer, the board also cut the salary of Mr. Baldwin, the sexton, from $150 to $100 a year. In fact, so severe were the church's financial affairs, that the trustees even decided to sell some of the church's mahogany chairs.

Early in 1824 the United Insurance Company was again approached for reduction of interest. The company declined, but offered

[9] Catharine M. Sedgwick to Mrs. Pomeroy in Albany, N.Y., January 10, 1823, in Henry D. Sedgwick Papers, Massachusetts Historical Society.

[10] For an account of Schuyler, see Appendix C, pp. 260–262.

[11] William Ware in a letter to the trustees, November 7, 1823, transcribed in the All Souls Minute Book, Volume I, p. 73. See also the trustees' response in the same volume, pp. 74–75.

to extend the loan of $14,000 at the same rate of interest, providing that, in addition to the security of the church building, individual trustees pledged personal bonds. Most of the trustees so pledged themselves, and in this way the original $14,000 owed to the United Insurance Company was extended for an additional six years. The imminent crisis had passed, and from there on the society was to set itself upon firmer financial footing.

Although it is nowhere noted in the minute book, during this year of financial crisis, on June 10, 1823, William Ware was married to

Mary Waterhouse Ware by Nathaniel Frothingham. Courtesy of Malcolm C. Ware

Mary Waterhouse, a daughter of Dr. Benjamin Waterhouse of Cambridge and a sister of the wife of Henry Ware, Jr. The Ware boys had known the Waterhouse girls since childhood, from the time they had moved from Hingham to Cambridge.

William and Mary after their marriage apparently set out to follow in the tradition of his father as regards the production of offspring. They had seven children, all except the youngest born in New York City.[12]

§ § §

One of the first evidences that the new society was interested in a social service project is contained in a letter from Catharine Sedgwick dated January 10, 1823. She wrote to her friend Mrs. Pomeroy in Albany,

> We are just now very busy about establishing a charity school and we hope soon to get it in operation. Our plan is to have it kept in one of the lower rooms of the Church, kept by a woman and superintended by the ladies. We mean to teach the children the rudiments

[12] Henry Ware (July 17, 1824–February 4, 1885); Louisa Lee Ware (April 18, 1826–October 2 or 3, 1890); Mary Harriet Ware (according to the Ware Genealogy born and died on September 21, 1828, but according to All Souls Records baptized on December 7, 1828); Helen Ware (November 3, 1830–April 21, 1835, according to the Ware Genealogy, but the date of death in the All Souls Records is given as March 16, 1835, at age four years and four months); William Ware (August 3, 1832–March 2, 1834); a second William Ware (April 3, 1834, born about a month after his brother William's death, died March 21, 1835); and Frederick Ware (June 3, 1843–1869), who was Doctor of Medicine in the Harvard Class of 1865. [Where these dates differ it would seem prudent to use the All Souls Records rather than the Ware Genealogy, for the All Souls Records are written in the hand of William Ware himself.]

Only three of the seven children survived their father. Only Henry had children, for Louisa never married and Frederick died at Soden, near Frankfurt-Am-Main, four years after his graduation. The sole survivor of William Ware is Mrs. Margaret Ware (Thayer) Lancaster, William's great-granddaughter, who lives (1973) in Cambridge and gave the William Ware Papers to Harvard and the Massachusetts Historical Society and who was married to Southworth Lancaster at Greenwich, Connecticut, on January 17, 1927. [See Emma Forbes Ware, *Ware Genealogy: Robert Ware of Dedham, Massachusetts, 1642–1699, and His Lineal Descendents* (Boston: Charles H. Pope, 1901), p. 335; and Book 2 of All Souls Records, p. 124.]

of learning, of how to mend and make their clothes — darn their stockings. Our society is small, and far from rich, but we hope to accomplish it.[13]

By March of 1823, the trustees received a petition "from some ladies of the Society" proposing that a basement room of the church be used for such a charity school, and the trustees complied. Later that same year, the trustees, perceiving a possible source of new revenues for the church, began to inquire about obtaining two lots behind the church, facing on Reade Street. They felt that possession of these lots would allow them to enlarge their yard space for the children and perhaps to get a subsidy from the New York State education funds.[14]

The cost of renting these lots proved too much for the budget, however, and no action was taken. When, in the fall of 1823, the operating and other costs to the church had stabilized and were found to be running at the rate of a $1,000 deficit per year, the hope of acquiring these lots died altogether, and the free school operated separately, obtaining such funds as it needed from other sources.

In February of 1824, however, Isaac Green Pearson was offered the lease on the lower lot and, fearing the loss of all options on the property if the opportunity was not seized upon at once, he took the liberty of purchasing the lease, bargaining the lessors down from $600 to $410. Arguing that as much as $200 per year might be charged for the basement schoolrooms if they were improved and the yard facilities expanded, Pearson persuaded the board to pass on the purchase. Meanwhile, a committee comprised of Henry Wheaton, Thomas Cary, and Pearson himself, visited the school and found that 68 pupils between the ages of four and fifteen were regularly enrolled. On this basis, the committee filed a petition for a subsidy with the State of New York in July of that year.[15]

Mention of the lots on Reade Street, so avidly desired by Mr. Isaac

[13] Catharine M. Sedgwick to Mrs. Pomeroy, Albany, January 10, 1823, in Henry D. Sedgwick Papers, Massachusetts Historical Society.

[14] Ever since 1801, the state had given money to various churches for the education of poor children. Even when the state organized its own public school system in 1812, it continued to fund the free-school work carried out by the various churches. It was a portion of this money which the trustees of the First Church hoped to receive. See Edward R. Ellis, *The Epic of New York City* (New York, 1966), p. 252.

[15] All Souls Minute Book, Volume I, pp. 79 and 81.

Green Pearson to add to the church property, evidently bothered William Ware, although he approved their purchase. There were cow stables on them and in the summer these did not help the atmosphere of the church. He also indicated that the purchase of these lots would enable the church to build an entrance to the basement rooms from the street. What evidently bothered Ware was that Mr. Pearson also conceived that the lots in a few years might provide a place for a parsonage, and Ware was not at all certain that the neighborhood was the right place for a parsonage; "Reed [*sic*] is a dirty unwholesome place where I could hardly take a house for a gift." [16]

Plans did not work out as neatly as Pearson had envisioned them. Just about the time that the free school was getting its start in the basement rooms of the church, a scandal broke out when it was discovered that some Baptist schools had padded their enrollment books in order to get more than their fair share of state funds, and forced teachers to kick back part of their salaries. By 1825, the state had stopped giving money to any church schools, but handed educational funds over to the city's Common Council, instead. Wheaton, Cary, and Pearson's application with the state was turned down.

Early in February of 1826, the trustees received the following letter from the directresses of the school:

The Directresses of the Free School of the First Congregational Church having understood that the rooms in the Basement of the Church in Chambers Street remain unoccupied and have not been the source of involvement that was anticipated when the School was removed from them, have decided to apply for the gratuitous use of one or both of them. In consequence of the new regulations respecting the School Fund, private free schools will no longer derive any aid from that source and it is thought by many that this appropriation of the rooms is as essential to the welfare of the School as it will be honorable to the Church to which the School belongs.[17]

[16] William Ware to Mary Ware, February 4, 1824, Henry Ware Papers, Massachusetts Historical Society. The name of the street was spelled "Reed" at that time.

[17] All Souls Minute Book, Volume I, pp. 102–103. We believe the directress of the Free School was Miss Maria Forbes. There are several entries in the cash book that Miss Forbes paid the rent on the school, and her occupation is listed in the *City Directories* as "school teacher." She is identified as the head of the school in 1838 by the All Souls Minute Book, Volume I, p. 260.

No doubt embarrassed, the trustees quickly resolved to grant the ladies' application. The Free School continued making free use of the basement rooms for three years, until November of 1829, when it began paying approximately $100 a year. In March 1831, the school's rent was increased to $150 and, two years later, when a letter requested that the church make certain repairs, it was raised finally to the $200 originally anticipated by Pearson in 1824.

It is difficult to reconstruct the history of the Charity School which Catharine Sedgwick spoke of as early as 1823. In the April 1826 *Christian Inquirer,* edited by Barnabus Bates, a member, and published in New York City, there is an interesting article about the annual exhibition of the Charity School. It was evidently supported and operated almost entirely by the ladies of the First Congregational Church. "We were not present, but understand, that the pupils made improvements during the past year, highly creditable to themselves and to their teacher." [18]

Ninety-four children had been educated during the past year and the expense was six shillings per quarter per pupil, or about 75 cents per pupil.

The writer continued,

> We consider this charity as one of the best within our knowledge. It takes children from the streets, where they learn little else but profaneness and vulgarity, and places them in a situation to acquire that kind of knowledge which will make them respectable and useful members of society.... Those who have witnessed in our streets, groups of dirty children, using profane language, and inhaling nothing but vulgarity from the atmosphere around them, may know what these ladies have done for the community by visiting the school..., and viewing the altered habits and decent behavior of the children under their charge.

There was also a library in the basement of the church building that evidently was something more than the typical church library. It also had a missionary purpose. In April of 1823 the *Christian Register* hailed the "flourishing condition of the New York Unitarian Book Society." The editor felt that it was "doing much for the cause of pure and rational christianity by the publication and distribution of

[18] *The Christian Inquirer,* April 15, 1826, pp. 233–234.

religious books." The editor termed it "the best collection in the country of Unitarian tracts and pamphlets as well as a considerable variety of well-chosen theological works of a larger kind." The Unitarian Miscellany for May 1823 added the names of the committee of five who were managing the library. "Elihu Townsend, Daniel Stanton, James Fox, Henry D. Sewall, Treasurer, and Benjamin Armitage, Jr., Librarian." [19]

The lot acquired by the church for the free school, which was supposed to expand the yard facilities for the children, was actually, because of inadequate drainage, marsh land. Upon this lot stood an abandoned, ramshackle house which the trustees promptly "rented" to Mr. Baldwin, the sexton who had been with the First Congregational Church since its earliest days in "the rooms of Mr. Anderson."

Now, in 1824, just after the purchase of the lot on Reade Street, Mr. Baldwin was given a raise of $25 a year. This raise may have been merely an inducement to Mr. Baldwin to move into the dilapidated dwelling, for once Mr. Baldwin took occupancy of the house, his total yearly wage of $125 was relinquished to the church as rent for his new home. Fortunately, Mr. Baldwin was able to stretch this income into food for himself and his family by doing various extra jobs around the church, such as blowing the bellows for the organ, cleaning the church, making various minor repairs, and so forth.

Mr. Baldwin had lived in this house for little more than a year, when he finally got up the nerve to beg the board to make some restorations. Seeing that improving the house might be an excellent way of improving the revenues to the church, the board readily agreed, and two committees were formed to look into the matter. Mr. Sewall headed the committee to inquire into purchasing the land, or at least renewing the lease, which was held by St. Mark's Church.

For the next five months, poor Mr. Baldwin and his family sloshed around in the undrained swamp behind the church until October 30, 1826, when Sewall and Robert Schuyler gave their reports to the Board. St. Mark's apparently had been wholly indisposed to discuss terms of sale or renewal, and, thus, Mr. Robert Schuyler had considered it useless to consider ways in which the property might best be improved. On the other hand, Mr. Schuyler reported, Mr. Baldwin

[19] *The Christian Register,* April 18, 1823; *The Unitarian Miscellany and Christian Monitor,* May 1823, p. 200. James Fox is listed in William Ware's Pew Book as owning Pew No. 32. He married Elisabeth Armitage in August 1822.

had assured him that the house simply would not *stand* if something wasn't done soon! So the board agreed to see what could be done about draining the property, at least.

Steps to ensure better drainage were taken that same fall, but if any other measures were taken for the next three years to repair the house itself, no record of it shows up in the minutes or financial accounts until early 1829, when a carpenter's bill for about $70 was paid for work done on the house.

§ § §

While the trustees were struggling through the church's financial straits in late 1823 and early 1824, young William Ware had his own problems. He was, for one thing, trying to support a new bride on a substantially reduced income. He was also continuing to wrestle with his anxieties over his pulpit performance. Catharine Maria Sedgwick, writing to her friend Eliza Lee Cabot (whom shortly she was to introduce to Miss Cabot's future husband, Dr. Charles Follen) told of her frustration in living in New York City where there was only a single Unitarian Church and compared it to the hub of the Unitarian faith in Boston where there was the possibility of listening to many preachers.

> You who live in Boston at the very fountain of intellectual pleasure and can have weekly access to Dr. Channing's or Henry Ware's preaching can no more estimate the value of a single sermon than the happy dweller in a land of *water privileges* can rightly appreciate the value of a fountain in the desert. I do not mean that we have a spiritual waste either, for William Ware is faithful and well-beloved — but poor dull sleepy mortals that we are, we now and then want an energy that will make our pulses beat quicker and give an impulse to our thoughts and affections.[20]

A revealing letter about the inner workings of William Ware's mind and emotions is one he wrote to his wife, Mary, who in February 1824 had gone to Cambridge to visit her dying sister, the wife of Henry Ware, Jr. Writing on a Sunday evening after the second service, he commented that the attendance "was lamentably thin this evening."

[20] Catharine M. Sedgwick to Eliza Lee Cabot, February 11, 1825, in Catharine M. Sedgwick–Eliza Cabot Follen Papers, Massachusetts Historical Society.

*Catharine Maria Sedgwick by C. C. Ingham. Courtesy of
the Frick Art Reference Library and Mrs. Harriet N. Minot*

The short sentence in which he told his wife that he "passed the day as
usual preaching & eating" is typical. Then he made this admission:
"Of neither shall I say any thing because it must be either in praise or
dispraise of myself, neither of which is pleasant to do. I don't know yet
which I dislike the most, to be praised or run down." [21]

[21] William Ware to Mary Ware in Cambridge, February 1, 1824, in Folder 2,
Henry Ware Papers, Massachusetts Historical Society.

This problem of church attendance was deeply troubling him. He was concerned that the congregation at the evening service was declining, and the only reason that he could find in his own mind for this decline was that he was not successful as a preacher. He could not make himself into a preacher like his brother and his father; he knew it, and it rankled.

While Mary was away visiting her dying sister in Cambridge, William was obviously being taken care of by the parishioners who saw to it that he was not lonely. He wrote to Mary that he had made many parish calls: Mrs. Rhodes, Mrs. James, Mrs. Dudley, Mrs. Hughes, and Miss Squire. He spent the evening at the Russels where he found that the Sedgwicks and the Schuylers were also guests. He remarked that the day before he had dined at "Uncles" (President William Harris of Columbia) and had had tea at the William Benjamin Baileys. He wrote to Mary, "What do you think of a ministers life, dear." [22]

The first indication that we get that William Ware was thinking of a new career other than the ministry is in a letter to Mary Ware dated February 4, 1824. This letter followed the one of the first of the month when he appeared so discouraged about the evening attendance. One of his parishioners had written a novel (probably Catharine Sedgwick's *Redwood*, although we do not know for certain since he does not mention the specific novel). He wrote to his wife, "It is well worth while for any one who thinks he has the knack to try his hand at a novel." This is the first intimation we have that Ware himself might have believed himself capable of writing novels, which was to prove to be his eventual career. [23]

In 1825 the trustees saw fit to put into print two sermons that William Ware had preached on March 6th in which he had elucidated his ideas about the importance of the communion service. It was a simple declaration of the importance of the service and listed nine reasons that kept men and women from participating. He felt that the observance of the communion was a commandment from "our Lord," and that Christians were obliged to participate. [24]

[22] This list of scarcely known women again emphasizes women's importance in the life of the church; William Ware to Mary Ware in Cambridge, February 4, 1824, in Folder 2, Henry Ware Papers, Massachusetts Historical Society.

[23] *Ibid.*

[24] William Ware, Sermon on *The Communion*, preached on March 6, 1825, in the First Congregational Church in the City of New York, published at the

These nine reasons give us rather deep insight into Ware's own religious thinking: (1) There are those who (like Emerson later) believe it was not a command. But Ware felt that the Scriptures are quite clear in this regard and appended a long footnote from Thomas Belsham to bolster up his opinion. (2) There are those who govern themselves by the opinions of others. They "follow on the track of the thoughtless and the worldly." (3) There are those who believe that participating in this observance "will lay new and heavier obligations and demand greater strictness of life," and this deters them. Ware pointed out that just being a Christian already imposed this strictness of life. "If the religion of Jesus does not demand of us a holy and unspotted life before partaking of the Sacrament, it does not afterward."

Point four was that there are many superstitions about the sacrament that deter Christians from partaking. Here Ware traced the history of the rite and showed the magic and superstition that had grown up around it. Going back to the Evangelists and observing the rite as they did brought no cause for fear or superstition. (5) Some Christians are deterred because of the necessary preparation for the rite. Yet Ware said, "There is nothing in the nature of the ordinance itself, to call for more careful preparation, than any other part of divine worship." He did not feel that the partaking of the communion ought to be "the seal of perfection" but that men ought to come around the table of the Lord "for the purposes of mutual edification and improvement, to meditate on the character and services of Jesus, to cherish good affections, to compare ourselves with the perfect pattern of the Savior's example, to note our deficiencies, and stir ourselves up to greater efforts."

That pride also holds men back, was his sixth point. "They do not like to be known among the world as religious people." (7) There is also indecision. People "believe in their duty in regard to it, but postpone the performance of it." (8) A prejudice exists against the rite "as a means of spiritual power." The numbers of communicants are often used to boast ministerial and personal success. (9) The last reason is

---

request of the trustees (New York: Clayton and Van Norden, 64 Pine Street). The Massachusetts Historical Society possesses a copy autographed by William Ware and presented to George Bond, Esq., of Boston. Ware wrote that it was actually preached as two sermons.

"inattention to the subject — and unconcern about it." And Ware concluded his sermon with this summary statement: "Remember, the true friends of our Lord, are they who keep his commandments, He that has my commandments, and keepeth them, he it is — saith the Savior, that loveth me."

William Ware supplied the intellectual background for an understanding of the communion service for the Unitarians of this period, but Catharine Sedgwick supplied the emotional description of what such a service meant for at least one of those who partook. She wrote in her *Journal:*

> Communion Day — I felt on this sacred occasion more than usual vividness in my perception of the love & benevolence of Christ. I think I felt a more intense desire to testify the sincerity of my love & my faith. We had heard a good sermon from Wm. Ware for Mr. Eckford, setting forth the worth & the necessity of religion. God grant that the experience of the emotions of this day may not be lost upon [me] but may increase my faith & increase my fidelity.[25]

So during these early years of Ware's ministry, the church was settling itself down and becoming an established member of the New York religious community.

[25] Catharine M. Sedgwick, *Journal,* March 3, 1833, Massachusetts Historical Society.

9. A Second Unitarian Church Is Begun

Sometime between Channing's preaching in the autumn of 1824 and the resolution to publish William Ware's sermons in February 1825, a development occurred which further encouraged William's agonizing self-doubts. A group began to formulate plans for erecting a branch church farther uptown. This group included a large part of Ware's congregation. It was reasoned that, if the present society erected such a church, not only would certain members find it "easier" to go to Unitarian services, but also, many potential Unitarians might be gained among those with similar ideas but no convenient place of worship to attend. No break with the parent society was intended.

It seemed sensible; so, advertisements were placed in the newspapers on March 18, 1825, announcing a meeting to be held the next evening, March 19th, in the vestry rooms of the First Congregational Church of those members who supported the plan. The manuscript records of the Second Church indicate that Philip J. Schuyler, who was currently president of the board of trustees of the First Church, was called to chair the meeting. There followed a discussion as to the expediency of founding a second Unitarian Church in the city. The meeting was told that all of the pews at the First Church were either sold or rented (which was not quite accurate). It also became very apparent that the Chambers Street church was now too far downtown for the members who had moved northward with the expansion of the city. The meeting unanimously resolved to buy some land to erect a church building and set up a committee to obtain subscriptions and raise funds. Members of the committee were Robert Sedgwick, Asaph Stone, and John Crumby. The secretary for the meeting was none other than Henry D. Sewall who had acted in the same capacity to found the First Church.[1]

The hope was that the two churches were to be of a collegiate nature, following the example of the Dutch Reformed churches in New York City; that is, there would be one church with two ministers, separate but united. The ministers would take turns preaching in each of the churches although each church would take care of its own expenses. It was in this happy frame of mind, with much optimism, that the Second Church was conceived.

Another reason for the founding of the Second Church was the mood of church expansion that was rife among Unitarians in the middle eighteen-twenties. Several more Unitarian churches were founded in Boston during that decade. The New Yorkers were echoing the desire shown in Boston for neighborhood parishes. There was an aggressive attitude about expansion abroad, and a proselyting fervor not now characteristic of Unitarians. These young New Englanders living in New York had no qualms about promoting their point of view. They did not wait for people to wander into their churches. They went about the city and distributed pamphlets. They tackled the orthodox, and did not hesitate to engage in debate upon all subjects of theological dispute.

On Thursday, November 24, 1825, the cornerstone of the Second Congregational Church was laid in the presence of six to seven hundred persons at the corner of Prince and Mercer streets. The *Christian Examiner* stated that "The Throne of Grace was addressed by the Rev. William Ware, Pastor of the First Congregational Church." In his sermon, Ware stressed that the new church was being built because of

> the increasing numbers of those who are believers in the strict unity of God and lovers of real christian liberty . . . the number of Unitarian believers has greatly multiplied, and . . . more ample accommodations for religious worship are needed. It is to meet this want that we have begun to lay the foundations of this house of prayer.

Ware stressed that when the First Church had been built four years

---

[1] Vestry Meetings 1825–1831, manuscript records, Community Church Archives, New York, pp. 2–4.

The Second Congregational Unitarian Church at Prince and
Mercer Streets. The J. Clarence Davies Collection,
Museum of the City of New York

previously, it was scarcely thought that the erection of a second edifice
would be necessary in so short a time.[2]

The Second Church cornerstone thus appropriately laid, a rather
elaborate edifice began to rise on the chosen site at Prince and Mercer
streets. Yet, as the walls of the building were going up, something
happened to disturb the plan for the collegiate union of the two
churches. Some hidden problems, which at first glance do not appear,
may have caused the failure to complete the collegiate relationship.

Some of the members of the Second Church had approached
Henry Ware, Jr., to see if he was interested in coming to New York
to be the minister of the Second Church. Ware tried to discourage
such overtures, and yet his temptation must have been strong to accept

[2] *The Christian Examiner*, September-October 1825 (obviously printed after
this date), p. 477.

the pastorate of the new church which continued to hope that he would accept their solicitation. But the very first article of Association of the two churches stipulated that "The Senior ordained Pastor in either Church shall be the Senior Pastor for both Churches." The dilemma facing both congregations was: who would be the senior minister if Henry Ware came to New York? Would it be William as the senior settled minister in the city, or would it be his older and more distinguished brother, Henry Ware, Jr.? Evidently the men who had drawn up the original plans of collegiate union had not considered this possibility. The members of the First Church had naturally assumed that no man senior in point of service to Mr. Ware would be called to the Second Church. But when it came to the point of getting a minister, the committee of the Second Church was very keen on getting a great preacher.[3]

It is very difficult to disentangle the events of this period, for even Dr. John Ware, the third brother, when he later wrote the memoirs of Henry, Jr., got the events somewhat oversimplified. He told of the dedication of Second Church which took place on December 7, 1826, and then said that "in the course of a few weeks after the dedication of the new church, my brother Henry received an invitation to become its pastor." That is technically true, but Henry had been considering the invitation for weeks if not months before this actual call took place. And it may very well be that he declined the pastorate because conditions had soured by this time with regard to the collegiate plan of union. Most likely this happened because the Second Church persisted in trying to persuade Henry Ware, Jr., to come to New York. The two sets of events, the seeking of Henry Ware to be the pastor and the vote to discontinue the collegiate union plan, seem to be connected, although there were other factors.[4]

All appeared to be going well on October 29, 1826. A terse report in the Minutes of the vestry meetings of the Second Church stated that "The Committee on the Union of the Churches reported, a 'plan for this purpose,' which after much discussion & some amendments, was adopted & ordered to be submitted to the Trustees of the First Church."[5]

[3] All Souls Minute Book, Volume I, p. 116.
[4] John Ware, *Memoir of the Life of Henry Ware, Jr.* (Boston, 1846), p. 194.
[5] Vestry Meetings, 1825–1831, October 29, 1826, Community Church Archives (miraculously preserved through several fires).

The next evening, October 30, 1826, the trustees of the First Church met; and Henry Sewall laid before the board the communication from the subscribers to the Second Unitarian Congregational Church "containing a plan of union for the Two Churches." The board felt that this was a matter which should be decided by the whole society, and since the annual meeting was to be held the following week, it was decided to present the matter to the society at that time. At this meeting on November 6, 1826, the congregation resolved to appoint a committee "consisting of three of this Society who are not subscribers to the Second Church to confer with the Committee of the Second Church on the plan of association." [6]

The society of the First Church met again on Monday evening, November 20, 1826. A report of the committee was read, but the congregation, after some discussion, immediately adjourned the meeting, to meet again on November 29th. At this meeting a printed plan, dated November 24th, was given to the congregation. After much discussion the society passed the following vote which is puzzling in the light of previous sentiments of accord:

> This Society, after much reflection and careful consideration, are fully convinced that the acceptance, *at this time,* of the proposed Plan of Association between the Two Churches, would not tend to promote the general diffusion of the simple and liberal opinions which we revere as Scriptural, nor be beneficial to the best private interests of this Society, and therefore that the plan of our Christian Brethren of the Second Church can only be efficacious by the feelings of interest which cannot but be the consequence of its proposal and of the similarity of religious views and hopes which unite us in one common object. [7]

A perusal of the conditions proposed for the union of the two churches indicates that they were well worked out and that each church retained its relative independence. Why the congregation of the First Church voted not to join in the plan has many facets. One possible answer is that members of the First Church were afraid that a possible "Senior Minister" in the Second Church might threaten their position as the "Mother Church." The members thought of the

[6] All Souls Minute Book, Volume I, pp. 107, 109.
[7] *Ibid.,* pp. 115-117.

Second Church as a daughter church, an offshoot from their own church in the hoped-for expansion of the Unitarian religion in New York City. There was also the knotty problem of finances in regard to the Second Church. The sale of pews, in the absence of a minister, had not gone well, and the finances were in a precarious state.

There can scarcely have been any serious rift between William Ware and the members of the new church, which has usually been overstressed by persons who have looked into the matter. Ware continued to be called into conference by the Second Church to help them in many ways, and the relationship between the pastor of the First Church and many members of the Second appears to have been one of warmth.

Ware continued to help the Second Church in its search for a minister, and he presided at its meetings. On September 24, 1826, Ware was invited to chair the trustees' meeting which was planning the dedication of the new church building. On April 25, 1827, Henry Sewall informed the trustees of the Second Church that he had paid for and presented to William Ware a portrait of his brother Henry by Frothingham of Boston, scarcely the act of men estranged from each other. The trustees of the Second Church agreed to compensate Sewall for the portrait. On May 30, 1827, Ware was reported to have written to Stephen Higginson, inviting him to become the minister of the Second Church, again indicating a very friendly atmosphere. The church had a difficult time finding a minister, and evidently Ware helped as much as he could in this regard.[8]

The timing of these events is very important in understanding them. The First Church voted on November 29, 1826, not to continue with the idea of the proposed collegiate church, and the new building of the Second Church was dedicated just a little over a week later on December 7, 1826. But in order to really understand the events, we must also see how the Second Church moved in its attempt to call Henry Ware, Jr., to be the pastor.

Obviously there had been some problems in this connection, for almost immediately after the abandonment of the collegiate idea the committee of the Second Church moved to formally call Henry Ware, Jr., as the pastor. The formal invitation issued on December 16, 1826, contained the following words:

[8] Vestry Meetings, 1825–1831, Community Church Archives, pp. 17, 52, and 57.

We beg leave to express our deep conviction that the prosperity of this church, and of the great cause to which it is devoted, is intimately connected with your acceptance of this invitation.

This official call was followed by a private letter from "H.D.S.," probably Henry D. Sewall, with an especial plea on behalf of the new church.[9]

But all of the Unitarians in New York had been aware long before this formal invitation that Henry Ware, Jr., was being approached by the committee of the Second Church. John Ware wrote that "Some intimations that a movement of this kind was intended had already been made to him, and in answer to them he had some time before thus expressed himself to his . . . brother in New York:

I wish you would think and say nothing about my removal. It is absolutely out of the question. I have looked, at it, turned it over, longed for it; if there is anything I should prefer in this world to any thing else, it is this. But it is impossible, and I will not deceive myself or you by any false hopes. I shall always come and see you when I can, and be with you as much as I can; but to live near you is not to be granted me this side of Heaven.[10]

After fulfilling a promise to deliberate further, Henry finally sent in a firm refusal to the Second Church on January 3, 1827. Although he had had a prolonged debate with himself on this matter, the reason he ultimately came to turn down the offer can be summarized in the last line of this letter to his sister-in-law: "If you and William had not been where you are, I doubt if I should have hesitated an hour." [11]

Catharine Sedgwick in a letter to her brother Charles immediately after the Second Church had again asked Ware to consider the pulpit, felt that the new church was "in quite a desperate state." Evidently

---

[9] Quoted in John Ware, *op. cit.*, p. 195. Two of the original founders of the First Congregational Church have the initials H.D.S.: Henry D. Sedgwick and Henry D. Sewall. Sedgwick was having personal difficulties at this time, however, and Sewall was now the only one active in church affairs. In view of Sewall's transfer to the Second Church, it seems reasonable to assume that it was he who made the personal appeal to Henry Ware, Jr.

[10] John Ware, *op. cit.*, Henry Ware, Jr., to William Ware, p. 194.

[11] Quoted in *ibid.*, January 6, 1827, p. 198.

the members of the Second Church had not considered any other possibility except Henry Ware. "They will not allow that there is any next best," said Catharine, "and they have today determined to give a second and louder call, to write to Mr. Ware, his people, and to the Boston Association." But she concluded, "I confess I cannot but shrink from urging him to leave that full congregation whose desiring eyes and hearts are turned towards him, for the Mercer Street Walls." [12]

A few days later she heard a sermon by the Rev. John Pierpont which she wrote to Eliza Lee Cabot,

> made us all cringe.... It is such men ... that make our cause repulsive to all serious minds. He is amiable and well meaning but he has not the *religious sentiment*. He is one of those negative Unitarians who show the world what Unitarianism is not — not what it is.

She wrote that she believed that Henry Ware had done right to refuse the call and spoke again of "the bare walls of Mercer Street." [13]

William Ware's attitude about the founding of the Second Church is ambiguous and puzzling. He evidently felt that this was a matter for the laymen, and he wanted to be detached from it all although it intimately affected him and his own career. While he was in Philadelphia in November 1826 for the ordination of William Furness he wrote several letters to his wife which indicated this ambiguity. "Let me hear if you learn anything about the new Church." He asked Mary to tell Robert Schuyler that "I beg to have no voice touching that question." He felt that he had been so diplomatic that evidently the people had not understood at all where he stood in the matter. This appears to have been the way that he wanted it to be.[14] Ware was also encouraged in his own work in New York, for he intimated to Mary that the people of Philadelphia were not of the same high quality as his New York congregation. "Indeed, I do not believe there is among Unitarians a choicer parish than ours in all good respects,"

[12] Catharine M. Sedgwick to Charles Sedgwick, January 7, 1827, in Catharine M. Sedgwick Papers, Massachusetts Historical Society.

[13] Catharine M. Sedgwick to Eliza Lee Cabot, January 10, 1827, in Catharine M. Sedgwick–Eliza Cabot Follen Papers, Massachusetts Historical Society.

[14] William Ware in Philadelphia to Mary Ware, November 13 and 17, 1826, in Folder 2, Henry Ware Papers, Massachusetts Historical Society.

and then his own self-effacement showed: "What a shame then they have not a better minister." [15]

The Second Church was dedicated just about a year after the laying of the cornerstone on December 7, 1826. The opening hymn was written by a member of the First Church, William Cullen Bryant. William Ware gave the prayer of dedication and read from the Scriptures, and the sermon was given by William Ellery Channing. The *Christian Register* indicated that the new church was erected "for the purpose of accommodating those who live in the upper part of the city." The two churches were actually fourteen short New York blocks apart, a fifteen-minute walk, and there can be no doubt that the new church was more convenient for those who were following the trend of development in New York and buying and building homes farther north in Manhattan.[16]

Channing's sermon, like the Baltimore Sermon of 1819, was widely printed in newspapers in the United States. Channing felt that this was an important address in the furtherance of Unitarian ideas. As a result his lengthy sermon was very much on the order of the sermon at Baltimore, and he elucidated further some of the arguments of the reasonableness of the Unitarian position over the Trinitarian. It was a good sermon, and it was an important milestone in the founding of a second Unitarian church in America's fastest growing city.

The sermon was called "Unitarianism: Most Favorable to Piety." In it Channing defined the belief of Unitarians as

That there is One God, even the Father; and that Jesus Christ is not this one God, but his son and messenger, who derived all his powers and glories from the Universal Parent, and who came into the world not to claim supreme homage for himself, but to carry up the soul to his Father, as the only Divine Person, the only Ultimate Object of religious worship.

Then came the doctrinal part of the sermon, and it can be easily summarized by listing the nine ways that Channing suggested as making Unitarianism conducive to piety: (1) because it presents to the mind, *one,* and *only one Infinite Person;* (2) because it preserves inviolate the spirituality of God; (3) because it presents a distinct and

[15] *Ibid.,* letter of November 17, 1826.
[16] *The Christian Register,* December 16, 1826.

intelligible object of worship; (4) because it asserts the unbounded perfection of God's character; (5) because it accords with nature and the world around us; (6) because it opens the mind to new and enlarging views of God; (7) because of the high place which it assigns to piety in the character and work of Jesus Christ; (8) because it meets the wants of man as a sinner; and (9) because it is a rational religion. These points were elaborated at great length with the usual proofs and appeals to the perfectibility of man. John Ware in the *Memoirs* of his brother Henry, said about the sermon: "It was one of those great efforts by which he many times produced so remarkable an impression." [17]

Catharine Maria Sedgwick was present for the events of the excit-

Unitarian Church, Corner of Prince and Mercer Streets, 1831
(Drawn by Charles Burton, Engraved by G. W. Hatch and
James Smillie, Published by Bourne). Courtesy of
the New-York Historical Society, New York City

[17] W. E. Channing, "Discourse preached at the Dedication of the Second Congregational Church, New York, December 7, 1826." See also John Ware, *op. cit.*, pp. 193–194.

ing week of the dedication and wrote about them both in her *Journal* and in a letter to her friend Eliza Lee Cabot in Boston. The *Journal* description is less enthusiastic than that contained in the letter. Evidently Channing read the sermon in its entirety to his sister, Mrs. Russel, and to Miss Sedgwick, asking their editorial opinion as to what parts of the written sermon he should omit in the oral presentation.

Miss Sedgwick wrote that Channing spoke for an hour and twenty minutes. She was not too happy with the sermon, for she felt that it did not show Channing at his spiritual best but as a controversialist. She felt religious controversy was a necessary evil, but preferred the spiritual Channing. She felt that Channing had "that rich confidence and touching tenderness that makes you imagine you can hear the voice saying, 'This is my beloved Son.' "

Channing not only preached the Sunday sermon and the dedication sermon on Thursday, but he also had several meetings with the members of the new church in the evenings. One of these meetings took place at Henry Sewall's and one at Lucy Channing Russel's. At Sewall's, the men of the congregation organized a "Society for the Diffusion of Unitarian Christianity and the Welfare of Society," and at Mrs. Russel's the discussion was, in the words of Miss Sedgwick, "a spiritual conversation," by which she was more deeply moved than by the more practical discussion at Henry Sewall's. Her brother was so moved by the sermon that his wife reported that he repeatedly wakened in the night and exclaimed, "Glorious Sermon." [18]

In the light of the intemperate responses from the clergy which developed in the period of 1819–1821 in the Feltus, Spring, and Mason controversies, it is encouraging to note that a layman in Providence, Rhode Island, wrote a pamphlet in reply to Channing's dedication sermon which was a model of diplomacy and tact, and a very intelligent statement of the typical Trinitarian position. This unknown layman took Channing's sermon point by point and attempted to show that the Trinitarian position was not any less reasonable than the Unitarian one. He maintained as against Channing, "that a doctrine is not to be rejected, because it cannot be fully comprehended. He

[18] This description of the dedication and the associated events is to be found in Catharine Sedgwick's *Diary* at the Massachusetts Historical Society, and in a letter dated December 8, 1826, from Catharine M. Sedgwick to Eliza Lee Cabot, in Catharine M. Sedgwick–Eliza Cabot Follen Papers, Massachusetts Historical Society.

tried to demonstrate that the Trinitarian position "is not an outrage upon our rational nature; that it neither degrades reason, nor discourages piety," as Channing had claimed.[19]

It became evident shortly after the establishment of the Second Church that what it needed more than anything else was a strong and devoted minister. The *Revivalist,* a fundamentalist publication, had made the statement that the establishment of a second Unitarian church in New York City was premature, that few pews had been sold, that services were ill-attended, and that the whole enterprise was in a desperate condition. The editor of the *Christian Examiner* responded to this attack by saying that the people who believed this about the Second Church were deceived.

> The letter before us from New York . . . shows that the step taken by the Unitarians of New York was a most judicious one. The church is built in a part of the city which is rapidly increasing in population, and bids fair at no distant period to be the centre of the metropolis. The pews sold have been as many as were sold in the same time either in the last Unitarian or last Orthodox church erected in this town; and that, too, without a settled minister. Its funds are in good condition, its numbers constantly increasing, and nothing is wanting to its complete success but the settlement of an able, enterprising, and devoted minister.[20]

In spite of the fact that two churches emerged from the founding of the Second Church rather than a single collegiate congregation, the members of the First Church who had promised money to build the Second Church largely carried through with their promises, and many members of the First Church continued to own pews in both churches for many years. For this reason, it is somewhat dangerous to attest as to which members of the First Church were actually members of the Second. It is true that some did maintain an exclusive membership in the new church, but many simply felt that they were helping the new society by owning a pew there. Names in the "Cash Book of the Second Church" include such as Henry D. Sewall, Henry D. Sedgwick, Benjamin Blossom, Robert Sedgwick, Isaac Green Pearson,

[19] *Review of the Rev. Dr. Channing's Discourse Preached at the Dedication of the Second Congregational Unitarian Church in the City of New York,* by a Layman (Providence, 1827).

[20] *The Christian Examiner,* July-August 1827, pp. 374–375.

Curtis Holmes, Benjamin Armitage, William Wheelwright, Oroondates Mauran, Augustus Greele, and Elihu Townsend.[21]

Unitarians in 1826 felt that Boston was too far away from them to be the central focus of the denomination. In April, in the *Christian Inquirer,* an anonymous writer who called himself only "A Unitarian" complained that he had attended the Chambers Street Church where he was informed about the new book publishing ventures of the American Unitarian Association. His chief complaint was that the whole project was centered in Boston, and that the books were to be published on good quality paper. He felt that Boston was too far away. "Do they expect that people will subscribe, and give their money to a society two or three hundred miles distant, to do what they please with it?" He complained that printing on good paper would make the books too expensive. The editor answered the letter and suggested "we see no good reason why Boston is not as suitable a place as Charleston S.C., or New York." The editor then listed the names of those responsible for the new tract publishing society (actually the American Unitarian Association) with the Rev. Aaron Bancroft of Worcester as president and one of the vice presidents being the Hon. Henry Wheaton, Esq., of New York, an honored member of the First Church.[22]

One of the ways in which the ladies of the church indicated their devotion to Mr. Ware at this time was to purchase for him a Life Membership in the new American Unitarian Association. This purchase of a Life Membership was long considered a great honor.[23]

Dr. Gardiner Spring, who in 1820 had earlier made a series of accusations against Unitarians which Henry Sedgwick had answered

[21] Second Church Cash Book, April 18–October 22, 1825. The churches were actually on good terms for many years. The Second Church had one minister, Samuel Osgood, who, after serving the church for twenty years as minister, became an Episcopalian, and another minister, the Rev. George Hepworth, who tried to take the church over into the Congregational denomination and was thwarted largely by First Church members who either owned pews at the Second Church or bought them to "save the church." It was only after the coming of John Haynes Holmes to New York City in 1907, espousing both Socialist and pacifist ideas, that the two churches were at loggerheads, a condition happily now resolved with an annual pulpit exchange.

[22] *The Christian Inquirer,* April 1826, pp. 234–235.

[23] For many years in the Worcester Church, Stephen Salisbury purchased a Life Membership for every child of the church as he or she was born!

with a pamphlet, evidently had not had enough of controversy. In the early part of 1827, he delivered a further series of discourses from his pulpit on the subject of the Trinity.

The Unitarians were not going to take this kind of criticism without a reply in 1827 any more than they were in 1820. A correspondent "S" writing in the New York *Christian Inquirer* took Dr. Spring to task.

Then a week later it appeared that it was not just the Presbyterians who were fulminating against the Unitarians. It was also being done by the minister of a Baptist church (unnamed), who said that "of all the people I ever knew or read of, the Socinians, I think are the worst, and if there is such a place as the hottest hell, I do think they richly deserve it, and no doubt will have it." [24]

It is thus evident that even eight years after the First Church had been founded, Unitarians were still being consigned to hell by local clergy, or at least the more bigoted representatives of the local clergy. The Unitarians — now two churches instead of one — were not any more anxious to give up without a fight than they had been in 1820.

[24] See *The Christian Register* for March 17 and 24, 1827.

10. Co-workers in the City

F REE AND CLEAR FROM OBLIGATION to the First Congregational Church and ostensibly backed by William Ware's blessings, the founders of the Second Congregational Unitarian Church had eagerly looked forward to gaining the eloquent and eminent Henry Ware, Jr., as their settled pastor. His final refusal must have come as a sore blow to the budding society. But there was no retreating now; it had built a church and had officially severed its affiliation with the original society. There was nothing to be done now but to find a pastor of its own.

The Rev. Ezra Stiles Gannett, a very close friend of Henry Ware, Jr., was the first to be approached (February 1827), after Ware's refusal; possibly Gannett was Ware's own recommendation. Gannett was William Ellery Channing's assistant at the Federal Street Church in Boston. But Gannett, too, declined the New York group, and ten months later — having marked time — the Second Church tried Orville Dewey, of the New Bedford Church. Dewey had preceded Gannett as Channing's assistant and had been with the Federal Street Church during 1821 and 1822, before accepting the New Bedford Church. The latter congregation was a demanding one, however, and Dewey was not entirely happy in his post. He often felt overworked, and was frequently impelled to take as much as five months away from his pulpit each year. He wanted to accept the New York Church, but was hesitant lest he jump from the frying pan into the fire. He sounded out his own congregation on the move, but the New Bedford Church was adamant about his remaining. Thus, Dewey, too, declined the New York offer. Neither realized then that a partnership between them would be established less than ten years later.

That the search for a minister for the Second Church was getting to the point of desperation is indicated by a note which Catharine

Park Place, New York, Looking West from Broadway, 1831
(Drawn by Charles Burton, Engraved by James Smillie,
Published by Bourne). Courtesy of the New-York
Historical Society, New York City

Sedgwick appended to a letter to Eliza Cabot in Boston, "Do you Bostonians know anything about the dismal state of the new church here? Have you not one young man of talent and piety among you?" The letter indicated a final kind of desperation when man after man had turned down the church's offers of its pulpit. It was not until the middle of that year that the Second Church found itself a pastor. He was William Parsons Lunt, none other than the young and recently graduated favorite nephew of Isaac Green Pearson.[1]

The ordination of the Rev. William Parsons Lunt as the first minister of the Second Church took place on Thursday, June 19, 1828.

Introductory prayer by the Rev. Mr. Colman of Salem; Selections

[1] Catharine M. Sedgwick to Eliza Lee Cabot, March 4, 1828, in Catharine M. Sedgwick–Eliza Cabot Follen Papers, Massachusetts Historical Society.

*William Parsons Lunt, First Minister of the Second
Congregational Unitarian Church. From the
Unitarian Universalist Association Archives*

from the Scriptures, by the Rev. Mr. Pierpont, of Boston; Sermon,
by the Rev. Mr. Greenwood, of Boston; Prayer of Ordination, by
the Rev. Dr. Kendall, of Plymouth; Charge, by the Rev. Mr. Frothingham, of Boston; Right Hand of Fellowship, and Address to the
Society, by the Rev. William Ware, of New York; Concluding Prayer,
by the Rev. Mr. Parkman, of Boston.[2]

In Ware's remarks he challenged the members of the new congregation to live up to their professions of religion, to become defenders
of the faith, and charged them to become missionaries for Unitarianism.
"Remember, that in spreading your tenets, you are engaged in the
great and dignified task, of restoring the gospel from the saddest cor-
ruptions, to what it was as it fell from the lips of its holy author." [3]

Many important members of the First Congregational Church
moved to the Second Church. Isaac Green Pearson's apparently limit-
less energies were transferred to work for the new society right from

[2] *The Christian Examiner*, May-June 1828, p. 273.
[3] *The Christian Register*, August 9, 1828.

the start, and with him went Asaph Stone, whose home was actually next door to the Second Church. Others who had worked diligently on the founding of the First Church remained to fulfill their present commitments, but then abandoned the Chambers Street church altogether; for example, Henry Sewall turned in his official resignation as Deacon in June of 1827.

Robert Sedgwick, Henry and Catharine Sedgwick's brother, was elected in Sewall's place; and William Ware was instructed to convey the society's appreciation to Mr. Sewall. Fortuitously, the original letter from Ware to Sewall has recently come into the possession of the church.

> I was appointed a committee of the Church in Chambers St. to communicate to you their acceptance of your resignation of the office you have heretofore held in that body, and to present you their "sincere thanks for the fidelity and zeal with which you have ever discharged the duties of that office." . . . [P]ermit me to expound in few words my own sense of obligation for the indispensable services you have performed. . . . I have always looked up to you as the real father of our church, and I will miss your presence and your directing hand. But whatever the cost may be to me and our Society, I hope you will cement yourself with the other church, when a head is much wanted, and God will assume the direction of its affairs. I have assured you before — I do it again — that I have no bitter feelings nor have ever had any in this matter. I cannot perceive the least differences in my sentiments in relation to the two societies. I have taken as deep an interest in the one as the other — whatever I can do for the lower church I am as ready to do for the upper. I care only for the principles of our Christianity, while that goes forward I am content, and desire that personal feelings and considerations may never have place.[4]

Benjamin Armitage, who had been elected president at the annual meeting in 1826, also left for the new church as soon as he had finished

---

[4] William Ware, personal communication to Henry D. Sewall, July 2, 1827. Original letter in All Souls archives. Advertised for sale by Goodspeed's Bookstore of Boston, it was thoughtfully purchased for All Souls by Mr. and Mrs. James Durgin in 1969. Shortly after this communication, Sewall moved to Watertown, New York, and remained there the rest of his life.

his final term of office. It may be that members such as Armitage and Sewall continued to hope for an alliance between the two societies, for they continued to hold their pews in the First Church for several years. But as the years passed and no further move was made to link the churches, they let their payments on their annual pew assessments lapse.

Other members who switched were Elihu Townsend and William Cullen Bryant, who had only just arrived in New York at about the same time as the early plans were being laid for the Second Church. After his arrival in New York, Bryant attended services at William Ware's church, but sometime after the church on Prince and Mercer streets was dedicated, he began attending there. Bryant definitely appears among the members of both the First and Second Churches after about 1835, until the arrival of Henry Bellows, when he returned to the First Church.

After the dedication of the Second Church the fates were kinder to the pastor of the First Congregational Church. Ware now had a Unitarian co-worker in the city, and it must have been a great help and comfort to him to have a colleague even though the collegiate plan had fallen through. But William Lunt was a very young man who evidently had not as yet displayed the qualities that later made him a beloved and competent pastor in the Quincy, Massachusetts, church.[5] He was but 23 years old when he was ordained and in some ways very ill-equipped to face this sophisticated New York congregation. Henry Bellows said about the young minister:

> Lunt brought no store of sermons; no *prestige;* no experience; and he came from the bosom of a sympathizing community to stand almost alone in a city that hated his creed and his denominational name. Delicate in constitution, and not yet hardened into complete manhood, with a temperament tending to melancholy, but with ... the foundation of a scholarship rare and exact, a nature lofty and modest, he had every qualification for success, except a maturer age and a less feeble body, and perhaps a more buoyant spirit. What he might have done in New York, if he had been more patient with himself and the people more patient with him, we may partly infer from the brilliant

[5] For a biography of William Parsons Lunt, see Samuel Atkins Lunt, *Heralds of a Liberal Faith* (Boston: Beacon Press, 1910), Volume III, pp. 232 ff.

career as a preacher and citizen he ran in Quincy, Massachusetts, for twenty-two years after he left this society.[6]

Lunt lasted barely six years with the Second Unitarian Congregational Church, but these were the happiest years of William Ware's ministry. Ware was now 31 and had behind him six years of experience with, and adaptation — if not adjustment — to the rigors of New York religious life. In Lunt, Ware had not only no serious challenge to himself; he also had a fellow Unitarian minister to share with him some of the antagonisms which were still felt by Unitarians in New York City.

§   §   §

In October of 1828 William Ware made a "Missionary Journey" to the western part of New York State. On Sunday the 12th of October, he delivered a series of three lectures on "Unitarian Christianity" in Utica. But it was more than a preaching assignment in Utica, for Ware also gave one or more of the sermons at other New York cities: Lyons, Rochester, Syracuse, Salina, and Watertown.[7]

Exactly what the results of this "Missionary Journey" are we do not know. But the occasion called for the printing of the sermons "by request" in Watertown, and it gives us some rather keen insights into the systematic theology and Unitarianism of William Ware.

Ware has not been considered an original thinker in theology but has been charged with aping his father, brother, and Channing in this area. However, the three sermons given in Utica were written in a lucid and convincing style, and the first and the third sermons were excellent expositions of what more conservative Unitarians were thinking in those early years of the nineteenth century.

Ware stated that everywhere the different sects of Christendom were warring for converts, but that no denomination has in its pos-

[6] Church of the Messiah, *Services in Commemoration of the Fifty-Fourth Anniversary of the Founding of the Church of the Messiah, and of the Recent Redemption of the Church from Debt*, March 18 & 19, 1879 (New York: Church of the Messiah, 1879), 102 pp.

[7] William Ware, "Three Sermons Illustrative of the Principles of Unitarian Christianity Preached in Utica on Sunday the 12th of October, 1828, published by request" (Utica: Northway and Porter, 96 Genesee Street, 1828). A note on the printed sermons indicates that portions were delivered at these other cities.

session "the whole and exact truth itself," including the Unitarians. He suggested that "God will accept the sincere pious believer, whether with the Athanasian he believes that Christ is God and worships him as such, or with the Unitarian that he is not God, and conscientiously restricts his worship . . . to the Father." Ware asked "How shall we know the truth since there are so many competing versions of it among Christians?" His answer was that each person must "inquire, therefore, for the truth . . . for this is our solemn duty, as it is our inalienable right."

Yet this right of inquiry has often been withheld from Christians by those in power in the Church. This right is too little missed by most Christians; said Ware, "He gave us our minds to be cultivated and filled with knowledge. . . . He has sent his Son into the world bringing his will, showing us how we may secure everlasting happiness, and presenting to our consideration the most interesting and important truths." Ware urged that men should not receive the Scriptures blindly, but should inquire as diligently as possible into their meaning. Free inquiry may terminate in error as well as understanding, yet "it will still have advanced the virtue of him who shall have engaged in it, if it has been conducted in a right spirit. Unitarian Christianity, like Protestantism, is the offspring of free inquiry."

Ware then proceeded to speak about Unitarianism or Rational Christianity although he admitted that he felt that the name was not very important. "A Unitarian is one who believes in the strict unity of God, in opposition to the Trinitarians, or one who believes in a three-fold or tri-personal God. So it is with Unitarians; though they substantially agree, they do not hold it essential to believe in all things alike. Each inquires and believes for himself, or ought to do so." Thus, almost a decade after the Baltimore sermon of Channing, a more open principle can be observed coming into prominence in Unitarian thinking; the right to diversity of belief, and the foundation of the institution of the church upon such a doctrine of diversity.

Ware still expressed in 1828 the concept that had been a cornerstone of early nineteenth-century Unitarianism: "We believe in Jesus Christ and his divine commission and authority, that he was the *Son of God* in the Scripture meaning of the words; that he was not *God the Son* in any sense of the phrase." Ware admitted that Unitarians "reject the doctrine of the Supreme Deity of Christ, we deny that he was Almighty God. . . . We reject the horrible idea that the creator and sustainer of the universe died upon the cross." But Ware was careful to point out that he and other Unitarians believed that

> the rank of Jesus in the scale of being has nothing to do with the authority and divinity of his religion. The authority of Jesus — the divinity of his mission — not his person, is the important point. . . . Jesus came and showed that he came from God, by the godlike works which he did. . . . In the Divinity of his religion, that it came from God and was attested by miracles, we are the firmest believers, and have ever been, as a sect, its staunchest defenders against the Atheist and Deist.

The second of the three sermons is a lovely little homily on religion as a practical sentiment and as a means of devotion. The third, titled, "The Characteristics of Unitarian Christianity," gives some further insights into William Ware's particular kind of Unitarian belief. Again he averred that Unitarianism is a scriptural religion. He said that many sects make up long lists of articles and creeds which they think better express the principles of their particular brand of the Christian religion than the Bible. And then they exclude others on the basis of these creeds. "Unitarianism admits of no such control over the faith of another. The Bible is its creed."

The second major point he made about the Unitarian faith was that it is rational. "How rational?" he asked, and then answered by stating that Unitarianism is not built upon reason independent of Scripture, but

> all the truths which it embraces, it receives from the scriptures alone, and values them only as they are revelation, and far beyond the reach of the human mind. It receives not a single doctrine which is not a revelation of Jesus, not one on the ground of its being a doctrine of reason and not of scripture.

Ware averred that Unitarians use their reason in forming their opinions and in learning the true sense of the Scriptures. He also felt that Unitarianism was "rational in a higher sense than the prevailing systems of Christianity." There are no doctrines which are required for belief even if the believer cannot understand the doctrine.

Unitarianism, he stated, is a liberal system. It is liberalism in the

sense that "we use it in opposition to exclusiveness, bigotry, unchari-
tableness, bitterness." But one must be careful not to use the word
liberal "in the sense of loose, free, easy and licentious." He expounded
the doctrine that the liberal must "allow to others the liberty which
we claim for ourselves." He also believed that Unitarianism is liberal
because:

> it does not hold that mankind will be condemned in the judgement
> of the great day, merely because they have not entertained a certain
> belief. We say that if a man is sincere in his opinions whatever they
> may be, if he has conscientiously searched for, and adopted them, and
> then acts according to his convictions, he is safe now and always.

But Unitarianism is not liberal in the sense that it is easy on the sinner
and gives him to understand that sin is a light evil.

> Unitarianism admits of nothing in the place of personal holiness. No
> other qualities — no other gifts or graces can compensate for its
> absence.

"The piety of Jesus," he said, "lay not in a fearful observance of
prescribed forms, but in the divine and holy and settled temper of his
soul." But Ware also felt that Unitarianism "teaches the truth of a
certain, dreadful, and universal retribution, taking place in the future
life and reaching on into the ages of eternity." He was undoubtedly
disturbed when Emerson preached that the retribution and the working out of the laws of compensation took place in the here and now.
Ware felt that:

> the consequences of sin are universal . . . inherent in the very nature
> of things, and that the law of gravity could no easier be dispensed
> with, or suspended . . . than that eternal law that binds sin and misery
> together, now and forever.

In concluding, Ware claimed as had his father and brother, that:

> Unitarian Christianity, we steadfastly believe, to be pure Christianity,
> as it came from Jesus himself divested of the errors which time, the
> superstitions, the hopes and fears and craftiness of man, have con-
> nected with it. We are therefore most anxious to see it prevail.

In the Annual Report to the American Unitarian Association in 1829 it was stated that the

> effects of [Ware's] services were immediate and great. It was scarcely known . . . that Unitarian preaching would be acceptable . . . [but Mr. Ware found] large audiences wherever he journeyed, and an impulse was given to religious sentiment which has already produced results that must be permanent. . . . In Rochester a society has been formed. . . . No other part of our country, at the present moment, offers more encouragement to the hopes of the Unitarian Christian.[8]

§   §   §

One of the most interesting and revealing insights into the character of William Ware as a family man is shown by the little book which he wrote and illustrated for his four-year-old son, Henry Ware III, in the year 1828. This charming handwritten book is fortunately preserved in the Henry Ware Papers in the Massachusetts Historical Society. Its publication run consisted of one copy. Ware called it *The Shrewsbury Book, 1828*. The father obviously chose short words to serve in a reader for his son. When a word of two syllables did appear, the father hyphenated it. The word thus used shortly appeared again to cement the idea in the young boy's mind. He also used childish dialogue. The illustrations are captivating, especially the simple line drawing of the boy at his desk. The landscapes are not as successful, for Ware tended to overdraw them. But his gift for caricature comes out extremely well in this little book.

In the content of the book there were two dominant themes. The most prominent had to do with equating good behavior with good study habits. William was telling his son that it was good to learn to read, and it was good to try very hard to learn. Fortunately, Henry III was a gifted child and had no academic problems. (His report card appears later in the Henry Ware Collection, and the son evidenced model deportment and academic achievement.)

A second theme in the book was William Ware's preoccupation with the poor. He was concerned with the poverty-stricken mass of humanity which inhabited New York City. In the early 1820s, as now, about one-seventh of New York's population lived on charity. He was

[8] Fourth Annual Report to the American Unitarian Association, May 26, 1829 (Boston, 1829).

Drawing by William Ware of His Son Henry at His Desk.
In "The Shrewsbury Book, 1828." Courtesy of the
Massachusetts Historical Society. Photograph
by George M. Cushing

trying to inculcate sensitivity on this subject of poverty to his son. It is interesting that William Ware stressed this particular aspect of the city's life to his son in this very simple little reader. Few modern books for four-year-olds would stress poverty. This book is perhaps more illustrative of the inner character and interests of William Ware than any sermon he ever preached.[9]

9 Edward R. Ellis, *The Epic of New York City* (New York, 1966), p. 218.

City Hotel, Broadway, 1831 (Drawn by Charles Burton,
Engraved by James Smillie, Published by Bourne).
Courtesy of the New-York Historical Society,
New York City

§   §   §

As we pass the first decade with which this history of All Souls
Church is concerned it is worthwhile to stop and take a look at the
nature of the culture of the times. In 1829, New York City had just
passed Philadelphia in population and commercial importance. The
Erie Canal had been completed in 1825 and had made New York
the actual seaport for the Great Lakes region. The *Savannah* had been
the first steamboat to cross the Atlantic in 1819, and although steam-
boats were common on lakes and rivers, still most of ocean transporta-

tion was by sail. Not until 1826 did steam become prominent as a means of locomotion on the oceans. The first locomotive in America was imported from England in 1829, and the engine was discovered to be too heavy for the tracks. The Baltimore and Ohio Railroad opened its first fifteen-mile section in 1830.

New York had become a city of 200,000 people, and immigration was increasing yearly. There were no street railways in the city; only the stages ran up Broadway. The tallest buildings were only five or six stories high. The streets were just beginning to be lighted with gas streetlights. Women still did most of the work of family care in the home: baking, washing, ironing, weaving, spinning, and tailoring. A skilled workman earned about a dollar a day, and an able-bodied seaman about $14 a month and keep. Hours of work were from twelve in the summer to fourteen in the winter. Bacon was 10 cents a pound, and private board ran $2 a week. Andrew Jackson had just been swept into the presidency in a wave of democracy. And the church on Chambers Street decided that the cost of $100 for replacing the stoves that heated the church with furnaces was not expedient.[10]

§   §   §

Ware's career with the church proceeded relatively smoothly throughout these years, and while he suffered some mild setbacks — such as having his jurisdiction over the disposal of the charity funds taken away from him and placed in the hands of the trustees — he also had some mild achievements. In 1827, he edited *The Unitarian,* a small periodical with a rather limited audience; and thereafter, he was fairly frequent in contributing to other periodicals, such as *The Christian Register.* In October 1830 he requested permission to use the church to deliver a weeknight lecture on behalf of the American Unitarian Association, and collected $50 for that organization. Shortly afterward, he conducted a series of lectures addressed to young men, which sufficiently impressed the trustees that they asked Ware for copies to publish.

William Ware's prosperity and contentment during these years can be discerned from certain passages in Henry Ware's letters to William. In these passages there are no hints, as there are earlier and later, that William was overcome by his anxiety and self-doubts. Most

---

[10] All Souls Minute Book, Volume I, p. 169.

of the congregation that had remained loyal to the First Church had grown to love their self-abnegating minister. In January 1828 Ware was finally awarded the full salary of $2,000 which he had relinquished in 1823, and in 1833 he was awarded a bonus of $250. At the annual meeting of 1833, Robert Sedgwick had called to the society's attention Ware's voluntary surrender of $500 annually, and reminded the members that they actually owed the surrendered amounts to Ware as a debt. But after further and perhaps strenuous discussion on the matter, Sedgwick withdrew his motion and substituted one which would give the minister a $250 dividend for the year 1833. The following year, the society awarded Ware a similar dividend of $200.[11]

§ § §

In July of 1832 a cholera epidemic hit New York City, and with it, panic. When William Cullen Bryant returned to New York on July 12th, he found his family suffering from what his wife Frances called the "premonitory symptoms," of the plague. The disease had made its way across Europe, and Bryant reported the crisis as news for his paper. He used large headlines, which at that time was most unusual practice, when the cholera struck London, and later, when it was reported in Quebec and Montreal. By July 3rd, the Board of Health had identified several cases of the plague. Immediately many people fled the city. "*The Evening Post* estimated by August 6th half the city's population had fled. Nearly 4,000 persons died. The plague departed as quickly as it had come, and on August 22nd the Board of Health announced that those who had left might return without danger." [12]

Ware sent his family to Bridgeport, Connecticut, to escape the cholera epidemic. He himself, having been detained in the city with necessary duties, joined Mary and the children a few days later. On August 7, 1832, he wrote a friendly letter to William Cullen Bryant, by now his close friend, and spoke of "the comfortable quarters," in a large upper floor which they had to themselves. He was somewhat concerned about the food that one should eat with a cholera epidemic raging in New York. "The table is a proper cholera table & therefore such as we should choose were our's the choice. I have seen nothing to contradict this except once, cucumbers, which only one was bold

[11] All Souls Minute Book, Volume I, pp. 133, 201–202, 212.
[12] Charles H. Brown, *Bryant* (New York, 1971), pp. 208, 209.

enough to touch. I looked daily to hear of symptoms in him, but none have yet developed themselves."

Ware wished that he had brought his paints, as he found the view in Bridgeport from the house "almost the most beautiful I ever believed anywhere. A landscape painter could not do better than to spend one or two months in coloring it." He found some Unitarians in Bridgeport, but when he wrote the letter, he had not preached to them. Instead he had gone to hear a Rev. Mr. Hewitt, a temperance man who "was engaged in defending old Calvinism against the encroachments of West Haven divinity." He went to hear him preach three times on one Sunday. Hewitt spoke for nearly four hours on a single text during the course of the three sermons, and Ware found it somewhat flat preaching. When the cholera scare had abated, Ware and his family returned to their city home. New dimensions to their work were ahead of them.[13]

[13] William Ware, Bridgeport, Connecticut, to William Cullen Bryant, New York, August 7, 1832, in Bryant–Godwin Collection, Manuscript Division, New York Public Library.

11. *The "Ministry-at-Large"*

IN THE EARLY EIGHTEEN-THIRTIES there are occasional references to a "ministry-at-large" which was being set up in New York City. This was a joint venture by the Unitarian churches of the city, and, like many other Unitarian social enterprises, it became an organization that did not remain completely within the confines of the church but moved outside of it. The money, the inspiration, and the management, however, came from within the established Unitarian churches.

The idea of a ministry-at-large was conceived by Joseph Tuckerman of Boston. Tuckerman (1778–1840) was graduated from Harvard College in 1798 as a classmate of William Ellery Channing, and in 1801 he was ordained to his first and only pastorate, in Chelsea, Massachusetts. During his ministry there, he started a society for the improvement of the lot of seamen, the first of its kind in the country. His interest in them was also duplicated by his interest in what he called "the neglected poor in our cities." He moved from Chelsea to Boston in 1826, giving up his parish because of poor health, and there began what he called a ministry-at-large. This was in effect a city mission for the poor, conducted by an ordained minister. In 1838 Tuckerman wrote a book in which he described his efforts in this area of work with the poor called, *The Principles and Results of the Ministry at Large in Boston*. But his health worsened and he died at the age of 62, worn out with his exertions. By this time, the idea had spread to England and to other American cities including New York.[1]

As in the case of the charity school which the ladies of the church began in 1823, we get our first inkling of a new project from the pen of Catharine Sedgwick. Her diary for February 4, 1833, tells of a meeting which she attended the evening before.

---

[1] *Dictionary of American Biography.*

Last evening we had a visit from Mr. Curtis, a philanthropist. He has a plan for districting the city & appointing persons in each ward who should know every inhabitant, their occupation, their wants. The plan in its details is a most interesting one & seems to be a feasible one. Mr. C. is a jeweller. He has a large Manufac'y about 7 apprentices & four in his employ. They, the boys, all live with him & constitute a domestic republic. During the cholera last summer he determined to remain in the City and keep up the establishment. The boys just then took a dramatic turn. He encouraged it; one wrote a play, another painted scenery, they were some of them musicians & while all the City was in consternation, the Spirits of health & cheerfulness hovered over this young band & withstood the Demon of Cholera.... Mr. C. had been principal in the house of refuge.... Today we have planned our Society in Aid of the Ministry at large.

Thus, we have the first glimpse as to how this amazing project was conceived by Joseph Curtis. In his *Autobiography,* Orville Dewey mentioned Joseph Curtis as a man whose "hand and heart were open to every call of charity." [2]

In 1832 an energetic and enthusiastic Unitarian gentleman in New York City wrote three long letters to the *New York American* in which he outlined the idea of a ministry-at-large. These letters were later printed in pamphlet form to be given to prospective donors to the program. Unfortunately, the writer of these letters and the pamphlet used a pseudonym, "Philo," so there is no exact indication as to who he might have been. He was probably Joseph Curtis as indicated by Miss Sedgwick's *Journal*. Both Unitarian churches immediately became active in seeking funds for a minister-at-large or several such ministers for the city. [3]

Social welfare concepts of the eighteen-thirties are well illustrated in these articles and this pamphlet. The ministers-at-large were to be ordained ministers (Unitarian, although the pamphlet does not specifically state this) who were to be assigned to a certain section of the

[2] Catharine M. Sedgwick, *Journal,* for February 4, 1833, Massachusetts Historical Society. Mary E. Dewey (ed.), *Autobiography and Letters of Orville Dewey, D.D.* (Boston, 1884), pp. 90–92. See also Catharine M. Sedgwick, *Memoir of Joseph Curtis a Model Man* (New York: Harper and Brothers, 1858).

[3] *The New York American,* late December 1832 and early January 1833. The pamphlet is titled, "Ministry at Large for the Poor of Cities" (New York, 1832).

city. The minister was to take under pastoral care in this area anyone who might need his services and would be willing to accept them. This was not to be a missionary effort in the sense that the poor were to be converted to the Unitarian faith, as was true in regard to the efforts of other denominations working with the poor, who conceived of their efforts as a missionary enterprise.

The minister was to be essentially a social worker, and the objectives of his ministry were to be far reaching. He was to give moral and religious instruction to the families, although it is difficult to see how this squares with the "no conversion" principle. He was to try to get as many of the children as possible to attend public school and to see that they remained in school. He was to see to it that those children who needed to go to "houses of refuge or reformation" should be sent there. He was to devise "measures which shall save the young from intemperance, dishonesty, etc.," and to try to secure for these children some useful employment by making sure that they were educated to qualify for employment.

It was suggested that there might be "rooms for public preaching." But the duties of the minister were "rather to be discharged by going from house to house — frequently visiting the poor in their homes and administering there to all their various necessities." The minister-at-large was to be an ordained preaching social worker. But he was to work solely with the poor in a particular section of the city and had no other duties. He was to be constantly on the move, a kind of priest among the poor. Bishop Cheverus' work among the poor in Boston was cited as a fine example of what was needed.

This was all to be supported "by voluntary associations among the rich . . . by the union of two or more of our religious congregations . . . in part by grants from city governments." The sum needed yearly for such a project was estimated to vary from twelve hundred to twenty-five hundred dollars, and the ministers were encouraged to make frequent and "minute reports of their doings to those who employ them."

In this field, as in many others, Unitarians were to be pioneers seeking ways to ameliorate the conditions of the poor. It was to be a personal kind of service. But it never worked out very well in practice when it was tried in New York. Undoubtedly, one of the reasons for this was that the training of a young man for the ministry in no way prepared him to operate in the field of social work. He was merely an amateur with good intentions, but it took a person of great dedication and special aptitudes even to want to engage in such work. There are evidences that, when Dr. Charles Follen was being approached to supply the pulpit in New York City in 1837, he hesitated because he thought that he might have to be a minister-at-large, and he did not feel qualified in this field of endeavor.[4]

In New York the project got off the ground shortly after the appearance of the article in the *New York American* and the publication of the "Philo" pamphlet. Some fifty-five persons, all but three or four members of the First Church, raised about $1,500. The salary of the minister-at-large was to be $1,200, and the remainder constituted his "poor purse" with which to help people in need (scarcely a munificent sum in the light of the great need that must have existed in the city, although there were some voluntary offerings during the year that increased the amount in the "poor purse").

This group of fund raisers also hired the first minister-at-large, the Rev. George B. Arnold, who was to report semiannually to the benefactors. Mr. Arnold worked for three and a half or four years at this task, and his reports were printed by "the Book and Tract Society of the First Congregational Church." They were models of what a report should be, full of exhortations to do more in the area of helping the poor and emphasizing the needs with a series of specific and personal examples of some of the conditions which were found among the people with whom the minister-at-large worked. The reports are long, the first, for example, running 23 pages, written in a flowing style and moving spirit. At the completion of his sixth report Mr. Arnold was appointed to an additional three-year term, for which vote of confidence he profusely thanked his backers.[5]

George Benedict Arnold (he was born "Benedict" and later became George B. Arnold) was born January 2, 1803, in Uxbridge, Massachusetts, the son of William and Hannah Arnold. His ministerial background is obscure. He was not graduated from either Andover-Newton or Harvard Divinity Schools, and unfortunately there are no records in the American Unitarian Association archives about Mr. Arnold. But he was an ordained minister and also an accom-

[4] See this book, page 213.

[5] George B. Arnold, "Reports of His Services as Minister-at-Large in New York," published by the Book and Tract Society of the First Congregational Church, New York, 1833–1836.

The Reverend George B. Arnold, Minister-at-Large
(Late in Life). Courtesy of Mrs. H. C. Borchardt

plished horticulturist, specializing in fruit-tree culture. His wife is easier to trace: she was the sister of Marcus Spring, a New York businessman and philanthropist. The Arnolds had several children, one of whom became a somewhat obscure poet, George G. Arnold.[6]

Arnold was called to be the minister-at-large in New York, and he evidently served faithfully, if we are to countenance his reports and his extended contract, from 1834 to 1837. Then, all of a sudden, he left New York City, accepting a pastorate in Allegheny City, now a part of Pittsburgh. But this pastorate was very short-lived. Arnold left for some property which he had purchased the previous year in Alton, Illinois, where he appears to have reentered the horticultural business, preaching occasionally to a mixed group of Quakers, Congregationalists, and Unitarians there. Later, he ran for the state senate as a Democrat and in 1848 was an electoral candidate on the presidential ticket. He was also treasurer of the Illinois Mutual Fire Insurance Company.

[6] *Vital Records of Uxbridge, Massachusetts* (Boston, 1916), p. 25; *Dictionary of American Biography.*

But his interest in idyllic communities was very strong, and in 1849 he and his family moved to Red Bank, New Jersey, to become part of the North American Phalanx, a successful Fourierite community with many Unitarian supporters. He came to the community as a nursery-man and orchardist. He informed officers of the community that he was an ordained minister, but the rules of the community forbade any kind of sectarianism.

Disagreements arose, and soon the Springs and Arnolds withdrew to form a second utopian community in New Jersey, the Raritan Bay Union at Perth Amboy. George Arnold became its first president, but his wife died shortly after the Union came into being, and he retired to Monmouth County, where he lived at Strawberry Farms and pursued a horticultural and inventive career. He returned to New York City about 1862, where he remained until his death in 1889, at the age of 86.[7]

§   §   §

In his seventh and last report about his work, George Arnold had stated that he had a colleague:

It is with sincere joy I inform you, that, within the last six months, another labourer has entered this ample field. The Rev. Mr. Channing [William Henry Channing] has been appointed by some members of the Second Congregational Society as a Minister At Large; and is already doing efficient service.

However, the young nephew of the founder of the First Church had come to New York not to replace Mr. Arnold but to be a second minister-at-large sponsored this time by the people of the Second Church.[8]

William Henry Channing (1810–1884) was William Ellery Channing's nephew. He had been raised with much advice from his uncle, for his own father had died when he was only one year old. Henry finished Harvard College in 1829, and when he was graduated from the Harvard Divinity School in 1833, he decided that he wanted to go to the West and be a Unitarian frontier preacher. To sway the

[7] Obituary in the *New York Times,* February 3, 1889.
[8] Seventh Report of Mr. Arnold, December 31, 1836.

young man from this idea, William Ellery Channing sent him on a tour of Europe. When he returned to Boston he came under the influence of Joseph Tuckerman, with his uncle's blessing. When he was offered the position of the second minister-at-large in New York City, Channing encouraged William Henry to take the post. Channing wrote to Dr. Charles Follen, then temporarily at the First Church, "I earnestly hope that he will enjoy sympathy and encouragement in his philanthropic work." [9]

Actually his work at the new undertaking proved to be very short-lived. His colleague, George Arnold, soon left for greener pastures. William Henry found that, among the workingmen of New York, his rather advanced intellectual ideas about religion did not make much of a mark. He also discovered to his chagrin that he could not compete with the existing agencies for social reform, and particularly he was swamped by the results of the Bank Panic of 1837 which began in May, just a few short months after his arrival.

Orestes Brownson, doing the same sort of work as Channing in Tuckerman's old parish in Chelsea, ran into similar difficulties; Brownson withdrew from his religious attempts to improve the workingman's lot and joined the Democratic Party to seek public rather than private solutions to the problems of poverty. Channing did not go this far. He merely left New York in August of 1837 when he became completely discouraged and returned to Boston where he came under the influence of James Freeman Clarke.

Fortunately, several letters from the young Channing to his mother are extant. Early in 1837 he wrote to his mother about some of the difficulties he was experiencing and why he was determined to give up his work in New York. He wrote that he had no one to advise him what to do except Mr. Arnold who "aided me as far as possible."

He took on as his district one of the poorest sections of the city and went through it street by street and house by house. He discovered in this survey that most of the children in the area already attended some sort of Sunday school. He had hoped to find an entrance into poor families through helping their children, yet he found 26 Sunday schools already operating in the area he had chosen for his territory. He had thought when he accepted the position that this would be a

[9] *Dictionary of American Biography;* Arthur W. Brown, *Always Young for Liberty: A Biography of William Ellery Channing* (Syracuse, 1956), p. 212.

*The Reverend William Henry Channing. From the
Unitarian Universalist Association Archives*

religious wilderness, but he found instead that the orthodox denominations were very hard at work.

So he began to conceive of new ways that the work he was supposed to do might become effective. He proposed

> that every family [presumably in the Second Church] shall take under
> their charge some one or more poor families, to be their spiritual and
> temporal friends; that such visitors should form a society to gain in-
> formation and concert [coordinate] measures for relieving poverty.

But evidently these suggestions were not thought to be practical by the people of the Second Church (if Channing stayed long enough to propose the suggestions to them).[10]

He also decided to do more in the way of actually conducting religious services, and he organized a chapel. The first service was held on May 27, 1837 (the month of the Bank Panic so perhaps religious services were in order), and ten people showed up. This shortly increased to twenty, and his wife constituted the choir. He expressed his disappointment, "the small hall near the Bowery was never full." When he decided to leave, he wrote his hopes to his uncle, "I had hopes that a society might be gathered there on a new plan, or in a new spirit." But, like Arnold, he became discouraged with the effectiveness of the role of the minister-at-large in the area of social change, and the depression of 1837 evidently clinched the matter in his mind for he fled back to Boston.[11]

Young William Henry Channing also kept in constant touch with his uncle William Ellery Channing. When he was the most discouraged his uncle wrote him a moralizing letter in an attempt to bolster his hopes and courage. But even this bit of support by his uncle did not keep young Channing in New York. With his departure from New York in 1837, the role of the minister-at-large in New York ceased, for there seem to have been only unsuccessful efforts to revive it.[12]

§　§　§

In his *Autobiography,* Orville Dewey told about another organization designed to help the poor, "The Employment Society," which still exists today as "The Society for the Relief and Employment of Poor Women."

---

[10] Letter of February 4, 1837, quoted in Octavius Brooks Frothingham, *Memoir of William Henry Channing* (Boston and New York: Houghton Mifflin Company, 1886), pp. 130–132.

[11] *Ibid.,* p. 141.

[12] William Ellery Channing, Boston, March 20, 1837, to William Henry Channing, New York; Pierpont Morgan Library, New York. Young Channing's later life led him back to New York again for another ill-fated experiment when in 1843 he founded an "Independent Society" which lasted for only two years. He went to Brook Farm but did not stay there long. He edited various journals, and most of his life after 1854 was spent in England. Henry Bellows tried to persuade Robert Waterston to take the position of minister-at-large but was unsuccessful.

To give help in a better way, an Employment Society was formed in our church [Second Church] to cut out and prepare garments for poor women to sew, and be paid for it. A salesroom was opened in Amity Street, to sell the articles made up, at a trifling addition to their cost. The ladies of the congregation were in attendance at the church, in a large ante-room to prepare the garments and give them out, and a hundred or more poor women came every Thursday to bring their work and receive more; and they have been coming to this day. It was thought an excellent plan, and was adopted by other churches. The ladies of All Souls joined in it, and the institution is now transferred to that church.[13]

Thus ended the experiment with the ministry-at-large in New York City.

[13] Mary E. Dewey (ed.), *op. cit.*, p. 92. This group still meets at All Souls on Thursdays, still hands out materials to be made into garments which are then given to the Friends Service Committee and hospitals.

12. The Last Years of Ware's Ministry

IF THE YEARS 1828–1834 were relatively smooth ones for William Ware, they were also relatively prosperous ones for the First Church, while its "sister," and now clearly rival, church was floundering. Ever since it had been founded, the Second Church had been having severe difficulties. The building of the church at Prince and Mercer streets had plunged the new society heavily into debt, and its pastor, William Lunt, was not drawing the crowds needed to aid its financial welfare.

In 1831, the Second Church suffered a severe blow when its building was damaged by fire. Two years later, Lunt's pastorate was terminated, and the society found itself once again searching for a suitable minister. Thus, when the members of the Second Church heard of Orville Dewey's availability, they lost no time in repeating their invitation of 1827 that Dewey should settle with the Second Church in New York.

Orville Dewey was a protégé of Channing and had filled Channing's pulpit at the Federal Street church much of the year 1822 while Channing was recovering his health in Europe. On Channing's return, Dewey had accepted a call to the New Bedford church. But, after only a few years there, he had found that pastorate extremely taxing. His labors became even more tedious to him after he declined the first New York offer, and Dewey found it necessary to spend more and more of each year relaxing at his country home in Sheffield, Massachusetts. In 1833, Dewey decided that the only thing that could help him recoup his strength was an extended trip abroad, and, through the help of some friends in New York who were originally from New Bedford, his plans became a reality. Messrs. Grinnell & Co., who owned a fleet of ships, offered Dewey a complimentary passage to and from

Orville Dewey, D.D.

Europe. Dewey sailed June 8, 1833, and returned a year later, feeling relaxed and refreshed.[1]

But Dewey had been back with his New Bedford parish only a month when he once again found the strain intolerable. Finding that he could no longer remain in New Bedford, he left his church without any plans for employment, expecting to retire for an indefinite period to his Sheffield home.

Perhaps through 31-year-old Moses Grinnell — who had only recently joined his family in New York at this time, and who attended the First Congregational Church — the trustees of the Second Church heard of Dewey's availability and made haste to invite him to preach in New York. Dewey agreed to preach temporarily; though he had long since run dry on new ideas for sermons and had preached each of his ideas at least five times over in New Bedford, Dewey realized that his stock of sermons would be new to New Yorkers. Moreover, his temporary term would probably not demand much in the way of

[1] Mary E. Dewey (ed.), *Autobiography and Letters of Orville Dewey, D.D.* (Boston, 1884), p. 66.

parish visiting, which Dewey disliked. Thus, Dewey came to New York in the early fall of 1834 to fill, temporarily, the pulpit of the Second Church.[2]

His success was immediate. The congregation which gathered to hear him on Sunday mornings and evenings grew rapidly. Dewey was just the tonic the Second Church needed. Before the year ended, the congregation begged Dewey to settle. But Dewey was still uncertain; he was afraid of having to face all over again the pressures that had besieged him in Massachusetts, and his eventual failure there. Dewey did agree to remain indefinitely while he thought the prospect over, however; and for the next twelve months he slid easily into his rising fame and prestige. The Second Church continued to iterate its pleas for Dewey to settle and, finally, in October of 1835 — "feeling stronger" — Dewey accepted. He was installed on November 8, 1835.

Moses H. Grinnell by George E. Perine. Courtesy of the New-York Historical Society, New York City

---

[2] *Ibid.*, p. 76. Moses Grinnell (1803–1877), a merchant shipowner originally from New Bedford, had been in New York from 1824. His firm became agents for a line of packet ships between London and New York and soon began building its own ships. Later he went into banking and insurance, then politics and public life.

Yet Dewey's relationship with the Second Congregational Unitarian Church was never a very secure one because Dewey's own personality was not secure. When he had first been approached to become the minister, it had been suggested that he might be only a preacher and be relieved from the parochial visiting, but the congregation decided that it could not support two ministers. Even a year later when he felt stronger and accepted the call, he was not happy about the physical situation of the church. He complained that

the church was on the corner of Mercer and Prince Streets; a bad situation, inasmuch as it was on a corner, that it was noisy, and the annoyance became so great that I seriously thought more than once of proposing to the congregation to sell and build elsewhere.

Yet he found the church agreeable in other ways and "it was easy to speak in." [3]

Dewey arrived in New York to take up the duties of his temporary pastorate just as William Ware was happily moving into a new brick parsonage on Reade Street. In February 1834 William Ware requested that the lease for the lot on Reade Street, now properly drained, be transferred to him so that he might build a brick house on the property. By this time the lease had finally been renewed by St. Mark's Church. The board agreed to Mr. Ware's proposal, providing that the house was built under the trustees' supervision "for the security or benefit of the Society." [4]

The Ware family moved into the new quarters later the same year. It is probable that the brick house of the Ware family replaced the rather ramshackle dwelling that had previously been occupied by the sexton, Mr. Gabriel Baldwin, and his family. Mr. Baldwin was a carpenter who moonlighted as sexton of the church, and he later set up his own building business and became quite successful. He resigned in the Spring of 1836 to devote his full time to carpentry. He was replaced by John Cochran in November of 1836. [5]

Even though William had long wanted to build his brick house on Reade Street, he had some premonitions that he would not be happy there. Writing to Bryant in Italy, he laid bare his reasons. He told

[3] Mary Dewey (ed.), *op. cit.*, p. 76.
[4] All Souls Minute Book, Volume I, p. 208.
[5] All Souls Cash Book, entry for November 5, 1836.

Bryant that their friends had furnished the house for them "in a very handsome & to me luxurious manner." But he "looked forward to the summer with some apprehension" because "of the extreme dirtiness of the street, and the high walls which so closely box us in on the rear which the south wind can neither get over nor through." But he recalled that the sexton's children "were always among the healthiest & heartiest we ever saw and he lived on the same street in an old shell of a house for over ten years. I dare say we shall do very well though there are not wanting prophets who predict the worst things." The worst things were to happen for two of his children, Helen and William, died in March, one month after Ware wrote the letter.

Ware was also concerned about the rundown condition of the city surrounding the church and his home. A number of projects for improvement of the area had been brought before the various city boards but nothing had been done. "I fear nothing will be done till one of our sweeping fires lays hold upon this whole quarter, levels it to the ground." [6]

Dewey's immediate success at the Second Church, particularly in the pulpit, must have disturbed Ware's temporary happiness, for although he respected Dewey and was delighted to have a colleague of this man's stature, he knew that his own weak spot in his ministry was in the pulpit. "Trouble," he wrote his brother Henry, "is hardly so familiar a thing to you, as it is to me." [7]

What was this "trouble" which bothered William? Obviously his feelings were mixed, for he appreciated his colleague and yet he wished that he himself were capable of the pulpit utterances of Orville Dewey which were drawing large crowds to the Second Church.

Even as late as 1835, nothing much had happened to increase the attendance at the evening service. Writing to Bryant, Ware said, "Our second service (now in the evening) is more forsaken than ever. I am greatly discouraged about it. It were much better to give it up entirely than to have it continue as it is." Ware went on to muster backing for his opinion. "Mr. Dewey is of the opinion that there ought not to be but one service on the Sabbath — that the better classes do not

[6] William Ware to William Cullen Bryant in Italy, February 3, 1835; in Bryant–Godwin Collection, Manuscript Division, New York Public Library.

[7] William Ware, quoted in John Ware, *Memoir of the Life of Henry Ware, Jr.* (Boston, 1846), p. 372.

want but one & will not generally attend upon but one." Ware added that, in Europe, Mr. Dewey said they had come to realize that only one service was important on a Sabbath, and other laymen in his own church had reported the same thing. He asked Bryant to report on the state of religion in Italy.

Ware also reported to Bryant about the conditions in the church of Orville Dewey,

> Our upper church is doing famously under Mr. Dewey who is there for a year — & perhaps for life — at least so I trust it will turn out. They have sold many pews and all have occupants. This is a quite refreshing change. He is a noble preacher. I do not know a better. He unites all the qualities it seems to me we must wish for in a preacher — seriousness, correctness, impressiveness . . . and yet liveliness in the matter which occasionally may be truly called eloquence.

But Orville Dewey lacked one quality which prevented his ministry in New York from becoming a lifetime profession. Eventually he came to grief at the Second Church simply because he could not go on preaching month after month.[8]

Ware's letter to Bryant was a prelude to tragedy that was to strike the Ware family within the next month. He had described recent illnesses from which the family had been suffering. Soon these proved fatal to two of the children. Helen died on March 16, 1835, at slightly over four years of age; and young Willie, who "has wholly conquered his humor" apparently had not, for he died six days later on March 21.[9]

There can be no doubt that the deaths of two of his children within a week deeply affected the spirits of William Ware. Perhaps this made the brick house on Reade Street and the position of pastor of the First Congregational Church less significant to him. Certainly the spirits of both Mary and William were distraught. This, as well as the other accumulated problems, may have caused him to begin to think of re-

[8] William Ware, letter to William Cullen Bryant in Italy, February 3, 1835, in Bryant–Godwin Collection, Manuscript Division, New York Public Library.

[9] All Souls Death Records, p. 28. As indicated on p. 137, these dates differ from those given in the Ware Genealogy. The "Register of Interments in the New York Marble Cemetery," Book 1, New-York Historical Society, gives the dates of interments: Helen Ware, March 18, 1835, and William Ware, March 23, 1835.

signing the pulpit at First Church, even as the general Unitarian movement in New York City was spreading.

§ § §

Although at least twelve organized churches had been established in Brooklyn by 1833 — one Dutch Reformed, two Episcopal, three Methodist, one Baptist, three Presbyterian, and two Roman Catholic — those who were of the Unitarian persuasion still took the ferry to lower Manhattan and attended either the First or the Second Unitarian Church.

It was even more irksome to attend churches nearer home which did not provide them with the kind of religious atmosphere which was amicable to their temperaments. (Brooklyn was growing and now contained more than 20,000 inhabitants.)

Steam Boat Wharf, New York, 1831 (Drawn by Charles Burton, Engraved by S. H. Gimber, Published by Bourne). Courtesy of the New-York Historical Society, New York City

The story is told that one Sunday as Captain John Frost, William H. Cary, and John Jewett, Jr., with various members of their families were returning in the ferryboat from Manhattan, Captain Frost remarked that it was high time that they had Unitarian preaching in Brooklyn. The idea was heartily seconded by the rest of the group. Other families of like persuasion were consulted, and steps were immediately taken to found a new church.

In response to an invitation from Mr. Josiah Dow, nine other gentlemen met at his residence on the 19th of June 1833 to take whatever action they thought might be best in this regard. The names of those present were: Josiah Dow, Seth Low, John Frost, W. H. Cary, Alexander H. Smith, William H. Hale, Charles Woodward, Henry Leeds, Thomas Woodward, and George Blackburn. Of these, only William H. Cary had been especially active in the early days of the First Church. Most of the others in 1833 owned pews in either the First or Second Church.

At this meeting, Josiah Dow, Seth Low, John Frost, and William H. Cary were appointed a committee to make arrangements as necessary. A week later, five more gentlemen had joined the group: George S. Cary, P. G. Taylor, Richard W. Dow, James Walters, and Joshua Jolferd. At a third meeting the number was increased to eighteen, and all pledged themselves to form a new Unitarian Society. They engaged "Classical Hall" as a place of worship, and a letter was sent to Boston asking that a suitable preacher should be sent to Brooklyn.

The reply, written by the Rev. Henry Ware, Sr., promised all possible encouragement, but expressed doubt whether a preacher could be secured as soon as was suggested. An advertisement was placed in the *Brooklyn Evening Star* for four successive weeks announcing divine worship. There being no clergyman present, the exercises were all conducted by laymen. Mr. Seth Low at one meeting read a sermon and offered a prayer. The Rev. David Hatch Barlow was secured for the fall preaching assignments, and on March 31, 1834, he was unanimously called to the pastorate.

The founders set up a Sunday school and provided some sort of music. They adopted Greenwood's collection of hymns rather than Sewall's. Mr. Barlow was installed on September 17, 1834, as the minister, and the two churches in New York sent delegates that met in an Ordaining Council along with several other churches. The Rev. William Ware was elected moderator. In the Service of Ordination and Installation which followed, Ware gave the charge and also the concluding prayer. After the service there was a sumptuous repast in the garden of Mr. Josiah Dow, which was interrupted by a drenching rain.

The new society prospered under Mr. Barlow. In 1835 it purchased for $8,000 the building of the Second Presbyterian Church in Adams Street, also known as Gothic Hall. During this year the society was incorporated under the name of the "First Unitarian Church of Brooklyn." The financial crash of 1837 greatly embarrassed the financial position of the new church, and, that July, Barlow left Brooklyn. During 1837 the church consulted with the Rev. Dr. Dewey and Dr. Charles Follen, and later in the year the Rev. Frederick West Holland became the second minister, ordained on April 11, 1838. Again the representatives of the New York churches were present, as was Ralph Waldo Emerson, who by invitation, sat on the council. Emerson offered the opening prayer in the services, and the prayer of ordination was by Dr. Follen.[10]

§ § §

During the period that the Brooklyn church was being established and while Dewey was beginning his work at Second Church, Ware initiated steps at the First Church which eventually led to his resignation. In a letter to the annual meeting of 1835, he devoted attention to the almost total loss of congregational attendance at the evening services. Less than "a quarter or a fifth of the morning number."

"The only probable solution to the evil" that he foresaw — since he had been there 13 years and his preaching would not change — was "my resignation and the introduction of some person into my place to whom a more willing and interested attendance would be given." [11]

This suggestion came as something of a shock to the society. They drew up an elaborate set of resolutions testifying to their "highest respect for the talents of our Pastor," discharging him of any blame for the poor attendance at evening services, and hoping that he was bound to them "by ties which we trust will never be dissolved." At the same

[10] A. P. Putnam, *Unitarianism in Brooklyn,* printed sermon plus additional material preached at the Commemorative Services held on April 25, 1869, on the twenty-fifth anniversary of the consecration of the church (Brooklyn, 1869).

[11] All Souls Minute Book, Volume I, pp. 222–223.

Nathaniel Currier Lithograph of the Great Fire of 1835
from Coenties Slip. Artist, J. H. Bufford.
The J. Clarence Davies Collection, Museum of
the City of New York

time they increased his salary by $500 to make their point explicitly clear.[12]

But with the relentlessness so characteristic of him, Ware wrote again to the trustees, declining the raise, thanking them for their reassurances, and still urging on them his suggestion that he should resign.[13]

Dumbfounded and perplexed, the trustees decided to lay the matter before the society and, on November 15th, another meeting of the society was held. But the congregation, equally dismayed and dumbfounded, merely referred it back to the trustees. The business must have been a little wearing on all concerned, but particularly on the trustees who had been the middle men in this rather unorthodox sequence of events. They met on December 7th and rescinded the raise,

---

[12] *Ibid.*, pp. 220–221.
[13] *Ibid.*, pp. 226–227.

*Merchants' Exchange, Wall Street, New York City, 1831
(Drawn by Charles Burton, Engraved by H. Fossette,
Published by Bourne). Courtesy of the New-York
Historical Society, New York City*

but accorded Ware the $200 dividend he had received the previous
year as repayment of the salary he had surrendered twelve years earlier.

§   §   §

A week later, a severe fire hit the lower part of the city. It began
during the early evening of December 16th, and by 9 P.M. had reached
serious proportions. It was a bitterly cold night, the temperature
dropped to about zero, but the flames generated intense heat, and
more and more of the buildings in Pearl and Front streets were soon
caught up in the spreading holocaust.

*Ruins in Exchange Place, December 17, 1835 (Garden Street Church
on the Left). Aquatint by W. J. Bennett after a Painting by
N. Calgo. Courtesy of the New-York Historical Society,
New York City*

By midnight the flames remained unchecked and were rapidly en-
gulfing buildings in adjacent blocks. The firemen continued to muster
their strength against the inferno all through the next morning and
afternoon, by which time the smoke was thick over the entire area that
comprised New York City. By December 18th, the tide turned, but it
took a good part of the day to extinguish every ember of the fire. In
the end, the fire had consumed thirteen blocks and the loss, including
the Stock Exchange and many office buildings, was estimated at thirty
million dollars.

Ware's sermon on December 20th was addressed to the event, the
text being from Jeremiah 22:8: "And they shall say every man to his
neighbor, wherefore hath the Lord done this to this great City?" That
Monday, the trustees thanked him for his "eloquent and appropriate
discourse" and asked to have it published. All of the trustees signed
the letter. Never in his ministry had Ware received from his church
so pointed an expression of commendation for one of his sermons. With

quiet dignity, Ware thanked the trustees for "the kind expressions you note," and submitted the requested copy.[14]

Catharine Sedgwick commented,

> Mr. Ware has preached an excellent sermon today from that most appropriate text, "who hath done this unto this great city?", & he has showed that being in exact obedience to the physical laws of Providence it matters not whether the hand that set the fire was a madman's, an incendiary's, or a careless match's. He admonished the merchants, the nobility of the city, that they needed this rebuke. He commented upon the progress of luxury, of vain silly expenditure within the last few years. He said we were the reproach of foreigners & a byword among ourselves. He confessed the impotence of the preacher who could urge only a precept against the energy of infectious example.[15]

But Ware saw — or, at least was convinced that he saw — the handwriting on the wall. And he was quick to perceive that his six years of relative calm and security had come to an end. Calm and security, success and contentment, were alien to Ware's character.

William Ware's true feelings about the profession of the ministry and his own inability to practice it in the ideal way that he desired are nowhere more clearly shown than in an address which he gave almost a year earlier than these events, at the installation of D. H. Barlow at the Brooklyn church in January 1835. Ware expressed his deep feelings about the ministry from which he was soon to take his leave. In a sense, it is a valedictory to the ministry, eloquently stated, and deeply felt.[16]

Ware contrasted the "useful, conscientious minister" with the "selfish, worldly man, who seeks himself and preaches himself." He bemoaned the fact that so many of the contemporary clergy seemed to despise their profession,

> abandoning it for some other, reaching after other things, aping the manners and ways of the world, covetous of some other and higher reputation than that which a quiet, faithful discharge of the duties of

[14] *Ibid.*, pp. 232–233.

[15] Catharine M. Sedgwick, *Journal*, entry for December 20, 1835, Massachusetts Historical Society.

[16] *The Christian Examiner*, January 1835, p. 402.

their great office would confer. This brings contempt upon the order and justly.

Then Ware got into the heart of his subject and the basis of his own unhappiness in the ministry. He stated that a minister must faithfully discharge his pastoral duties, but that

the pulpit must claim your principal care.... Think not to make up for deficiency here by increased familiarity with your people. ... No matter how much you may go from house to house, you will obtain scarce any thing better for your pains, than the reputation of a clerical gossip, except your character as a sound and learned, an eloquent or a useful preacher, make you welcome by making you respected.

Here in a few sentences we find the basis of Ware's disillusionment with himself. Try as hard as he could he could not communicate from the pulpit even though he was an excellent writer. This sermon gives us insight into his own restlessness.

§   §   §

At a meeting of the board on September 12, 1836, Andrew Snelling, who had been elected to the board in 1833, announced that Mr. Ware wished to address the trustees, and a special meeting was called for the next evening. Ware used the intervening time to change his mind about appearing personally and to commit his thoughts to writing. Seven members of the board were present to hear the secretary, Charles Francis, read William Ware's long letter, which announced his resignation as of "last Sunday," adding this was done "with great pain" but "without a single feeling of regret."

He was "so dissatisfied with my success in my profession" and so convinced that his decision was the best not only for his own peace but for the general welfare of the congregation itself, that he wanted their earliest acceptance of his resignation so that he could complete "the necessary arrangements for my removal." The essence of the statement was his feeling that it is "impossible that you should do otherwise than decline under my ministry." [17]

The following Friday, the board met again to approve a formal

[17] All Souls Minute Book, Volume I, pp. 239–242. For the trustees' response, see pp. 243–245.

response to Mr. Ware, and on Sunday, September 18th, the Rev. Mr. Barlow, the minister of the Brooklyn church, read from the pulpit Ware's resignation and the trustees' reply.

The congregation was severely shocked by their minister's resignation and self-abnegation, for the members had truly come to love and respect him. The trustees deeded over the lot on Reade Street and the house to Ware and his family, requesting only that should Ware retire from the city, he would allow them first option on the sale of the house. It was only a fortnight later when Ware did exactly this, and after all of the arrangements had been made, the Wares quit the city which had never fully been home to them despite their 15-year residence.

Writing to Bryant after leaving New York City permanently, William Ware wrote that he had read an extract from the *New York Herald* in one of the Northampton papers giving some rather fallacious reasons for his leaving the First Church. The story which appeared in the *Hampshire Gazette* read as follows:

> PLAIN LANGUAGE — The New York Herald states that the Rev. Mr. Ware, in that city, in his recent farewell sermon, gave his congregation rather a severe lecture. "I have," said he, "labored here for years to save souls — but my hearers are so negligent and inattentive, that I find it is no use. — The fashions and vanities of this world overpower the word. I have been offered an increase of salary — but increase of salary is not my object. It is an increase of grace — increase of salvation. I am going where my salary will be less but where I hope there will be more piety and more religion.[18]

The garbled report by James Gordon Bennett, the flamboyant editor of the *New York Herald*, exceedingly irritated William Ware. He detested the "penny paper" of Bennett, and the article expressed sentiments about his leaving the New York pulpit which had no basis in fact. If there was anything that had not been distorted in his relationship with the church it had been the problem of money. The trustees were constantly pressing upon him money either to repay what they felt he had relinquished in the early years, or to increase his salary.

The Wares settled for a brief period in Brookline, Massachusetts, where William devoted his energies chiefly to writing. In June of 1837

---

[18] *Hampshire Gazette,* November 16, 1836, p. 2.

he moved to Waltham, Massachusetts, where he supplied the pulpit of the Second Church for nearly a year. The Wares then moved to Jamaica Plain, where they purchased a small farm, and William devoted most of his time to writing, although preaching occasionally. Ware also edited the *Christian Examiner* for a period of two years, from 1842 to 1844. He accepted a call from the West Cambridge Church in 1844, and there he hoped to settle permanently. But very shortly he was stricken with what was diagnosed as epilepsy. He resigned from his pastorate a few months after his settlement. For a short period of time he was involved with the ministry-at-large program in Boston.

In the spring of 1848 he went to Europe, where he traveled alone for more than a year, passing most of his time in Italy. He lived chiefly in Florence and Rome, where the antiquities interested him exceedingly and the art brought out his incipient artistic nature. When he returned home he prepared a series of lectures on his European experiences which he delivered in Boston, New York, and other places in the winter of 1849. In 1851 these lectures were published in a volume titled *Sketches of European Capitals*.[19]

In February 1852, he was stricken with an attack of such intensity that he was unconscious for nine days, and died on February 19, 1852, at the age of 54 years.

Early in his ministry William Ware had looked for another field of endeavor than the pulpit in which he felt uncomfortable. Probably encouraged by both William Cullen Bryant and Catharine Sedgwick he had begun to write a series of imaginary letters for the "Knickerbocker Magazine" which published them serially under the title of "Letters from Palmyra" in 1837. These were so highly successful that they were published two years later under the title of *Zenobia*.[20]

Thus the remaining years of William Ware's life after leaving the pastorate of the First Church were spent not primarily in the ministry, although he did some preaching, but in the writing of three lengthy novels which gained him something of a reputation in the field of American literature. These three novels, *Zenobia*, *Aurelian*, and *Julian*, were so long that they were often published as two volumes. The first

---

[19] See William B. Sprague, *Annals of the American Pulpit* ..., Volume VIII (New York, 1865), pp. 511–512.

[20] *The Christian Examiner*, September 1837, pp. 99–121, gave a lengthy review and praised the letters highly.

of these, *Zenobia, or the Fall of Palmyra,* and the last, *Aurelian, or Rome in the Third Century,* are concerned with the life and exploits of Zenobia, a third-century queen of Palmyra, who set up a kingdom in the Middle East with Roman encouragement, but whose capital was subsequently destroyed by Aurelian because the Roman emperor became convinced that Zenobia meant to take over the entire Middle East and Egypt and set up her own rival empire.

Julian is a novel of an entirely different sort, being set in the time of Jesus, in the locale of Palestine. Julian is a Roman who travels in the Holy Land and eventually meets the historic Jesus in much the same way that Lew Wallace's "Ben Hur" was later to do. There are some amazing descriptions of life and times in the first century A.D. in the city of Caesarea on the Palestinian coast, which are even more remarkable considering the knowledge of Roman times available when William Ware was writing. All three novels are well worth reading. They have a scholarly precision often lacking in historical novels and were published by Charles S. Francis, who had become active in the New York church during the latter years of Ware's New York ministry.[21]

The memorial plaque which the congregation of the First Church commissioned to honor the life and contribution of William Ware in 1855 is one of the most beautiful, executed with an artistry and sense of craftsmanship that would have pleased him exceedingly, except that in his modesty he would never have consented to its erection. Henry Bellows remarked toward the end of his ministry that there were, alas, very few in the congregation in 1879 who remembered William Ware. "But," he said, "in the memory of a few of the children of some of his best friends there still lingers the fragrance of his rare and exquisite purity, elevation, and culture. Happily, we keep the record of his ministry in monumental beauty upon the walls of this church." [22]

In summary, one must say that the fifteen years which he spent as the first pastor of the First Church were productive years in spite of his own feelings of insecurity. He was as young a man as William Lunt when Lunt first came to Second Church. He did not have the

---

[21] *Zenobia, or the Fall of Palmyra* (New York: C. S. Francis Company, 1839); *Julian, or Scenes in Judea* (1841); and *Aurelian, or Rome in the Third Century* (1849).

[22] Henry W. Bellows, Fortieth Anniversary Address, January 5, 12, 1879, p. 11.

WILLIAM WARE
Born Aug. 3 1797 Died Feb. 19 1852
First Minister of this Congregation
Ordained Dec. 18 1821
Resigned Sep. 16 1836
Author of
ZENOBIA AVRELIAN JVLIAN
His Ministry planted
VNITARIAN CHRISTIANITY
In this City
His life commended it
His memory endears it
ERECTED MDCCCLXIII

HE BEING DEAD YET SPEAKETH

*The Plaque Erected in Memory of
William Ware by the Congregation
in 1863. In the Unitarian Church
of All Souls. Photograph by
Rita E. Jamason*

style of Orville Dewey. Yet he gave the First Church a sense of stability in his pioneer work in the city that assured the permanent establishment of the Unitarian religion in New York City.

13. *Follen Comes to First Church*

Axooooooooooo

After the resignation and departure of William Ware,
the society was faced with finding a new minister to lead the church in
what Ware himself considered to be its greater destiny. In the manner
of most churches looking for a replacement for their pastors, the First
Congregational Church expected to find a new minister who had
exactly those qualities which Mr. Ware lacked. Although the minutes
of the society during this period reflect very little of the society's concerns with finding such a man, an apparent candidate, Charles Theodore Christian Follen, preached for two weeks shortly after Ware's
departure in early October 1836.

At the end of the two-week period, the congregation was not entirely satisfied with Follen, but they asked him if he would serve as
temporary minister until May 1st. Delighted to have even a temporary
pulpit of his own, and hoping to be called permanently, Follen agreed.
He returned to Massachusetts to collect his family and belongings and,
never having been ordained, called upon his friend William Ellery
Channing to perform this rite before he went back to New York. On
October 30, 1836, in Channing's church in Boston, the service was
performed.

Who was this new "Acting Minister" of the First Church? Charles
Follen was the second son of a German judge, Christoph Follenius,
of Giessen and Hesse-Darmstadt. He was born on September 4, 1796,
in the village of Romrod, to which his mother had fled to escape
Napoleon's armies during the turmoil of the French occupation of
Giessen. His mother died when Charles was only three, and the family
was scattered among various grandparents, only Charles remaining
with his father. After several years, his father married again. Fortunately for Charles the stepmother was devoted and sensitive, and

204

took the boy, now seven, into her nurturing care. He was intellectually precocious, but emotionally timid; later in his life, Follen recounted how he had forced himself to sit in a graveyard each night in order that he might overcome his fears. This eerie project and other practices of self-discipline helped him to attain the self-control which became a distinguishing trait of his personality.[1]

Charles was sent to the public schools where his precocity was recognized, and, after passing brilliantly through these years of his education, he entered the gymnasium where he distinguished himself in both ancient and modern languages. A teacher at the gymnasium aroused Charles' interest in politics, inspiring him in the cause of German freedom and hatred for the French domination under Napoleon. It was at the gymnasium, too, that Charles discovered the great German philosopher and poet of German freedom, Johann Schiller. Schiller had believed that freedom, in the Kantian sense, was synonymous with the moral nature of man, an ideal which Follen chose as the theme of his life.

At about this same time, Charles underwent a profound personal experience which was further to influence his chosen philosophy of life. Parts of Germany were virtually atheistic at the time of his birth, and Charles grew up with no religious education of any import. Cultivated people of his milieu looked upon Christian tenets as absurd and nonintellectual, as superstitions which no rational person could accept unless it be purely hypocritically. Thus, when Charles was once shut up in a room by himself to take a school examination, the object of which was to write a theme explaining how a man could willingly die for a cause, he was totally at a loss.

As he searched his mental store of historical events and considered those which might lead a man to give up his life, Charles began to perceive that there was something within a man which could *not* die, and which emerged to sacrifice what was purely temporal and vastly less important than this ultimate Self. "That there was something immortal in the human consciousness was proved by the fact that there

[1] The sources of the early life of Follen are in Eliza Cabot Follen, *The Works of Charles Follen, with a Memoir of His Life* (Boston: Hilliard, Gray, and Company, 1842); George W. Spindler, *The Life of Karl Follen* (Chicago: University of Chicago Press, 1917); William B. Sprague, *The Annals of the American Pulpit ...*, Volume VIII (New York, 1865); and *The Dictionary of American Biography*.

Dr. Charles Follen. From a Woodcut in the Possession of the Church of All Souls

was something mortal that could be separated from him and given away by it." Having finished his theme, Follen was profoundly impressed with what he called a "living communion with my Creator [which] gave me a flood of light."[2]

In 1813, Follen was graduated at the age of 16 from the gymnasium and entered the University of Giessen to study law. But immediately, he became active in the growing German patriotic movement which was mustering support among liberals against the Napoleonic domination of Europe. The King of Prussia appealed to German youth to take up arms against Napoleon and, in response, Follen, not yet 17, and two of his brothers, joined a corps of student riflemen volunteers. When this campaign came to a close in 1814, the brothers returned home safely, Charles to continue his studies in jurisprudence at Giessen. He received his doctorate in civil and canon law in the spring of 1818.

Upon his graduation, Follen began to lecture on jurisprudence at the University of Jena, and undertook, at the same time, a careful study of revealed religion. He could not accept dogmas on the "simple faith" espoused by the church, and proceeded to investigate all heretical arguments as well as all orthodox tenets. But his final decision in favor of the truth of Biblical teachings and revealed religion came almost entirely as a result of his own personal revelation.

Later in 1818, Follen was employed as a counselor to defend small counties and villages in the province of Hesse against what they felt were unfair taxes imposed upon them by the government. Follen won his case, but at an enormous cost; he lost his right to practice law as well as to teach because of his radical political activities. He was finally offered a position at Jena, only to be removed from it almost immediately for the same reasons. A popular German dramatist of conservative political tendencies was assassinated by a young liberal fanatic, and Follen was accused of being an accomplice in the murder. A target of suspicion and under constant police surveillance, Follen moved to Strasbourg, then to Paris. But in Paris, too, the murder of the Duke of Berri resulted in the issuing of an order by the French government requiring all foreigners to leave the country, and Follen was thus forced to go to Switzerland.

There, he received an invitation to become a professor at the

[2] Sprague, *op. cit.*, p. 546.

Cantonal School of the Grisons in Chur. He accepted, but in his history lectures, he expounded upon what were essentially Unitarian views, which created a Calvinistic reaction. Again, Follen had to move on. He went to Basel, where he was appointed public lecturer at the university. He remained in Basel until 1824, when a demand for his arrest was made by the Prussian government for what it considered revolutionary activities. Although Follen, in keeping with his personal philosophy, consented to being arrested, his numerous friends had cooler heads and convinced him to flee to America.

He arrived in New York City on December 19, 1824, accompanied by his friend Karl Beck. He was strongly moved by his first glimpse of the "promised land" of freedom, as he peered at it through the heavy fog. He was almost afraid that the splendid city might vanish like a dream. So powerful was his emotion, when he finally landed, that, he afterward stated, he wanted to kneel upon the ground and kiss it.

Follen arrived with little money and no visible means of gaining employment. Fortunately, General Lafayette, who was in this country at the time, was a friend of Follen's, and through the General's influence, Follen went to Philadelphia, where he spent most of a year learning English and the customs of America. Follen was so pleased with what he saw in this country and the outlook for American democracy that he immediately made application for citizenship.

Through the efforts of Mr. Du Ponceau of Philadelphia and Professor George Ticknor of Harvard, an acquaintance of General Lafayette's, Follen received an appointment to teach the German language at Harvard. Follen arrived in Cambridge in December 1825, and found that he was completely at home in the academic life there. Germanic literature had never been taught at Harvard before Follen's arrival, but there was a great interest in Goethe, Schiller, Herder, and others of the Weimar School of German literature. Follen also gave lectures on civil law and gained some popularity in Boston social circles because of them. In his spare time, he worked on the preparation of a German reader and a German grammar.

Sometime just before he settled in Cambridge, Follen had visited New York for a few weeks. There he looked up Catharine Sedgwick, whose recently published novel, *Redwood*, had served as Follen's first textbook in the English language. Her writings had deeply impressed Follen, and he had resolved to meet their author if possible. Catharine

*Eliza Cabot Follen. Portrait in
the Follen Church, East Lexington,
Massachusetts. Photograph by
Duette Photographers*

and her brother Henry, in turn, took warmly to the German immigrant, and a strong friendship developed.

The Sedgwicks armed Follen with letters of introduction to their friends in Massachusetts, including one to Catharine's good friend Eliza Lee Cabot in Boston. Miss Cabot was the daughter of Samuel and Sarah Cabot, nine years Follen's senior, and a member of one of the best New England families. Catharine's letter to Eliza urged her to "forgo all German prejudices and speak kindly to the man." She had found him very agreeable and thought Eliza might too. "I don't believe he is afraid of wetting his feet or driving a horse provided it be not rampant." Eliza and Charles soon formed a warm relationship which culminated in their marriage on September 15, 1828.[3]

[3] Catharine M. Sedgwick to Eliza Lee Cabot, December 12, 1825, in Catharine M. Sedgwick–Eliza Cabot Follen Papers, Massachusetts Historical Society.

Eliza Cabot, now Follen, had received an excellent education, and had become a cultivated woman with marked intellectual attainments. She was living at the time of her marriage with two of her sisters in a home of their own, both parents being dead. She was interested in literary, cultural, and religious enterprises, particularly the education of children. She taught Sunday school at William Ellery Channing's church on Federal Street in Boston. It was Channing's custom to meet with his Sunday-school teachers on Thursday evenings to consider the Biblical passages which were to form the basis for the children's Sunday lessons, and then afterward to hold a spontaneous discussion on some subject of interest to the members of the group. At Eliza's invitation, Follen attended one of these sessions, and that particular evening the subject turned to the significance of the death of Jesus.[4]

At first, as the regular members of the group participated enthusiastically, Follen remained quiet and unobtrusive, though listening intently. Hoping to draw the shy visitor into the discussion circle, Dr. Channing asked Follen if he had anything to say on the matter. Dr. Follen was taken aback, but without hesitation recounted his own experience of revelation that had occurred during his boyhood. All present were deeply impressed with Follen's intense enthusiasm, the high degree of articulation with which he expounded, and the obviously edified and enlightened ideas he set forth. One person went so far as to suggest that Follen become a minister.

Channing was so deeply struck by Follen's story that he dismissed the group earlier than was usual, detaining only Follen. The two men began a heartfelt conversation that was to set a precedent for many more like them in a close friendship that was to last for many years. Channing saw in Follen a man "whose religion was not an inheritance, nor an imitation, nor a convention of society, but the covenant of a consciously finite being with God, begun with the spirit, and made manifest in knowledge of Jesus Christ."[5]

The more that Follen thought about the idea of becoming a Uni-

[4] For Mrs. Follen's career, see *The Dictionary of American Biography.* A short but lively modern account of her appears in Elizabeth Bancroft Schlesinger, "Two Early Harvard Wives: Eliza Farrar and Eliza Follen," *New England Quarterly,* June 1965, especially pp. 156–166.

[5] From a letter by Elizabeth P. Peabody, quoted in Sprague, *op. cit.,* pp. 544–547.

tarian minister, the more warmly he felt about it. Channing not only encouraged him to pursue this vocation, but offered to help him attain it. So, under Channing's tutelage, Follen prepared himself to preach. He entered the ministry in the summer of 1828 and, though not yet ordained, became an active guest preacher and substitute minister for the next five years. He first preached for the Rev. Mr. Francis William Pitt Greenwood, minister of King's Chapel, and was immediately asked by the church at Nahant to fill the pulpit for several Sundays during his vacation from his college duties. At the end of the summer, Follen was appointed instructor in ecclesiastical history and ethics in the Divinity School at Harvard. Added to the other courses he was teaching, this appointment kept Follen actively engaged for the next two years.[6]

In March 1830, Follen received his American citizenship, and the event filled him with pride and ecstatic joy. His wife wrote later that "he brought me the certificate that he was an American citizen with a glow of joy in his face, and declared that the naturalized foreigner alone had the right to boast of his citizenship, for with him it was choice." All of the patriotic zeal young Charles had held for his native Germany was transferred to his love of America, and his patriotism and love of political freedom were inextricably bound up with his religious views.[7]

Follen was eager to have his own pulpit and when, in the summer of 1830, he was invited to become the permanent minister of the Unitarian church in Newburyport, he was strongly tempted to accept it. The president of Harvard College was opposed to Follen's leaving the college, however, and, according to Mrs. Follen, promised Follen a full professorship. Such a professorship in the Department of Latin had been offered earlier, but, as this was not in Follen's field of interests, he had declined it.

Finally Follen was assured of a faculty position at Harvard. He was offered a full professorship in Germanic literature. Although the chair was established on only a temporary basis, to be reviewed in five years, Follen eagerly accepted it because one of his interests was to open the treasure-house of German culture to New England. This, as much as the salary and prestige, led to his decision. The professorship

---

[6] Sprague, *op. cit.*, pp. 541–542.
[7] Eliza Cabot Follen, *op. cit.*, p. 267.

would demand much of Follen's time and energies, so Follen resigned from the Divinity School.

Follen is sometimes credited with introducing to New England the charming custom of a decorated Christmas tree. Harriet Martineau, the English novelist, was present the first time he did it for his young son, Charley, then only two years old. For Follen it was the happiest day of the year. A young fir had been planted in a tub and the base ornamented with moss. The branches of the tree sparkled with gilded egg-cups, gay paper cornucopias filled with comfits, lozenges, and barley-sugar. "Smart dolls and other whimsies glittered in the ever-green, and there was not a twig which had not something sparkling upon it." Then the candles were lit, the doors were open, and the children poured in. At the sight of the glow, all voices hushed. "Nobody spoke, only Charley leaped for joy." Soon, the children discovered the sweets, and "the babble began again." [8]

While conducting his lectureship at Harvard, Follen also began a course on moral philosophy which he gave to the public in Boston. In these lectures he spoke out against slavery, and in 1834 he joined the New England Anti-Slavery Society. At its first convention held in Boston he drafted "The Address to the People of the United States." At a hearing before a committee of the Massachusetts legislature in January 1836, he vigorously protested the proposed attempt to prevent the publication of Abolitionist writings.

Follen's friends at Harvard and in proper Boston society tried to advise Follen against publicly espousing the cause against slavery, but Follen was too strongly drawn to the movement to resist it. When the trial period for the chair in German literature had about one year to go before it was to be decided whether it would become permanent, Follen asked if it was to be continued. The college informed him that it was not since the special subsidy by friends was not renewed. Left with only the position of teacher of the German language, which paid him no more than $500 a year, Follen was forced to start planning for other means to supplement his income.

During the winter of 1834–1835, Follen preached from time to time to a small group of people in East Lexington, Massachusetts, who were trying to form a Unitarian society in that community. However,

[8] Harriet Martineau, *Retrospect of Western Travel* (New York: Charles Lohman, 1838), Volume 2, pp. 178–179.

he was not asked to be its permanent minister. His relations with Harvard were becoming increasingly difficult, and, in January, he severed his ties with the college entirely, attempting to eke out his and his family's existence by taking in pupils.

In the summer of 1836 Follen and his family made a western journey with a number of friends including Harriet Martineau, the distinguished English writer and sister of James Martineau, the famous English Unitarian preacher. The party intended to go down the Ohio River in order to visit a German colony in Missouri, but "on account of the proslavery animosity against Miss Martineau, this visit was abandoned." They took a more northerly route, traveling by way of Niagara Falls and the Great Lakes as far as Chicago. In Chicago, Follen was asked to address a small group of Unitarians who were completely isolated and wanted to found a church. His preaching was so powerful and so "impressed them . . . that they raised a subscription of $20,000 to build a meeting house and extended to him an urgent invitation to become their pastor." Follen, however, did not accept their offer. He undoubtedly felt that he too would be intellectually and culturally isolated in a place as far west as Chicago.[9]

Follen returned to Stockbridge at the end of the summer and, shortly afterward, was invited to fill in as temporary preacher for the First Congregational Church in New York City. Evidence indicates that Dr. Follen at first rejected the offer of the New York society in August of 1836 because the parish indicated that it was interested in ministerial work among the poor. Dr. Follen felt that this was a problem that he knew very little about. His interests were literary, and as we know — Abolitionist.

Mrs. Follen wrote from Stockbridge to Samuel Cabot in Boston that her husband

> thinks that he has not that practical knowledge of the physical wants of the poor & the best way of providing for them which is very important for them in New York. . . . Then all the precious study of his whole life would be thrown away in such an occupation as no other pursuit would be compatible or possible with this one . . . I know that our anti-slavery feelings being what they are are so in the way of our interest.[10]

[9] George W. Spindler, *op. cit.*, p. 91.

[10] Eliza Follen to Samuel Cabot, August 13, 1836, in Samuel Cabot Papers, Box 6, Massachusetts Historical Society.

But eventually Follen accepted the call to New York. The First Congregational Church and its trustees were, at the time of Follen's arrival, too much concerned with locating new premises for a church building to pursue diligently the choice of a new permanent pastor. Almost from the time of occupancy, the church on Chambers Street had been a source of trouble and financial outlays for repairs. Although the building was constantly undergoing repairs of one sort or another, the particular difficulty was associated with the roof.

When the building had been standing for only four years, it had to be closed altogether during the summer of 1825 for masonry repairs, and only the following year, the roof required more work. Relatively minor repairs on the roof were made in 1827 and 1828, and major ones in 1829. In 1830, the church building again underwent major repairs, particularly on its roof.[11] These lasted for three years but, in 1834, extensive masonry work was required yet *again,* and minor repairs were needed the two following years. Now, in 1836, the congregation had become so exasperated with the building that they decided to try to sell it and find another suitable place on which to build a better house of worship.

To finance the new building, the regular collections for the poor, which had been initiated more than ten years earlier when the church's finances began to get on firmer ground, were discontinued and replaced with collections taken up "for the benefit of the general funds of the Church."[12] The rent on the basement rooms which housed the free school was increased from $200 to $250, and efforts to sell pews, and to dun those who were in arrears on their pew assessments, were stepped up. The society also procured a loan from the Phoenix Bank. But no suitable buyers for the building came forward, as it was a time of financial distress in the country; and so, for a while, the congregation resigned themselves to make do with the present church.

Follen plunged into his new duties with enthusiastic optimism. After some years of facing an uncertain future, at last he had a splendid opportunity for fulfillment and success, and in no less than the great metropolis of New York. His sermons were well-received, and he seemed to be personally greeted with warmth and cordiality. Follen's prospects looked bright indeed — until Thanksgiving Day 1836.[13]

[11] All Souls Minute Book, Volume I, p. 165.
[12] *Ibid.,* p. 250.
[13] From this point in the narrative until the Follens left New York there is

Follen had been politely warned, when he was invited to remain for six months with the New York congregation, to refrain from exposing his antislavery sentiments; if possible, to dissolve his connections with the Antislavery Society, but at least to refrain from acting in its behalf. In conscience, Follen could not do this, but he did proceed cautiously. On one of the first Sundays after his ordination, Follen preached on the duties of a Christian minister and explained, in well-reasoned and acceptable terms, how important it was for a minister to associate himself with and to encourage all benevolent and Christian-oriented associations. He named by way of example several such associations, the Antislavery Society among them. In this rather tame context, the sermon was accepted without incident. As Thanksgiving Day approached, therefore, Follen decided to use the occasion to build upon this foundation to try to engender further support for the cause against slavery.

Follen decided to use a sermon that he had preached several years earlier at Cambridgeport which contained a fairly strong passage on slavery. Lest he offend his new congregation, he decided to wait until he was in the pulpit before making any decisions about whether or not to change the passage in doubt. Follen was good at extemporizing, and as he believed firmly in the power of the Spirit of God, he felt that his inspiration of the moment would be his best guide as to how to treat the subject. The Thanksgiving Day service was to be a special occasion, with Dewey's congregation joining the First Church for the celebration. Although Dewey would share the pulpit with Follen, Follen would be giving the sermon.

When the day arrived, the church was filled to capacity. The service proceeded smoothly, and when the time for the sermon came, Follen rose to the pulpit with mixed feelings of anxiety and eager optimism. He spoke deliberately and eloquently, increasing his animation as the inspiration of the moment overcame him. The congregation seemed to be entirely with him, excited and intent upon his every word. Then Follen came to the part about the slavery issue. He began to choose his words carefully but honestly. Yet the large audi-

---

very little evidence to corroborate the story told by Mrs. Eliza Cabot Follen about the reasons for leaving New York. Whatever other sources are available have been used. The great lack is in the failure to locate the letters or diaries of Dr. Follen.

ence seemed to be so much with him! After an imperceptible hesitation, Follen proceeded with confidence. Barely had he launched on the topic, when suddenly there was a great stir throughout the congregation. Two men rose and stalked out with great indignation. But Follen showed none of his former apprehensiveness; he did not pause in his delivery for even a moment, but completed what he had to say on the subject and then went on to conclude his sermon.

Follen realized he had alienated a large number of the members of both societies with his Thanksgiving Day service. He wrote to Dr. Channing on January 12, 1837:

> Mrs. [Follen] has told you of what happened on Thanksgiving Day at my church. I shall give to my friend Mr. Spring, who brings you this, a copy of the remarks made on that occasion. The greatest part was extempore, but written down immediately after service, as it was fresh in my memory. It is possible that the excitement produced by this homeopathic dose may have an influence on our remaining here; but I cannot judge. In case we should not remain, I should like to have the temporary care of some parish, or the supply of a pulpit, in the neighborhood of Boston.[14]

Follen was not immediately fired, nor was he officially reprimanded in any way. But many people were frank enough to tell him that though what he said might be true enough, he should not have aired his views so strongly. Among these persons was Dewey, who admitted being rather shocked at his colleague's outspokenness.

The members of the New York congregation undoubtedly had an attitude toward slavery that was more moderate than Follen's mild Abolitionism. Neither William Ware nor Henry Bellows in more critical years had had much of a problem with their parishioners about the issue of slavery. It may be that many agreed with Follen but were made the devil's advocate because of the way that he presented things with his abrupt and dogmatic assurance.[15]

[14] Quoted in Eliza Cabot Follen, *op. cit.*, p. 431. None of this sequence of events is alluded to in the All Souls Minute Book, but is based upon Mrs. Follen's memory as documented by her deceased husband's papers.

[15] In *The Liberal Christians* (Boston: Beacon Press, 1970), Conrad Wright has a chapter, "The Minister as Reformer," which delineates very well the positions of Unitarian ministers on the slavery issue. Even the so-called Abolitionists were not very radical, and Wright describes Bellows as a moderate and Orville Dewey as one of the most conservative.

The trustees were thus in something of a dilemma: Follen had too much of a following to warrant letting him go, and there were few competent Unitarian clergymen available to settle in his place. Dr. Follen had won himself a fine reputation as a scholar in the fields of Germanic literature and of law. He was also renowned for his erudition in theology. Further, Follen had proved himself capable of drawing crowds. Some of the trustees may have hoped to convince Follen to refrain from speaking on the slavery issue so that the church could capitalize on his many other talents. Toward this end, they encouraged Follen to undertake a series of Sunday-evening lectures upon his views of Christianity, and advertised the week's subject in the newspapers. The enterprise turned out to be a great success, and the second service on Sundays, which had always been very low in attendance, soon was filled to capacity with many strangers.[16]

But the popularity of the Sunday-evening services did not resolve the membership's conflict over Follen and his views, and Follen remained in doubt as to whether he would be asked to settle permanently. Early in March 1837, Follen received an invitation from Judge Cranch in Washington, D.C., to come to the Unitarian church in that city for the month of April, to preach and particularly to repeat the series of lectures for which he was now acclaimed. He happily accepted.

Aware that Follen's temporary term of service had only a little more than a month to go, the society had convened after Sunday worship service on March 19, 1837, to discuss retaining him. While a majority, 27 members, were in favor of continuing with Mr. Follen, at least for a while, as many as 16 votes were cast for letting his term expire. A vote was then taken to ascertain for how long Mr. Follen should be retained. Twenty-eight members decided that one year would be quite sufficient; they were probably hoping that a more suitable man could be found in that time. Six felt that Follen should be asked to serve for another two years, but at least nine people abstained from voting on this question.[17]

For months, Follen had half expected to be informed that his services were no longer needed; on the other hand, he had not been able to squelch his private hopes of being asked to settle permanently.

[16] The cost of newspaper advertising in 1837 was 25¢ per advertisement.
[17] All Souls Minute Book, Volume I, p. 254.

Upon receiving the report of this meeting, therefore, he responded to the standing committee with sweetness and serenity, as if it were quite what he expected. But inwardly the news hit him hard. When he was alone with his wife, he could scarcely contain his strong emotions:

> Surely it is not wrong here to confess my disappointment. O how bitterly I feel it. Through my whole life I have labored for the highest objects, and have been actuated by the most elevated purposes, and in all things I have apparently failed. I cannot help feeling this deeply.[18]

Follen was sorely tempted to decline the temporary offer altogether, and to pin all his hopes upon the Washington church. But a few of Follen's most loyal friends convinced him that his nonadmirers in the First Church were a very small minority and that he should accept the proposition.

Follen was determined to fulfill his commitment to the Unitarian church in Washington and thus spent the month of April there, achieving a satisfying success. He wisely refrained from making explicit reference to the antislavery issue in that slave-holding city, but preached instead "on the dignity and rights of human nature, on the great texts, 'Honor all men,' 'All ye are brethren,' and 'Pray for the oppressed' " in hopes of making his heartfelt views reach their mark in this oblique way. The Washington church, which had been struggling along mostly without a pastor since 1821, quickly filled up, and many who heard him sought Follen out personally to tell him how deeply he had impressed them. The Follens' child, young Charles, now just seven, became gravely ill on this trip, putting a blight on what was otherwise a happy moment in Follen's career. The boy recovered, however, and the Follens returned to New York to pick up where they had left off.[19]

---

[18] Eliza Cabot Follen, *op. cit.,* p. 440. This sequence of events, too, is taken primarily from his widow's biography of Follen, but this case is corroborated by the minutes.

[19] *Ibid.,* p. 443. While Follen was in Washington the New York congregation heard young John Sullivan Dwight, but he had left them unimpressed with his pulpit performance.

14. Follen Resigns

I was under severely inauspicious circumstances that Follen resumed his interim pastorate at the First Congregational Church on May 1, 1837. In contrast to Follen's insecure reputation, Dewey was continuing to draw crowds to the Second Church. Dewey's preaching constituted heavy competition for the First Church, and once again the church was faced with an exodus of its members. In November 1837, John Balch, the treasurer, served notice upon ten members for defaulting payment on their pew assessments. Henry Sewall, who ten years earlier had been in Balch's position of trying to collect arrears, was on the list, as were Henry Wheaton and George Dummer, two of the society's remaining founding fathers. William Taggard, James Fox, and Daniel Stanton were also among the many people who were delinquent in their accounts to the church. Each was served with a formal notice, but Henry Sewall wrote back, shocked that the trustees could treat *him* that way after all he had done for the church in past years. The trustees' response to Sewall's letter was polite but pointed:

> The board feels deeply sensible to the obligations of the Society to Mr. Sewall for the interest which he has always taken in its welfare ... in its foundation; but they cannot perceive why an exception in Mr. Sewall's favour should be made in regard to the operations of the laws which must be administered without respect of persons. If Mr. Sewall was not acquainted with the circumstances of his pew it was not the fault of the Trustees — and the Board cannot now perceive that the loss which Mr. Sewall is likely to sustain will be attributable to anything but his own neglect.[1]

[1] All Souls Minute Book, Volume I, pp. 256–257 and 260–261.

There must have been others who defected to the Second Church at this time and who canceled or sold their pews. William Cullen Bryant was definitely among Dewey's congregation now, though he may have switched from the First to the Second Church long before Dewey arrived on the scene. Elihu Townsend, who owned a pew in the First Church as late as 1829, was among those who gathered at Dewey's church during this period.

This exodus represented a serious loss of revenue to the society. To add to the society's financial troubles, in April 1837, the Phoenix Bank wanted its loan paid up, and the trustees borrowed $2,000 on a bond, and also remortgaged the church. Just when things looked blackest, Follen requested that he be paid with greater regularity. William Ware had never made such demands and his salary had been paid most casually. The financial records in the Minute Book during Ware's ministry reveal that one month he might have received $50, another $200 some months later, and perhaps over $1,000 all in one lump sum at another time. Follen was paid with similar irregularity. Nevertheless, the trustees pooled their personal financial resources in order that Dr. Follen might be paid up to date.

§ § §

Meanwhile, Charles Follen's hopes that he be asked to settle permanently continued to spur him to his finest efforts. Revitalized from his successful sojourn in Washington, he had plunged into his second year in New York with renewed vigor. He was careful to avoid explicit reference to the slavery issue, and poured all of his intensely earnest energies into instilling a true Christian attitude in his parishioners. He pleaded that the essence of Christianity is not blind belief, but skepticism.

As soon as he had returned to his pulpit, he had immediately initiated a course of lectures on infidelity in which he praised the conscientious skeptic, and even the atheist, who lives his life upon the best principles of religion though he may not be convinced of the irrational justifications of his ethics as put forth by orthodox Christianity. Follen advocated the diligent examination of those thinkers and writers who opposed Christianity, especially those to whom the foundations of Christian belief comprised the focal point of their studies: the French Encyclopedists as well as Hobbes, Hume, Paine, and others. True faith, said Follen, is the result of such diligent and conscientious skepticism:

> For myself, I can certainly say that, next to the Gospel itself, the books that have been written against it have been the most efficient promoters of my belief in its divine truth. Every difficulty we leave unexamined will become a cause of doubt to us, whereas, through a faithful investigation, it might have become an additional ground of conviction.[2]

For his sermons, Follen spoke on the various attributes of Jesus which modern men could apply to their true advantage. But his emphasis was upon dedication to the one God and the natural divinity of man: "The world is governed by laws not all calculated for man, but man's nature is fitted for all changes and chances. The essential wants of every man are secured not by bread alone, but by every word. — Why? The universe is the word of God, it is his book." The natural and true self of every human being knew well these principles of God's universe, but the external man was blind even to his own true nature. "Men are afraid to see spirits," said Follen, "because they are so little acquainted with their own spiritual self." [3]

Partly because his convictions were so integral with his living style, and partly to further his acceptance among the congregation, Follen began a series of open-house socials shortly after his return from Washington. Wednesday evenings, especially, were set aside for anyone who cared to call. The Follens made no plans, but merely left the lights on in the house from 7:00 to 11:00 P.M. No refreshments were served save a glass of water to anyone who asked for it. Follen and his wife were convinced that people should mix in friendly fellowship, and they hoped by these socials to break the barriers of affluence and class which pew arrangements in the church served to encourage. Many people came, and Mrs. Follen writes that even in stormy weather, there were always some who faithfully put in an appearance.

The late spring of 1837 passed successfully; Follen's lecture series was well attended, and many members of the Society of Free Inquirers

---

[2] Quoted in Eliza Cabot Follen, *The Works of Charles Follen, with a Memoir of His Life* (Boston, 1842), pp. 446–447.

[3] *Ibid.,* pp. 457–458, 456.

who heard him at his lectures soon began coming to the Sunday-morning services. At the end of the series, one orthodox Christian who came to church for no other reason than to observe the "unbelievers" of Unitarianism told a trustee that he would secure $1,500 for Dr. Follen, if he would repeat the series before Tammany Hall. Instead of reporting this to Follen, the trustee replied to the gentleman that it would be better for him to purchase a pew in the church and to bring his family to services. The man did exactly that!

However, the spiritual climate within the First Church was not improved in May of 1837 when the bottom dropped out of the economy of the country in what is known as the Panic of 1837. States had piled up huge debts to build canals and railroads. People had speculated recklessly in buying land in the West and even on the remote stretches of Long Island. In order to try to check speculation Andrew Jackson ordered that all payments for public land would have to be made in silver or gold. This served to stop the speculation but cramped the usual banking operations. And the banks overextended themselves in giving credit, interest rates were much too high, imports exceeded exports in the country as a whole, crops were ruined by bad weather, and British bankers called in their loans.

The result was economic disaster. The values of real estate collapsed. It is difficult to know exactly how the members of the First Church were affected by the collapse. Several of them had dealt heavily in real estate. Yet foreign shipping was not seriously affected and Jonathan Goodhue somehow emerged unscathed.

§ § §

At the end of June 1837, the Follens left for Stockbridge on their vacation, which, according to the contract, was to extend for nine weeks. Dr. Follen relaxed in the warm and friendly atmosphere provided by his many friends in that town and, at the same time, prepared his notes for his next season of preaching, that he might truly excel and be offered the permanent pastorate.

Yet, by September of 1837, Dr. Follen felt very confident that the church in New York was really "my" church, and expressed the hope that the congregation would provide him with a new parsonage to replace the old one. He wrote to Samuel Cabot, from Oyster Bay, that they were returning to New York "to take up winter quarters.

*Dr. Charles Follen. Portrait in
the Follen Church, East Lexington,
Massachusetts. Photograph by
Duette Photographers*

A busy season it will be for me. As business and confidence are re-
viving [after the panic of 1837], I hope that the members of my society will carry into effect their long cherished plan of selling the old
house, and building a more commodious one in a more convenient
quarter of the city." [4]

When he returned in September, he picked up his professional affairs, not as if they were a duty, but rather as though they represented
a joyful challenge which he had missed. He and his wife resumed
their custom of opening their house to all who cared to come on
Wednesday evenings, and Follen became even more active on behalf

[4] Charles Follen to Samuel Cabot, September 26, 1837, in Samuel Cabot
Papers, Box 6, Massachusetts Historical Society.

of the poor than he'd been the year before. German immigrants flooded to the Follen residence in hopes of sharing a meal or getting a handout, and Follen spent so much time with them that he was frequently exhausted when the time came to give his Sunday-morning sermon. He wrote less and less of his sermons down and relied more and more on extemporaneous preaching.

The fall months went smoothly and successfully. Had it not been for a single event which occurred late in the autumn, Follen might, indeed, have been offered the permanent pastoral charge of the First Church.

On November 7, 1837, Elijah Parish Lovejoy, a notorious Abolitionist newspaperman, was killed in Illinois while defending his press. The nation was stirred by the news, but the Antislavery Society was in an uproar. This Society immediately set about making arrangements to capitalize upon Lovejoy's martyrdom for its cause. Unfortunately for Follen, its members put his name on the committee of arrangements for a great rally they planned to hold at the Broadway Tabernacle.

They had not consulted Follen first, and Dr. Follen was greatly displeased. He did not believe that exploiting so gruesome an event could further a truly Christian cause, and he wanted no part of the affair. No doubt, he also feared that this publicity would damage his career in New York. On the other hand, he feared that by withdrawing his name, he would create even greater controversy by appearing to be a hypocrite, and he thus quietly let the measure stand.

For the same reason, he felt obliged to attend the rally, which he described in a letter to Harriet Martineau on December 11th:

We had here in New York, at the Tabernacle, an anti-slavery celebration of the martyrdom of Lovejoy. There were nearly five thousand persons present. A disturbance was threatened, and attempted by a small number, who counted upon the sympathy of the assembly. The noise of the few was rendered audible by the profound silence of the assembly, upon which the constables took courage, and arrested two, and this put an end to all disturbance. The exercises were dull, except [for] the mere recital of the facts, and the concluding prayer. We should have gained more, perhaps, if the defence of the liberty of the press had been made the principal ground of the celebration, rather than the anti-slavery principle which he [Lovejoy] advocated; at least, so it appears to me. Still, one thing seems established, that no antislavery mob can be excited again in this city, notwithstanding the rage of the merchants connected with the South.[5]

Most of the "merchants connected with the South" who had once made up an influential portion of the First Congregational Church were now worshiping at Dewey's church; nonetheless, there remained in the Chambers Street church those who were sorely dubious of Follen's antislavery activities. Follen had been warned that his attendance at the rally would do harm to his chances of remaining in New York, and now Follen resigned himself to the possibility — or rather, probability — of his being asked to leave, at least when his present contract expired at the end of April 1838.

Shortly after the rally, Follen preached a sermon based on the text, "I have come not to destroy, but to fulfill," in which he pointed out that both the conservative and the reformer have valid points of view, and that the true follower of Jesus would work as hard to uphold what was good about the existing society as he would to correct what was wrong.

Now, the true conservative, after the example of Jesus, set out with the view to preserve whatever, in established opinions and institutions, is sound and salutary, and not, as his prejudiced antagonist may suppose, to support the existing order of things from a superstitious belief, that whatever is is good. And, on the other hand, the reformer, who has the spirit of the chief of reformers, is not prompted by a restless desire, such as his prejudiced antagonist imputes to him, to make all things new, as if their newness alone was sufficient to establish their superiority over old things; but he proceeds on the supposition, that all that is human, whether it be a speculative or practical character, is susceptible to improvement, and therefore needs reform.

The prejudiced reformer forgets that the great object of change is stability. We strive after truth that shall prove truth not only to-day and to-morrow, but at all times.[6]

On November 26, 1837, the Second Congregational Unitarian Church was totally destroyed by fire. Orville Dewey wrote that all that was saved was his library "which was flung out of the vestry window and the pulpit Bible, which I have — a present from the Trus-

---

[5] Quoted in Eliza Cabot Follen, *op. cit.*, pp. 464–465.
[6] Quoted in *ibid.*, pp. 467–468.

tees." George Templeton Strong noted in his diary that he walked uptown that morning of November 26th to see the destroyed church. The members of the congregation were shocked and dismayed; but undaunted. They hired a hall for temporary worship in the Stuyvesant Institute, a public hall on Broadway, and Dewey continued his preaching there to even larger crowds, both morning and evening.[7]

Dewey records that the congregation immediately got into a discussion as to what kind of a new church they wished to build, and where the new church was to be located. "At length it was determined to build in a semi-Gothic style, on Broadway, it being the great city thoroughfare, and ground very expensive; but it was thought best to build there. It was contended that a propagandist church should occupy a conspicuous situation, and perhaps that view has been borne out by the results." [8]

It is worth noting, perhaps, that nowhere in All Souls Minute Book is this tragedy recorded. And yet what a potentially bright opportunity now presented itself for the merger of the two churches. The First Church had a building, if an unsatisfactory one, but had what many in the congregation felt to be an unsatisfactory minister. Follen's term had only another five months to go, but after this time, the society would be free to avail itself of Dewey's services by the time a merger had been completed.

The Second Church had an excellent minister, but no building. A merger at this point would have provided the Second Church with at least suitable temporary quarters until the merged societies could relocate. Both churches would have increased their memberships and their finances and, together, they could have found an excellent new place on which to build a fine new church. Certainly, if the two societies had really been on such fine terms with one another as is implied by the sources concerning the establishment of the Second Church, such a merger would surely have been attempted soon after the fire.

But if any members of either of the two societies probed into such a possibility at this time, there is not the slightest hint of it in the

[7] Mary E. Dewey (ed.), *Autobiography and Letters of Orville Dewey, D.D.* (Boston, 1884), p. 79. Some of the church records, perhaps in a safe, also were preserved. See also Allan Nevins and Milton Halsey Thomas (eds.), *The Diary of George Templeton Strong* (New York: The Macmillan Company, 1952), Volume I, p. 78.

[8] Dewey, *op. cit.*, p. 79.

minutes for this period. Instead, the trustees of the First Church decided to advertise the church building for sale again early in January.
They may even have tried to sell the building to the Second Church.

Dr. Follen's Sunday-evening lectures had consistently been an unqualified success, and had drawn many people to the church. William
Cullen Bryant had attended the lectures, and one lecture that Dr.
Follen had delivered on the German poet Friedrich Schiller had inspired a poem by Bryant. After the antislavery rally at the Tabernacle,
however, the trustees had deemed it wise to discontinue advertising
them, and attendance in the evening fell off markedly.[9]

Taking this as a sign that his contract would not be renewed,
Follen agreed to deliver a lecture at the Brooklyn Lyceum on "Re-
publicanism," in which Follen again came out boldly against slavery.
He was becoming impatient with the way Americans abused the
precious principle of freedom upon which their — and Follen's —
country had been founded, and his repeated censure had greatly disillusioned him about Americans. But he did not lose faith in the country, and decided to use what he believed were his last days in New
York to expound fearlessly upon his religiopolitical convictions, in
order that his fellow countrymen might come more sincerely in line
with the precepts they so glibly claimed.

He heard no complaints about his renewed outspokenness, however, and no one alluded one way or another to his prospects with the
society. The suspense was agonizing, and he probably mentioned something to Benjamin Wheelwright of the standing committee. For, at a
trustees' meeting on January 16, Mr. Wheelwright announced that he
had made an informal survey of the membership on the subject of
renewing Dr. Follen's contract.

Follen, it had to be admitted, had gained a strong following, despite the controversy and hostilities waged over him. Believing that the
society could do worse by turning Follen out at this point, Wheelwright
assured his fellow trustees that the members had evidenced a willing-
ness to keep Follen on for another year, at least until they had a chance
to look over any available candidates. Thus, the board resolved that
Follen should be asked to stay provisionally. Robert Ainslie, who was

---

[9] Charles H. Brown, *Bryant* (New York, 1971), p. 258. The All Souls Cash
Book supports this fact. There had been extensive newspaper advertising from
September 1836 through November 17, 1837, in as many as five papers.

now the president, and Wheelwright were appointed a committee to wait upon Follen to communicate this resolution.[10]

According to Mrs. Follen, when Follen returned from his conference with these gentlemen, his face was flushed with emotion and he appeared to be overcome with depression. Attempting to gain control of himself, Follen said to his wife:

> I am sure no insult was intended to me; but a proposition has been made to me, which if I were to accept it, would degrade me in my own eyes, and in the opinion of all who know me. They wish me to retain my place here, but to supply the desk only a part of the time myself and to invite other candidates to preach as often as I can, that they may be able to ascertain whom they should prefer to me. They have a right to their choice, and I well know that the gentlemen who brought me the proposal from the whole committee meant me no wrong; but the situation in which it would place me, and whomever I put into the desk, would be as awkward and unpleasant as it would be undignified. I shall, of course, refuse and, as soon as is proper, resign my place here.[11]

No doubt Follen would have been far less upset by an out-and-out termination of his services; as it was, he was being asked to remain in limbo for yet another year — and to help his society find a man they would prefer in the very place he himself coveted so much!

Mustering every bit of dignity his depression could afford, Follen wrote on January 25th the following notice to Mr. Ainslie:

> I have taken into full consideration the proposal of the Standing Committee.... The Committee proposes to reengage my services for one year from the first of next May, with the understanding that during that time other clergymen should be occasionally invited to supply the pulpit, in order to gratify those members of the Society who desire a more ample opportunity of comparing different preachers before they proceeded to a permanent settlement.
>
> Yet, consulting with a number of my friends, I have come to the conclusion respectfully to decline this proposal. However far my attainments have fallen below my earnest desires, I cannot promise to do more or better than I have hitherto endeavored to do in my

[10] See Appendix C, for sketches of Ainslie, p. 253, and Wheelwright, p. 265.
[11] Eliza Cabot Follen, *op. cit.*, p. 475.

ministry, and . . . I cannot but think that another experiment, so far as I am concerned, would be unprofitable either to myself or to the Society.[12]

When Follen's supporters heard of the kind of proposal the board had made to Dr. Follen — and that, of course, he had declined it — they were outraged, and immediately informed the board that only a formal meeting of the society could resolve such an issue. The trustees had no choice but to call a meeting of the membership, and Follen was instructed to announce it from the pulpit beforehand. The meeting was held on February 18th.

Follen himself did not attend, but those anti-Follenists who had remained in the church turned out in their full number — far more than even Follen himself had suspected to exist. By contrast, many of Follen's most devoted supporters were not yet members of the society and could not be present for the vote.

Mrs. Follen claims in the biography of her husband that there was an attempt to stifle the opposition to Dr. Follen and to "pack" the meeting. But to understand the legal nature of this meeting one must realize that many who attended the Second Church still owned pews and paid annual pew rentals in the First Church, and thus they had a right to vote at any meeting of the society. A complete and detailed survey of the pew rental lists of both the First and Second churches has been made for this period to see if Mrs. Follen's claims are accurate. It shows that 36 names appear on both lists, and these included many of the most prominent members of both churches. The 36 names may represent as much as half of the legal membership of the First Church at this time. The meeting was so vitriolic that no vote was taken, and the meeting was appropriately adjourned to March 4th. But it was apparent to everyone that the opposition to Dr. Follen's remaining at the church was in a precarious balance, probably about an even number for him and against him.

When Follen heard of the extent of the opposition expressed against him and the sentiments the members were expressing about him to each other at the meeting, he decided to take immediate action to prevent a recurrence at the March 4th meeting. On March 1st, he wrote to Robert Ainslie:

[12] Transcribed in All Souls Minute Book, Volume I, pp. 264–265.

Will you be so kind as to lay before the adjourned meeting of our Society, on Sunday, the 4th instant, the following communication previous to any vote being taken in relation to the object of the meeting.

I have learned that a number of persons belonging to this congregation, think it expedient that they should have an opportunity of hearing several preachers before the Society proceeds to the choice of a pastor. This desire on their part seems to me very reasonable. It is, therefore, my decided wish . . . that the Society would postpone the choice of a pastor until this opportunity has been afforded to all who may desire it.

The committee on supplying the pulpit, which had been appointed in January, before these distressing events took place, immediately set to work, and Follen spent the remainder of his contracted term.[13]

Even so thorough a scholar and biographer as George Spindler did not know the full story of Follen's New York disappointment. Spindler says simply,

The success with which he had met in his pastorate caused him to believe that he had at last found his proper and most useful sphere of activity, but when after a year and a half of devoted service to the cause of religion and philanthropy in New York his congregation became displeased with his bold and fearless attitude toward the slavery question he resigned his position and returned to Boston with his family in the Spring of 1838.[14]

It really wasn't that simple; there were many factors that prompted the congregation not to renew Follen's contract. There can be no doubt that his unequivocal stand on the slavery issue was unsettling to many persons in the church. Mrs. Follen asserts that this was the main reason, and William B. Sprague had this to say, "he took leave of the church . . . chiefly on account of the opposition to him which had been excited by his intense devotion to the cause of Anti-slavery." [15]

But even some of Follen's friends talked about his Germanisms,

[13] Quoted in full in Eliza Cabot Follen, *op. cit.*, p. 477; cited in All Souls Minute Book, Volume I, p. 269.

[14] George W. Spindler, *The Life of Karl Follen* (Chicago, 1917), p. 92.

[15] William B. Sprague, *The Annals of the American Pulpit* . . . , Volume VIII (New York, 1865), p. 543.

by which they meant certain traits of character, such as stubbornness, which did not endear him to some of his parishioners; and some felt the same kind of stubbornness in Eliza Cabot Follen. The trustees of the church obviously wanted a permanent pastor who would unite rather than divide the church, and although some of them may have been able to understand his position on slavery, and some may even have agreed with him, they knew well that a man with such a position who was convinced that he was right would end up with a divided church. There were enough problems already without asking for that additional one. In addition the church already had the reputation in the city for being radical in matters of theology. It is perfectly understandable that the parishioners did not want also to be known as a church that was radical in political matters also.

15. End of a Beginning

FOLLEN'S REFUSAL TO CONTINUE FOR ANOTHER YEAR apparently gave some members, at least, the notion of merging with the Second Church. The idea was only tentatively and most cautiously explored, and a committee was appointed to do no more than "confer with any gentlemen not belonging to this Society, who may be inclined to unite with us in the erection of a building for public worship, and to report upon the practicability and expediency of an incorporation of a new Society to which the funds of this may be transferred." [1]

This committee, composed of Robert Sedgwick, Robert Schuyler, and Daniel Low, made its report the following week. In a nutshell, the report stated that the committee had conferred with an "influential member" of the Second Congregational Church, who had shown not the least interest in joining with the First Church; and that, while financial assistance from members of the Second Church might be forthcoming to help the First Church to build a new house of worship, it would only be as a profitable investment for those members. In other words, the First Church would have to prove that it was fully capable of repaying the loans.

The committee also pointed out that, under the laws of New York State by which the First Congregational Church had been incorporated, no one was permitted to vote without having been a member (attended divine services) for at least one year; consequently, only by disbanding the First Congregational Church could any merger take place, as the members of the Second Church would have to wait for a year before being able to vote in a union of the two present societies. The committee admitted that it was legally practicable to dissolve

[1] All Souls Minute Book, Volume I, p. 266.

232

the existing society, to form an entirely new one, and then to transfer the assets of the First Church to the new society, but they did not deem this measure an expedient one: "Your Committee cannot recommend to that Society who were the earliest and foremost of the Unitarian Congregations in this City to surrender that distinction, nor even with the aid of warm hearts and liberal hands to embark in an enterprise not entirely without peril in itself." [2]

There was nothing left for the First Church to do, therefore, but to struggle on as best it could with the present building and under the present unhappy financial circumstances, in the hope of finding a permanent minister who could help the church to compete successfully with Orville Dewey. To alleviate somewhat the problem created by the diminished funds of the church, the trustees converted all loans owed to creditors outside of the institution to loans owed to some of the wealthier members of the society. Robert Schuyler supplied $1,500, while other members loaned amounts ranging from $65 to over $100. The committee on supplying the pulpit reported, on April 2, 1838, that it had invited William Henry Channing, William Ellery Channing's nephew, and Henry W. Bellows to preach at their own convenience after the first of May. [3]

Channing's nephew had been in the city during 1836–1837 and had regularly attended the ministerial meetings held on Monday mornings that year with Dewey, Follen, and Mr. Arnold. Both Arnold and the young Channing had left the city by this time, however; and Mr. Channing was now in the vicinity of Boston, preaching at various churches in the area. Bellows had been graduated from the Divinity School at Cambridge only the year before, and was now in Mobile, Alabama, helping a Unitarian Society to get established there. Bellows would not be available in May, but Mr. Channing agreed to take over the New York pulpit for the month of May.

The Follens were once more faced with the task of packing their belongings and looking for a new home. Follen wrote to the senior Channing, hoping that the great master could find some pulpit for him in Massachusetts, and, in the meantime, he sadly prepared his many books — which he had so optimistically put on their shelves in New York two years earlier — for travel back to Boston. He refused to

[2] *Ibid.*, pp. 267–268.
[3] *Ibid.*, p. 270.

let his depression get the better of him, however, and vowed to speak freely and vehemently upon any subject he chose during his remaining Sundays. He also undertook to give a lecture series on Schiller's contributions, and was somewhat gratified to see that these last lectures were well attended.

After giving their last Wednesday-evening open house — at which there was scarcely a dry eye after the gathering had sung "Auld Lang Syne" — the Follens moved into the home of the William T. McCouns after their furniture and belongings had been packed and stored, and until a place to send them had been found in Boston. Mr. McCoun was an attorney who had been a pew owner in the First Church during Ware's ministry and who had remained loyal to the church, and to Follen, throughout the very difficult past two years.

For his final and farewell sermon, Follen outdid himself. During one of the frequent conversations he and his wife had on the blindness of the city's people to the very religion they professed to follow so purely, Eliza happened to say that, if Jesus were to come back to earth at that moment, he would be crucified all over again by the very Christians who held him to be chief in their religion — just as he was murdered by adherents of his own Jewish faith for merely trying to get them to follow sincerely the law and the prophets which Judaism claimed to hold as central. "Yes," said Dr. Follen, "they do not know him; and that shall be my text for my farewell sermon. . . . 'Have I been so long with you, and have ye not known me?' " [4]

He had little time to prepare the sermon, and when the day came to preach it, Follen entered the pulpit with nothing more than his Bible and his own profoundly heartfelt convictions. His only intent was to say, as plainly, as clearly, as cogently as he could put it, what seemed to him to be the very obvious and realistic truth which Jesus had seen and exposed; and to show that, despite the wide acceptance of Christianity in the world, men were still as ignorant of this truth 1800 years after Jesus' death as they had been in Jesus' time.

Yet, despite Follen's earnestness, his plainness of language, his

[4] Quoted in Eliza Cabot Follen, *The Works of Charles Follen, with a Memoir of His Life* (Boston, 1842), p. 483. Note on the date of Follen's "Farewell Sermon": by deduction I assume this to have been delivered on April 30, 1838. The records of the treasurer (All Souls Minute Book, Volume I, pp. 274–275) show that Follen's contract was paid through May 1, 1838, and that William Henry Channing began to preach on May 6th for five Sundays.

many practical analogies and lucid examples, there were many among those who heard him who thought Follen was referring to *himself;* that he was telling his congregation that he, Follen, had been so long with them and they had not known *him,* Follen!

Not everyone missed the point, however, and when the service was over, Dr. Follen — who had delayed deliberately in the pulpit so that he would not have to face last good-byes on this emotion-ridden occasion — was greeted by a man and his wife who had waited patiently for him to come out. The couple's eyes were streaming with tears, and the man, who pressed Follen's hand with his own in deep communication of his sentiments, said, "You have, Sir, during your ministry here, changed an unhappy atheist into a happy, believing Christian." [5]

Again, without any immediately foreseeable means of employment, Follen undertook the completion of his book on psychology which he had started some time previously. He had barely begun to settle down to this business when he was asked to fill in temporarily for the Rev. Mr. Cunningham in Boston, who was to be absent for several weeks. When his term there came to its end, Follen planned a trip to Europe to visit his friends.

Just as he was completing his arrangements to leave, however, an urgent request from East Lexington enjoined Follen to postpone his trip and to come and take charge of the Unitarian Society he had helped to form there in 1835. The appeal was so earnest that Follen could not deny it, and again he moved his family to take up what was once more only a temporary position. As urgent as was the East Lexington Society's appeal, it did not include an invitation for Follen to remain permanently.

Nevertheless, his efforts in East Lexington were highly accepted by the congregation there, and he designed and helped them to build their own church. The society proudly and eagerly looked forward to moving into their first house of worship, and scheduled the dedication for January 15, 1840. Of course, they expected Follen to deliver the dedication sermon.

At the end of 1839, Follen was invited to deliver a series of lectures on Germanic literature before the Mercantile Library Association in New York City, and, affairs at East Lexington not demanding

[5] Quoted in Eliza Cabot Follen, *op. cit.,* p. 484.

The Follen Church in East Lexington, Massachusetts.
Photograph by David A. Marlin

Follen's attentions until the dedication in January, he accepted. It was a prestigious lectureship, and one Dr. Follen could not turn down.

Though he was to be gone for little more than a month, Follen brought his wife and son with him to New York. It turned out to be an unwise decision, for in the midst of the lecture series, Mrs. Follen fell gravely ill. As the days wore on, Follen began to fear for her life. Even if she lived, she certainly could not be expected to recover enough to return to East Lexington with him for the dedication.

Not daring to leave her side, Follen wrote to the society in East Lexington, begging them to postpone the dedication. But they would not; they had been looking forward to it for too long, and they wished Follen to return without his ill wife, temporarily, in order to officiate at the service. Reluctantly, he left Eliza and Charles in New York. Follen booked passage for himself on the S.S. *Lexington* for the trip to Boston.

The boat was owned by the New Jersey Steam Navigational Transportation Company. Two of the company's directors were Moses Grinnell and Elihu Townsend, who maintained their pews in the First Church, but who had attended Dewey's church during Follen's interim pastorate. When the steamship *Lexington* made her maiden voyage from New York to Providence in 1835, one New York newspaper expressed the belief that she was the fastest boat in the world.

With his dedicatory sermon not fully written, Follen boarded the boat on January 13, 1840. The boat pulled out of New York Harbor at 3:00 P.M. that afternoon and sailed peacefully through the wintry seas until about half-past seven, when it was discovered that the chimney and some bales of cotton placed nearby were aflame. The crew promptly set about attempting to extinguish the fire, but to no avail. When it was clear that the lives of the passengers were in danger, an alarm was sounded. The lifeboat and some smaller boats were lowered, but the lifeboat was shattered when it hit one of the paddle wheels. Panic spread. The small boats were swamped as too many passengers raced to fill them.

As it happened, the *Lexington* was not too far off Eaton's Neck, Long Island, so the pilot decided to head straight for the shore. Suddenly the engines stopped dead. Now all hope for the passengers was cut off. The members of the crew and the passengers, alike, raced for the bales of cotton which the ship was carrying as cargo, and for any other debris that would sustain them. But few people could withstand the icy waters. The pilot of the ship and three other crew members survived; only two passengers did. Although many bodies were later recovered, all that was ever seen of Follen again was his trunk, which drifted eventually to shore. It had been rifled of everything but his papers.

For a short time it was believed that Mrs. Follen went down with her husband. She lived to write a biography of his life and to publish many of his writings. She was famous as a writer of children's stories including the classic, "Three Little Kittens." She died in 1860 at the age of 70 and was buried in Mount Auburn Cemetery in Cambridge. Their son, Charles Christopher Follen, graduated from Harvard in 1849 and became an architect in Boston.[6]

The disaster of the *Lexington* prompted the diarist George Templeton Strong to make some rather strong comments. He heard of the disaster on Wednesday, January 15th. "A more horrible business I never heard of, nor of any disaster in which the ruinous effects of terror and confusion, the importance of presence of mind are so clearly marked." Strong deplored the terrible mistakes that had been made by the captain and the crew in trying to get the lifeboats overboard: "The tiller ropes were burnt — and for the illegal use of ropes, I hope someone is answerable — for had chains been used, they could have run her ashore." [7]

Orville Dewey also was prompted to preach about the subject, and his sermon was published in the *New World*, for January 25, 1840. Strong described the sermon as a "somewhat prosy moral essay on the shortness of life, the valuableness of fortune, the propriety of being duly shocked on so melancholy an occasion, the importance of presence of mind, and the virtues of Dr. Follen, together with certain consolatory remarks, intended I suppose, for the friends and relatives of the victims of the disaster." [8]

It was not until two and a half months later that the news of the tragedy of the *Lexington* reached Catharine Sedgwick in Naples. She wrote to her dear friend Eliza:

> We wonder at the dispensation of Providence. We look with dismay upon the removal of a human being in the midst of holy & unexecuted purposes, gifted with the will & the power to advance society, & enjoying in perfection the sanctified relations of life. . . . We know nothing of the significance of a life beyond its presence with us, of an

[6] See *The Monthly Journal of the AUA*, April 1860, Volume I, No. 4, for a sermon on her life and character.

[7] Allan Nevins and Milton Halsey Thomas (eds.), *The Diary of George Templeton Strong* (New York: Macmillan, 1952), Volume I, p. 123.

[8] *Ibid.*, p. 125.

Nathaniel Currier Lithograph of the Burning of the Steamship Lexington.
The Harry T. Peters Collection, Museum of the City of New York

inextinguishable thought that has come from the fountain of a mind
divinely kindled.[9]

The intensity of the feeling against the Abolitionism of Dr. Follen
can be understood in the realization that even the Federal Street
church refused to open the meetinghouse for a eulogy on Dr. Follen
which was to be delivered by his friend, the Reverend Samuel J. May,
a Unitarian reformer and Abolitionist. This attitude led Dr. Channing
to feel that "the Unitarians, as a sect, were indifferent to the question
of slavery, and when his meetinghouse was refused to the eulogist of
Charles Follen, [he] doubted the efficacy of his ministry, and was dis-
posed to think that he had poured out his soul in vain, if this was the
result of his endeavors." [10]

---

[9] Catharine M. Sedgwick to Eliza Cabot Follen, Naples, March 24, 1840, in
Catharine M. Sedgwick–Eliza Cabot Follen Papers, Massachusetts Historical
Society.

[10] Octavius Brooks Frothingham, *Boston Unitarianism, 1820–1850: A Study
of the Life and Works of Nathaniel Langdon Frothingham* (New York: G. P.
Putnam's Sons, 1890), p. 49.

It is an interesting coincidence in the history of All Souls that the dramatic tragedy of the *Lexington* assured the success of the New York artist, Nathaniel Currier, who owned a pew in the First Congregational Church, bought that same year, and later was to serve as a trustee (1847–1866). Mr. Currier had studied lithography in Massachusetts, where he had been born and raised. At the end of his apprenticeship, he had tried to set up his own shop in Philadelphia but, when these efforts failed, he came to New York. The great fire in December 1835, on which William Ware had expounded shortly before his resignation, had been the subject of a lithograph which Currier had made within a few days of the incident. This achievement laid firm foundations for Currier's later success. But it was the burning of the *Lexington* which really made the reputation of Nathaniel Currier (the firm became Currier and Ives in 1850). Only three days after the tragedy, Currier came out with his lithograph and an up-to-the-minute report. This was one of the first pictorial scoops in the history of American journalism.

§   §   §

Charles Follen lived intensely, and he died intensely. Certainly it must be said that he died in the path of his duty, for it was in an effort to fulfill his responsibility to the East Lexington Church that he met his fate. Had he stayed at the side of his wife, as he was inclined to do and as his wife had begged him to do, the burning of the *Lexington* would not have taken his life. But his was not a hero's death in the strict sense of self-sacrifice.

Follen had spent most of his life espousing unpopular but supremely moral causes; he had even consented to his arrest and possible death by the Allied Powers for his political activities before his friends had urged him to reconsider. Certainly he had been martyred in the cause of the freedom of truth and service of Jesus by many in his own congregation — the very people who professed these ideals. Yet, though he was persecuted throughout his life, it was a relatively mild persecution. And now his end was not heroic, but only tragic.

Despite the antipathy which Follen engendered among many people, he was not without his beloved friends — particularly in New England, but even in New York. Charles Sumner, who had been Follen's pupil at Harvard, said that Follen had "a heart throbbing to all that is honest and humane." Elizabeth Peabody, who came to know Follen largely through Eliza Cabot and William Ellery Channing, said, "I never knew any foreigner who seemed to be so easily and widely understood and appreciated by Americans. In fact, he was less of a German than a Christian cosmopolite." And William Cullen Bryant, who had come to New York from Boston at the encouragement of their mutual friend, Henry Sedgwick, came to love Follen (though he remained with Orville Dewey's congregation). Said Bryant of Follen, "The world has not had a firmer, more ardent, a more consistent friend of liberty." [11]

But perhaps the best epitaph of Charles Theodore Christian Follen is contained in the poem written in his memory by John Greenleaf Whittier:

> Friend of my soul! — as with moist eye
>   I look upon this page of thine,
> Is it a dream that thou art nigh,
>   Thy mild face gazing into mine?
>
> That presence seems before me now,
>   A placid heaven of sweet moonrise,
> When, dew-like, on the earth below
>   Descends the quiet of the skies.
>
> The calm brow through the parted hair,
>   The gentle lips which knew no guile,
> Softening the blue eye's thoughtful care
>   With the bland beauty of thy smile
>
>   . . .
>
> Thou livest, Follen! — not in vain
>   Hath thy fine spirit meekly borne
> The burthen of Life's cross of pain,
>   And the thorned crown of suffering worn.
>
>   . . .
>
> 'Tis something to a heart like mine
>   To think of thee as living yet;

[11] Charles Sumner, *Life and Letters* (London, 1878), Volume II, p. 133; Elizabeth Peabody, in Sprague, *The Annals of the American Pulpit* . . . , Volume VIII, p. 547; and Parke Godwin, *Life of William Cullen Bryant* (New York, 1883), Volume I, p. 377.

> To feel that such a light as thine
> Could not in utter darkness set.[12]

A more important aspect of Follen insofar as All Souls is concerned is that he was the only Transcendentalist minister in its history. Henry Bellows, his successor, was in so many ways non-Transcendentalist. Indeed, there are few churches outside of New England which can boast a Transcendentalist among its ministers, as the movement was confined almost solely to New England.

Although Follen generally has been omitted from the lists of Transcendentalists — or, at best, has been considered as only an incidental figure in the movement — he certainly belongs among the great names of this school: Ralph Waldo Emerson, Bronson Alcott, Henry David Thoreau, Margaret Fuller, George Ripley, and Theodore Parker, to mention just a few. One reason that Follen is not usually included is probably that when the so-called "Transcendental Club" was organized in Boston in 1836, Follen came to New York to preach and was unable to be an active participant in the most fruitful years of the movement.

In its broadest sense, Transcendentalism held that there are realms of knowledge and understanding which cannot be grasped through ordinary worldly experience, but can only be intuited directly through mystical experience and communion with God or Being. This idea was chiefly associated with Immanuel Kant, the eighteenth-century German philosopher whose idealism was a rebuttal of the materialism of the empiricists. In New England, with the rise of the Unitarian emphasis on freedom in reaction to Trinitarian dogmatism — coupled with the introduction of Oriental philosophy and religion into this country — Transcendentalism received a new twist. Personal search and discovery for mystical communion directly with God, as opposed to the mediation of Christ, became the foundation of New England Transcendentalism.

Charles Follen was not only intimately familiar, through his own intellectual discovery, with the German idealists; he had himself undergone a personal revelation of extreme intensity, and at a time in his life before intellectual and religious conditioning had predisposed him in that direction. His entire mode of living was centered on that

[12] John Greenleaf Whittier, *Poetical Works,* Riverside Edition (Boston: Houghton Mifflin, 1882), pp. 290 ff.

personal revelation, and on the subsequent intellectual inquiry he made into revealed religion. Two years before Emerson delivered his Divinity School Address, Follen had said that the intuitions of the mind must form the basis for religious reforms; yet, Ralph Waldo Emerson rocked Harvard Divinity School with essentially the same notion in 1838.

With the other Transcendentalists, Follen was eager to see a wide-sweeping reform occur in Christianity — indeed, in all religions. While he in no way tried to impose his ideas upon others, in 1836 he brought out a book entitled *Religion and the Church,* which he hoped would be the first installment in a comprehensive study of all religious institutions. Using the syncretic method, Follen drew heavily upon the work of Friederich Schleiermacher, a German of the Romantic School who maintained that religion was independent of knowledge and morality, and Benjamin Constant. Follen made particular use of Constant's belief that religious institutions must undergo repeated modification as society advances.

Follen conceived a new theology which would contain not simply the best insights but the true and permanent elements common to all earlier faiths. He considered religion to be neither theological speculation nor belief in dogma, but a serious and personal contemplation of the harmonious workings of the universe. Every human being, he felt, was innately endowed with an impulse to feel reverence for and dependence upon an Infinite Spirit in whom we live and move and have our being.

William R. Hutchison has suggested that Charles Follen was one of the leaders of this movement within Unitarian ranks, that,

> Follen had made the human "religious sentiment" the starting-point of the theological system he intended to elaborate. The intuitions of the mind, he said, rather than "those records, which, by different portions of mankind, are considered as of divine origin," must form the basis for reforms in religion; and the new theology, when completed, must contain not simply the best insights of the Christian religion, but an historical synthesis of the true elements in all earlier faiths.

Hutchison suggests that Follen is usually eliminated from the listings of the Transcendentalists because he was preaching in New York and

*Plaque Erected to Dr. Charles Follen by the Congregation of
All Souls, 1972. Photograph by Rita E. Jamason*

the West during the early years of the Transcendental Club, and he
died in 1840.

> So it is difficult to say precisely what his position would have been
> in the controversy of the 1840's. It is plain, however, that in certain
> respects — notably in his emphasis on the intuitional basis of religion
> and in the syncretism of his theological method — he contributed to
> the structure of Transcendentalist reforming thought.[13]

Dr. Follen has never been listed as one of the "ministers" of the
Unitarian Church of All Souls. He is listed only as an "acting minister." In 1957, for the first time, a portrait of him was placed alongside the other eight ministers of All Souls in Fellowship Hall. And in
1972 a project which had been conceived in the anniversary year of
1969 was brought to completion with the erection of not only a plaque
in the church sanctuary to William Ellery Channing, the founder of
the church, but also one alongside it, appropriately, to Dr. Charles
Theodore Christian Follen, D.C.L. The present-day membership of
All Souls has not forgotten him.

[13] William R. Hutchison, *The Transcendentalist Ministers* (New Haven:
Yale University Press, 1959), pp. 49–50.

George Templeton Strong, an ardent Episcopalian and an opponent of Unitarianism (although many Unitarians eventually became his closest friends), commented in his diary immediately after noting the death of Dr. Follen:

> People may say what they like about the spread of Unitarianism. It can never be general. In wealthy cities it will be the fashionable and aristocratic faith (if that term can be applied to a system which is the negation of faith). Imposing no unpleasant restraints, requiring nothing but what decency and regard for the opinion of others also demand, involving no points of belief above the reach of common sense, it will be very likely to become the favorite creed of those who want a religion at once convenient, compressible, and fashionable, for show — not use. But with the great mass of people, this cold-blooded system of combining the minimum of belief with the maximum of license will not *take*. It never can be a popular religion. Men are carried into it by the impulse that takes them out of the church into dissent in general, though with by far greater numbers the impulse is not strong enough to carry them beyond the first stage.[14]

George Strong's gratuitous comments made just after the death of Charles Follen and just over a year before the time that Henry Bellows was to become the minister of All Souls is a good indication of the standing of the new faith among a certain group of New York intellectuals. Twenty years of controversy had not yet established the faith in the city of New York. George Strong represented not the bigots like Spring, Mason, and Feltus, but the lay intelligentsia. There was a great deal of work yet to be done, and after William Ware resigned and Charles Follen left and died in a shipwreck, it was to be up to Henry Whitney Bellows, who had newly arrived in New York, to put Unitarianism in its proper place in the city.

[14] Nevins and Thomas (eds.), *op. cit.*, pp. 125–126.

245

Appendix A—The Signers of the Covenant as They Appear in the Original Book

January 30, 1821

R. G. Van Polanen
Benjamin Armitage
H. D. Sedgwick
H. Wheaton
Henry D. Sewall
Phinehas S. Whitney
William W. Russel
William Glaze
Adelaide Van Polanen
(Mrs. R. G. Van Polanen)
Jane Armstrong (widow of
David Strong Armstrong)
Catharine P. Chambers
Jane Sedgwick (Mrs. Henry
D. Sedgwick)
Lucy C. Russel (Mrs. William
W. Russel)
Eliza Pearson (Mrs. Isaac
Green Pearson)
Isaac Green Pearson
Mary C. Sewall (Mrs. Henry
D. Sewall)
Catharine Wheaton
(Mrs. Henry Wheaton)
Arthur Kinder
Abigail Perkins (Mrs.
Cyrus Perkins)
Alice Low (Mrs. Daniel Low)
Sarah Orne (probably a sister
of Mrs. Daniel Low)
Sarah Hough

McDowall Pate
Henry Spear

January 31, 1821

Hugh Armstrong

February 4, 1821

Mary Anna Schuyler
(Mrs. Philip J. Schuyler)
Sarah Atterbury
Henry Watkinson

February 10, 1821

Sarah Byers (Mrs. James Byers)
Gibbs Sibley

June 9, 1821

Anne Eliza Rodman

July 10, 1821

Mary Baynham

December 12, 1821

Mary C. G. Allanson

December 18, 1821

William Ware

April 7, 1822

Lydia Prentiss

April 24, 1822

John Campbell

May 14, 1822

Thomas G. Cary

June 20, 1822

George W. Lee

December 13, 1822

Anna Brooks

January 1823

Abigail Sewall (probably a sister of Henry D. Sewall. His mother's name was Abigail Devereux)

January 29, 1823

Anne Dickey

April 29, 1823

Mary Regina Norton (probably Mrs. Henry D. Sewall's mother)

July 27, 1823

Francis Carnes

November 1, 1823

Sarah Chase

April 29, 1824

Stephen Schuyler

May 2, 1824

Mary W. Carnes

December 9, 1824

Barnabas Bates

February 21, 1846

Henry W. Bellows

This list, aside from the names of the two ministers, William Ware and Henry W. Bellows, contains the names of 21 men and 25 women, which probably gives a more accurate picture as to the makeup of the congregation, in which the women undoubtedly outnumbered the men.

Appendix B—Officers of the Unitarian Church of All Souls

*Year of
Election   Officers and Ministers*

1819   PRESIDENT: James Byers, 1819
       TREASURER: Isaac Green Pearson, 1819–1822
       CLERK AND SECRETARY: Henry D. Sewall, 1819–1823
       TRUSTEES:
           John Shepard, 1819–1820
           Frederick Sheldon, 1819–1820
           David Strong Armstrong, 1819–1820
           Benjamin Armitage, 1819–1821
           Daniel Low, 1819–1821
           Oroondates Mauran, 1819–1821
           James Byers, 1819–1822
           Elihu Townsend, 1819–1822
           George Dummer, 1819–1822

1820   PRESIDENT: R. G. Van Polanen, 1820–1822
       TRUSTEES:
           R. G. Van Polanen
           Henry Dwight Sedgwick
           I. P. Whittelsey

1821   MINISTER: *WILLIAM WARE,* 1821–1836
       TRUSTEES:
           Benjamin Hustace
           Henry Wheaton
           William W. Russel

1822   PRESIDENT: Henry Wheaton, 1822–1823
       TREASURER: Benjamin Armitage, 1822–1824
       TRUSTEES:
           Thomas G. Cary

249

Year of
Election Officers and Ministers

Isaac Green Pearson
Henry Sewall, 1822–1824

1823 PRESIDENT: Philip J. Schuyler, 1823–1826
CLERK AND TREASURER: Isaac Green Pearson, 1823–1824
TRUSTEES:
Robert Sedgwick
Elihu Townsend
Philip J. Schuyler

1824 TREASURER: Henry D. Sewall, 1824–1828
CLERK AND SECRETARY: Robert Schuyler, 1824–1830
TRUSTEES:
John Crumby
Cyrus Perkins
Benjamin Armitage

1825 TRUSTEES:
Robert Dickey
Daniel Stanton
Curtis Holmes, 1825–1827
Augustus Greele, 1825

1826 PRESIDENT: Benjamin Armitage
TRUSTEES:
Henry Sedgwick, 1826–1827
Augustus Greele
Calvin How

1827 PRESIDENT: R. G. Van Polanen, 1827–1828
TRUSTEES:
Thomas G. Cary
Richard R. Hough
William Taggard
R. G. Van Polanen
Robert Sedgwick

1828 PRESIDENT: Thomas G. Cary, 1828–1830
TREASURER: William W. Russel, 1828–1830

250

Year of
Election Officers and Ministers

TRUSTEES:
Oroondates Mauran
James W. Otis
F. G. Carnes

1829   TRUSTEES:
Thomas Tileston
Charles Walker
George A. Ward, 1829–1831

1830   PRESIDENT: William W. Russel, 1830–1833
TREASURER: Benjamin F. Wheelwright, 1830–1836
CLERK AND SECRETARY: Charles Francis, 1830–1868
TRUSTEES:
William W. Russel
I. P. Whittelsey, 1830–1832
George Baxter

1831   TRUSTEES:
Benjamin Hustace
Joshua Brooks
William S. Fearing

1832   TRUSTEES:
Benjamin F. Wheelwright
Hercules M. Hayes
Charles S. Francis
Samuel F. Dorr, 1832

1833   PRESIDENT: Benjamin F. Wheelwright, 1833–1834
TRUSTEES:
George A. Ward, 1833–1834
Robert Ainslie
Josiah Lane, 1833–1834

1834   PRESIDENT: Robert Ainslie, 1834–1836
TRUSTEES:
John T. Balch

Year of
Election *Officers and Ministers*

        David Lane, 1834–1836
        David Hustace
        Andrew S. Snelling, 1834–1835

1835   TRUSTEES:
        Robert Sedgwick
        Jeremiah Smith
        Samuel F. Dorr
        John Wheelwright, 1835–1836

1836   ACTING MINISTER: *CHARLES FOLLEN*, 1836–1838
       PRESIDENT: William W. Russel, 1836–1837
       TREASURER: John T. Balch, 1836–1839
       TRUSTEES:
        William W. Russel
        Benjamin F. Wheelwright
        Charles S. Francis
        D. Godfrey, 1836–1837

1837   PRESIDENT: Robert Ainslie, 1837–1843
       TRUSTEES:
        Robert Ainslie
        Thomas Tileston
        Daniel Low, 1837–1838

1838   TRUSTEES:
        Joshua Brooks
        George Winston Gray
        Robert Schuyler
        Joel Stone, 1838–1840

1839   MINISTER: *HENRY BELLOWS*, 1839–1882
       TREASURER: William F. Cary, 1839–1841
       TRUSTEES:
        William F. Cary, 1839–1841
        Joseph W. Haven
        Edward Anthony

Appendix C — Some Prominent Laypeople

THERE HAS BEEN A VERY SERIOUS ATTEMPT in this history of All Souls to make it not just a history of the ministers but also of the laymen and laywomen. In addition to the 34 men who were earlier discussed as founders there are others who played a prominent part in the life of the church during the first twenty years of existence, but who were not actually founders. These men and women are treated in alphabetical order as this appears to be the simplest way.

Robert Ainslie (*c.* 1775–1851), a member who became prominent at this time, was a transplanted Scotsman who became a wealthy merchant, banker, and real estate operator. He became active in the church when he was elected a trustee in 1833. He served as president of the board from 1834 to 1836, very crucial years in the history of the church and of William Ware, personally. He was again elected a trustee in 1837, reelected in 1840, and served again as president of the board in the crucial years of 1837–1843, when Charles Follen was having difficulties with the church, and during the period when Henry Bellows was called and during his early ministry. He was president of the North American Fire Insurance Company, which must have had its troubles after the fire of 1835. But he also owned extensive real estate in the city. His wife was Elizabeth Ann Ainslie, and he had three daughters, Elizabeth Ann, Catherine Johnson, and Margaret, as well as many grandchildren. He died on January 14, 1851, at the age of 73, and lived at 174 Hudson Street at that time.

The Cary brothers. Three brothers who were active in the First Church were Thomas G. Cary, William F. Cary, and Henry Cary. Thomas was active from the eighteen-twenties until his removal to Boston, and the two other brothers from the eighteen-thirties on. These three brothers were the sons of Samuel Cary of Boston, who went to the West Indies and made a fortune. He returned to Boston, married, and sired eight children. The sons came to New York in the early eighteen-twenties and engaged in commerce and trade, in which all of them flourished.[1]

[1] See C. G. Cary, *The Cary Letters* (Cambridge: Riverside Press, 1891).

*Henry Eckford by
Robert Fulton. Courtesy
of the Frick Art
Reference Library and
Mrs. John L. Baber*

Thomas G. Cary was elected a trustee in 1822, again in 1827, and served as president of the board of trustees from 1828 to 1830.

William Armstrong describes Thomas's brother, William, as

a descendant of the "Boston Tea Company," a "Boston boy" and a regular Simon Pure from down east, as keen as a rock, with a remarkable stock of go-a-headness in his composition. He commenced business peddling combs, the proceeds of which small traffick were carefully hoarded and went to the gradual enlargement of his stock in trade until he finally got himself located as a dealer in Fancy Goods, and as one of the first to commence that immensely profitable business, amassed thusly the principle [*sic*] portion of his large fortune. He is respected for his many good qualities and is worth, as we are informed on good authority, not less than $500,000.

Thus goes the gossip of the times. The Cary brothers were all prominent in the church, and our baptismal records attest to their large families.[2]

Henry Eckford (1775–1832), unlike most of the other early participants, did not come from New England. Eckford was born at Irvine,

[2] William Armstrong, *The Aristocracy of New York,* p. 17. See also *Dictionary of American Biography.*

Scotland, in 1775. At the age of sixteen he emigrated to Quebec, where he began to study the art of shipbuilding in the yards of his uncle, John Black. In 1796, at the age of twenty-one, Eckford settled in New York City and began shipbuilding on his own. His early yards were on the Long Island side of the East River. Because of the abundance of timber in the country, he could easily outsell the British and French shipbuilders, for he could build ships for $35 a ton whereas the British needed $50 a ton and the French $60. Henry Eckford's ships came to be known for their quality, their strength, and their speed.

He prospered during the War of 1812, and after the war from 1817 until 1820 he became the chief of naval construction at the Brooklyn Navy Yard. He resigned this position because of differences of opinion with some of the officials of the Navy Department. Thereupon, he resumed work in his own yards and built the *Robert Fulton,* which made the first voyage by steam from New York to New Orleans and Havana in 1822.

In the eighteen-twenties he also became keenly interested in Democratic politics in New York City, and he controlled the *National Advocate* which sponsored the candidacy of William Harris Crawford for President of the United States, who lost to John Quincy Adams in the Senate vote. Eckford owned a large country estate on Manhattan Island between Twenty-first and Twenty-fourth streets and Sixth and Eighth avenues and was noted for the entertaining that he did there. In his later years the failure of an insurance company in which he had a large interest took away a large part of his fortune. In 1832 he built a corvette for the Turkish Navy. He sailed the ship to Turkey, where he was put in charge of naval construction, and he died there on November 12, 1832.

Writing to her niece, Kate, at Lenox, Catharine Sedgwick told her that Mrs. Henry Eckford was going to Constantinople where her husband

> is admitted to greater intimacy with the Sultan than any European has ever been, walks about the palace with perfect freedom, & is often seen side by side with the Sultan on the most familiar terms. . . . The Sultan is a man of sense & knows how to appreciate so clever a man as Eckford & makes it worth his while to stay there.[3]

Meanwhile, news came of Henry Eckford's death, and just a month later, Catharine wrote in her *Journal,* "The body of Mr. Eckford arrived today. The Sultan paid him a just compliment when he said America must be rich in character to afford to spare so great a man."[4]

[3] Catharine M. Sedgwick to her niece, Kate, January 7, 1833, Massachusetts Historical Society.

[4] Catharine M. Sedgwick, *Journal,* entry for February 11, 1833, Massachusetts Historical Society.

In 1839, when Henry Ware, Jr., wrote a letter to Henry W. Bellows who had just become the new minister of the church, he urged Bellows to look up Mrs. Henry Eckford, "Mrs. Eckford in North Moore Street will be glad to see you. A very silent family, but warm hearted. They have gone through a world of affliction of all sorts." Mrs. Eckford was Marion Bedell, the daughter of Joseph Bedell and Miriam (Dorlon) Bedell.[5]

Charles Stephen Francis (1805–1887) was another very important member of the First Church who held many offices during his lifetime. His father, David Francis, was a member of the publishing firm of Munroe and Francis of Boston, which brought out the first New England edition of Shakespeare. Young Charles learned about the printing business and the selling of books from his father. He came to New York at the age of twenty-one and launched a business for himself. His first store was on lower Broadway near the residences of many wealthy citizens. Later, he moved to 252 Broadway and then to 554 Broadway. In 1838 his brother entered into partnership with him, and in 1842 the firm became known as C. S. Francis and Company. He published many guide books to the city, sermons by Bellows and Dewey, William Ware's *Zenobia* (1839), and the work of other Unitarian authors. He had an agency in London and thus was able to fill orders for British publications promptly. The firm was dissolved in 1860, but Francis continued in business for another ten years until he retired to Tarrytown.[6]

In 1830, he married Catharina Rebecca Jewett, who died in 1841; he married Averic Parker Allen in 1849.

In the church he served as clerk of the board of trustees from 1830 to 1868, so that 38 years of the minutes of the board are written in his hand. He was elected a trustee in 1832 and served as treasurer of the society for thirteen years, from 1844 to 1857, the only person to serve as both secretary and treasurer at the same time.

Jonathan Goodhue (1783–1848) was one of the most respected citizens of New York City and thoroughly established as a merchant trader. Fortunately we know a great deal about him, for his personal diary is in the New York Society Library, which his family was instrumental in founding. He has written the only personal account that we possess of Channing's visit and of the first meetings of the newly founded church. Jonathan Goodhue was born in Salem, Massachusetts, the son of Benjamin Goodhue

[5] Henry Ware, Jr., to Henry W. Bellows, January 9, 1839, Henry W. Bellows Papers, Box 2, Massachusetts Historical Society.
[6] *Dictionary of American Biography.*

Jonathan Goodhue (Painted in 1819) by James Frothingham.
Courtesy of the New York Society Library and the
Frick Art Reference Library

and Frances Richie Goodhue. His father had been a United States Senator from 1796 to 1800. Jonathan joined the firm of John-Norris, a local counting house or merchant's bank in Salem, which sent him to the Far East twice and to New York in 1807. His Diary tells us that when he came to New York he first stayed at the City Hotel.[7]

Two years after his arrival he founded Goodhue & Company, which prospered considerably as a commission house for commercial firms everywhere and which underwrote insurance as well. In 1813 Jonathan Goodhue married Catherine Rutherford Clarkson, the daughter of General Matthew Clarkson, who had distinguished himself during the American Revolution and was one of the most influential men in the city. So far as we have been able to determine, Goodhue and George Dummer were the only men among the early members or founders who married New York girls. Their circle of friends included the Sedgwicks and the Sewalls, partly because Jonathan's father had had political connections with the fathers of Henry Sedgwick and Henry Sewall.[8]

The Goodhues were practicing Episcopalians, and Catherine and her family were particularly loyal to the Episcopal Church. Jonathan dutifully bought Pew No. 8 in Trinity Church for $230 from Patrick G. Wildreth. But he also visited other churches. His Diary records that he paid a visit to a Congregational church in Burlington, Vermont, in August of 1814 while visiting there, and that he liked the "great evidence of good spirit in the service." He was constantly asked by the Episcopal Bishop of New York to serve on various diocesan committees which he usually politely refused, although he did agree to serve on a committee in 1817 to establish a Sunday school.[9]

Goodhue attended all of the early meetings of the new church. But in deference to his wife's and father-in-law's religion he did not immediately join the new society. Henry Bellows said many years later at Goodhue's funeral service,

He was not among those who started the first Unitarian congregation in New York. It was not till the spirit of persecution arose in this city, and he saw men and opinions he knew to be pure charged with infidelity, and branded with social opprobrium, that he felt his spirit stirred within him. Then his sense of duty, his love of truth, and his abhorrence of intolerance all combined to make him cast his lot with a sect everywhere spoken against....

[7] Goodhue Diary, entry for November 9, 1807, New York Society Library.

[8] See Jonathan E. Goodhue, *History and Genealogy of the Goodhue Family in England and America*... (Rochester, N.Y.: printed by E. R. Andrews, 1891), pp. 33–34, 56–57; *Dictionary of American Biography*.

[9] Goodhue Diary, August 12, 1814; March 1, 1817.

Mr. Goodhue was a firm believer in the doctrine of Unitarianism, and rejoiced in every evidence of the spread.

Within a few months after the founding and the building of the new church, Jonathan Goodhue occupied Pew No. 51 for the rest of his life.[10]

Goodhue's business prospered, and eventually he possessed a line of crack ships with regular schedules. When he died in 1848, the whole city mourned and the ships in the harbor all flew their flags at half mast. William Ware was fortunate, indeed, to have a man of Goodhue's calibre in the struggling new society.

Benjamin Hustace (1765–1849), the progenitor of the Hustace clan, was considered one of the early "pillars of the Church" by Henry Ware, Jr. He was a merchant with a sales outlet at 176 Front Street. He was twice elected a trustee, first in 1821, and again in 1831. He had at least four sons: John, William, Augustus, and David, and three daughters: Maria, Emily, and Mary.

His son *David Hustace* (1802–1841) was also prominent in the church until his early death at the age of 39. David Hustace was elected a trustee in 1834 and served one term until 1837. Henry Ware, Jr., also spoke about the son when he wrote to the young Bellows about some of his parishioners.[11]

David Lane (1801–1885) was born in Maine on May 25, 1801, and died on January 27, 1885, at his home at 11 Park Avenue (which is exactly across from the present site of the Community Church). As a young man, he went to Boston to start a career in business. He eventually became a senior partner in Boston in the firm of Lane, Lamson and Company, was married to the daughter of John Lamson of Boston, and his wife predeceased him by only two years. Moving to New York, he set up his own business and prospered. He soon joined the First Church. In his latter years he resided for a time in Paris. He had four children, of whom one, Mrs. O. P. C. Billings, became active in the church. His two sons moved away from New York. David Lane's funeral was at All Souls with Mr. Williams in charge, and the burial was in Mount Auburn Cemetery, Cam-

---

[10] Henry W. Bellows, *Funeral Sermon of Jonathan Goodhue*, pp. 20–22. Copy in the New York Society Library.

[11] Henry Ware, Jr., Jamaica Plain, Massachusetts, to Henry W. Bellows, New York, January 9, 1839. Box 2, Henry W. Bellows Papers, Massachusetts Historical Society.

bridge. He was first elected a trustee of the church in 1834, again in 1854, and again in 1861.[12]

Dr. Cyrus Perkins (1778–1849) was the only physician among the early members of the church. William Ware listed him as a physician and the *City Directory* for 1819 listed him as a surgeon. Actually he was both. The son of Isaac and Joanna (Edson) Perkins, Cyrus was born in Middleborough, Massachusetts, on September 4, 1778. He was graduated from Dartmouth College in 1800 with an M.A. degree. He continued on at Dartmouth and was graduated with an M.B. (medical bachelor's) in 1802. He began his medical practice in Boston and also taught in Boston at the Hawkins Street School. An interesting story of his career is that when Daniel Webster, also a Dartmouth graduate, who had dabbled in reading law in several small New England towns and had taught school, went to Boston to "find himself" in 1804 he met his friend Cyrus Perkins who got him a teaching position.[13]

Perkins returned to Dartmouth and received his M.D. in 1810, immediately joining the faculty, where he became a professor of anatomy and surgery at Dartmouth from 1810 to 1819. He moved to New York in 1819, arriving in the city in time to take part in some of the early activities of the new society. He was married to Abigail Smith, the daughter of Professor Dr. John Smith of the Dartmouth faculty, in 1800.[14]

It was appropriate that there should be a prominent physician in the membership of the church. In February 1820, Dr. Perkins chaired a congregational meeting. Harvard gave him an honorary degree in 1823. In 1824 he was elected a trustee of the church, and in 1840 he still owned Pew No. 77. He died at Rossville, Staten Island, on April 23, 1849.

The Schuyler family. It was during the period from 1823 on that the name of Schuyler became very prominent at All Souls. Like few others in the church, the Schuylers were an old-line New York State family.

Philip Jeremiah Schuyler was the son of the famous soldier, Philip John Schuyler, who served in the French and Indian War and was a major general in the Continental Army during the American Revolution. After the Revolution, he entered the political scene and was a member of the

[12] Obituary, *New York Times,* January 28, 1885, p. 5.

[13] *New England Genealogical Review,* Volume 21, p. 5.

[14] George T. Chapman, D.D., *Sketches of the Alumni of Dartmouth College* (Cambridge, 1867), pp. 101–102.

Dr. Cyrus Perkins by James Frothingham. Courtesy of Dartmouth College

Continental Congress from 1778 to 1781. He was elected one of the first two Senators from New York State.[15]

Philip Jeremiah Schuyler, the son (1768–1835), settled in New York City and became interested in the church in the early eighteen-twenties. He was born at Albany, was tutored privately at home along with ten brothers and sisters, and pursued agriculture and land development. He served in the New York State Assembly in 1798 and a term in the United States Congress (1817–1819), not seeking reelection. He then moved to New York City where he became a "Gentleman," which meant that he dabbled in land and all kinds of investments.

Schuyler, like many others in New York State, belonged to the Dutch

---

[15] *Dictionary of American Biography.*

Reformed Church. But when his first wife died he married Mary Anna Sawyer of Newburyport, a Unitarian, who signed the Covenant on February 24, 1821. Philip himself never signed the Covenant but was elected a trustee in 1823 and served as the president of the board from 1823 to 1826. William Ware listed him as a "Gentleman."

Robert Schuyler (–1855) was the son of Philip Jeremiah Schuyler and his first wife Sarah Rutsen and was important in the life of the church for many years. William Ware listed him as a "lawyer," but his real interests were in business management; we shall have something to say about him in the later history, during the ministry of Dr. Bellows, for he was instrumental in the building of the second edifice on Crosby Street, was involved in a fracas with Henry Bellows about the architecture of the third edifice, was the president of the New Haven Railroad, and finally fled the country after perpetrating a great business scandal.

His half brother, *George Lee Schuyler* (1811–1890), was the son of Philip Jeremiah Schuyler and his second wife, Mary Anna Sawyer, of Newburyport, Massachusetts. It was no doubt her influence which swayed Philip from the Dutch Reformed religion of his birth to Unitarianism. He married Eliza Hamilton, the daughter of Alexander Hamilton. George Schuyler was engaged in various business enterprises during his lifetime, among which were organizing transportation on the Hudson River and Long Island Sound. He later became a yachtsman, and won the "America Cup." After his wife died, he married her sister, Mary M. Hamilton. Two of his children, Louisa Lee Schuyler and Georgina Schuyler, were active in the church from before the Civil War until the nineteen-twenties. Louisa Lee ran the New York Chapter of the United States Sanitary Commission for Henry Bellows, founded the School of Nursing at Bellevue Hospital (the first in the United States), and founded the State Charities Aid Society. Her sister, Georgina (1840?–1923), also had a distinguished career, and in 1923 she was elected the first woman trustee of All Souls Church.

Catharine Sedgwick. Perhaps the most famous of the Sedgwicks was Catharine Maria Sedgwick (1789–1867), Henry and Robert's younger sister. She was born in Stockbridge, the ninth child of Theodore Sedgwick and Pamela Dwight Sedgwick. Although not a founder, she attended the church shortly after its founding. It was she who introduced Charles Follen to the people of New York and Boston, and it was she who persuaded William Cullen Bryant to write five original hymns for Henry Sewall's hymnbook in 1820. Bryant recalled that Catharine "was well formed, slightly inclined to plumpness, with regular features, eyes beaming with benevolence, a pleasing smile, a soft voice, and gentle and captivating manners." [16]

She made a reputation in the field of literature and became one of the first woman novelists in America, and certainly one of the most famous. Her novels were introspective enough to indicate that she had renounced Calvinism as early as 1821, and she became a Unitarian in that year because she appreciated the greater religious freedom offered by such a church. Although it is said that she had many suitors throughout her life, she often voiced a decision not to marry in favor of looking after her family. Her mother died in 1807, and Catharine, then 18 years of age, felt that it was her duty to look after her father and her 16-year-old brother, Charles. When Henry and Robert left for New York there was no other female in the family to tend to things in Stockbridge. She was constantly in and out of New York and Stockbridge visiting her brothers, and after 1821 spent a good part of each year in the city.

Catharine Sedgwick occupies a disproportionate role in this history because she kept a Journal (most of which is extant at the Massachusetts Historical Society) and she described with personal feelings many of the events which occurred in the history of the church.

Robert Sedgwick (1787–1841), her older brother, was also not an actual founder, having joined the church about the same time as his sister in 1821 after being disillusioned by Dr. John Mason's attack against the Unitarians. He was three times elected a trustee of the church, in 1823, in 1827, and in 1835. He was an attorney, counselor, and notary, and was in partnership with his brother Henry. They became famous when they defended the Greek government in the famous "Greek Frigates" case. He had an attack of illness while arguing in court, and returned to Stockbridge to the ancestral home to try to regain his health. But like Henry he died at an early age, 54 years.

Roger Gerard Van Polanen (1756–1833) in point of view of his chronological age was one of the oldest of the members, being 63 when the church was founded. Although not present at the earliest meetings of the society, he very quickly became one of the leaders. It was natural for the younger men to look to him for leadership. William Ware, in his Pew Book, listed him simply as a "Gentleman." With a Dutch name like Van Polanen, it would be natural to assume that he was a member of one of

---

[16] *Dictionary of American Biography;* from *The Life and Letters of Catharine M. Sedgwick,* quoted in Charles H. Brown, *William Cullen Bryant,* p. 93.

Roger Gerard Van Polanen by James Frothingham.
Courtesy of the New-York Historical Society, New York

the old Dutch families of New York, but this was not the case. He stated in his will that he was born in Rotterdam, Holland, emigrated to America, and became a naturalized citizen. He first appears in the city directories in 1817–1818, just two years before the founding of the church. His will, written on June 20, 1833, incidentally was witnessed by Dr. Cyrus Perkins, a fellow Unitarian who obviously was acting as his physician. He left his books and pamphlets on religion and theology to William Ware "as proof of my high esteem." His wife survived him and continued to occupy the pew at the church on Chambers Street.[17]

Roger Van Polanen was elected a trustee in 1820, was president of the board from 1821 to 1822 in the earliest period of William Ware's ministry. He was elected a trustee again in 1827, and again served as president in 1827–1828. He was one of the three men along with Sedgwick and Armitage who were instructed to prepare a statement to correct the erroneous

[17] Will of Roger G. Van Polanen, liber 71, p. 87, New York County Surrogate's Court.

impressions that were going the rounds in New York as to what Unitarians believed. He died in 1833 at the age of 77 years.

Benjamin Franklin Wheelwright was a layman who became very prominent in the church in 1830, when he was elected treasurer. He was born in Boston on October 18, 1803, and died on October 7, 1875, at his home at 12 West 17th Street. He was a descendant of the Rev. John Wheelwright who was a friend of Oliver Cromwell. Benjamin Wheelwright moved to New York in 1825 when he was twenty-two years of age, went into the mercantile business as an independent dealer, and continued in this business until 1837, when he retired with a fortune. He must have been a shrewd business man, indeed, for 1837 was the year of a financial panic and he survived it in good financial shape. Two years later, in 1839, he was elected president of the Greenwich Bank and remained its president until his death 36 years later. He was also the president of the Greenwich Savings Bank, a trustee of the United States Trust Company, and a director of the United States Life Insurance Company. Dr. Bellows conducted the funeral service at the Wheelwright home in 1875, and Benjamin Wheelwright was buried in Woodlawn Cemetery.[18]

Wheelwright was often considered by many to be one of the founders of the First Church, but this was a mistaken idea because he was only sixteen years of age when the church was founded. But he held so many positions in the church that it must have seemed as if he had always been around. As early as 1829, he refused appointment as secretary of the board of trustees. He accepted the appointment as treasurer of the church, which position he held for six years from 1830 to 1836. Elected a trustee for the first time in 1832, he was elected again periodically throughout his life until 1865. He served as president of the board of trustees in 1833–1834 and again in the very difficult days of the Civil War from 1859 to 1866. He was a pillar of the church for over 45 years.

[18] Obituary, *New York Times,* October 9, 1875.

Acknowledgments

SINCERE THANKS are due to the following individuals and organizations for permission to reproduce pictures and to quote from material on which they hold copyrights:

Mrs. H. C. Borchardt for permission to reproduce the portrait of George B. Arnold.

Arthur W. Brown for permission to quote from his book *Always Young for Liberty* (Syracuse: Syracuse University Press, 1956).

Charles H. Brown for permission to quote from his book *William Cullen Bryant* (New York: Charles Scribner's Sons, 1971).

Coward-McCann and Geoghegan, Inc., for permission to quote from *The Epic of New York City* by Edward Robb Ellis (New York: Coward-McCann, Inc., 1966).

The Trustees of Dartmouth College for permission to reproduce the portrait of Dr. Cyrus Perkins by James Frothingham, from the Hopkins Center Art Galleries.

The Follen Church for permission to reproduce the portraits of Eliza Cabot Follen and Dr. Charles Follen.

The Frick Art Reference Library and Mrs. Elizabeth Sturgis Paine for the portrait of Elijah Paine II, by A. G. D. Tuthill; the Frick Art Reference Library and Mrs. Katherine W. Sawford for the portraits of Mr. and Mrs. Benjamin Blossom, by J. H. Larazus; the Frick Art Reference Library and Charles J. Sewall for the portrait of Henry Devereux Sewall by William Dunlop; the Frick Art Reference Library and the National Academy of the Arts for the portrait of William Cullen Bryant by Samuel F. B. Morse; the Frick Art Reference Library and Mrs. Harriet N. Minot for the portrait of Catharine Maria Sedgwick by C. C. Ingraham; the Frick Art Reference Library and Mrs. John L. Baber for the portrait of Henry Eckford by Robert Fulton;

and the Frick Art Reference Library and the New York Society Library for the portrait of Jonathan Goodhue (1819) by James Frothingham.

Mrs. E. R. Gay and Mrs. Edgar J. Brower for permission to reproduce the portraits of Mr. and Mrs. Benjamin Armitage.

Mrs. E. L. Gwynn for permission to reproduce the portrait of Lucy Channing Russel by Washington Allston.

Harvard University for permission to reproduce the portrait of Henry Ware, Sr., copied by George Fuller from an original by Frothingham (?) from the Portrait Collection; and the portrait of Henry Wheaton by John Wesley Jarvis (?), from the Law School Collection.

The Macmillan Publishing Company, Inc., for permission to quote from *The Diary of George Templeton Strong,* edited by Allan Nevins and Milton H. Thomas (copyright 1952 by Macmillan Publishing Company, Inc.).

The Massachusetts Historical Society for permission to reproduce the drawing by William Ware of his son Henry and to quote from Catharine Maria Sedgwick's *Journals,* the Samuel Cabot Papers, the Henry D. Ware Papers, the Henry W. Bellows Papers, and the Henry D. Sedgwick Papers.

The Museum of the City of New York for permission to reproduce the pictures of Broadway and the City Hall, 1819, and the Second Congregational Unitarian Church at Prince and Mercer streets, and the Nathaniel Currier lithograph of the Great Fire of 1835 from Coenties Slip (all in the J. Clarence Davies Collection); and the Nathaniel Currier lithograph of the burning of the steamship *Lexington* (from the Henry T. Peters Collection).

The Newark Museum for permission to reproduce the portraits of Mr. and Mrs. George Dummer by Samuel L. Waldo and William Jewett.

The New Haven Colony Historical Society for permission to reproduce the miniature of Elihu Townsend by Elkanah Tisdale.

The New-York Historical Society for permission to reproduce the portraits of Dr. Joseph Priestley by Rembrandt Peale, of Daniel Stanton by Charles L. Elliott, of the Reverend Edward Everett (engraved by J. C. Buttre after a photograph by Brady), of Roger Van Polanen by James Frothingham, of Moses H. Grinnell by George E. Perine, and of Mr. and Mrs. Philip Jeremiah Schuyler by Gilbert Stuart; the pictures of the City Hotel, Park Place (New York), City Hall, Broadway (1831), Steam Boat Wharf (New York, 1831), Merchants' Exchange,

Wall Street (1831), New York from Brooklyn Heights, and the ruins in Exchange Place, December 17, 1835; and William Ware's sketch of the First Church, from his "Pew Book."

The New York Public Library, Astor, Lennox, and Tilden Foundations for permission to reproduce the painting of clipper ships at South Street Wharf, New York City, by William I. Bennett, from the I. N. Phelps Stokes Collection, Prints Division; and for permission to quote from correspondence between Henry D. Sewall and William Cullen Bryant and between Bryant and William Ware, in the Manuscripts and Archives Division.

The New York Society Library for permission to quote from the *Diary* of Jonathan Goodhue.

The Pierpont Morgan Library for permission to quote from letters of William Ellery Channing to Mrs. Susan Higginson and to William Henry Channing.

Edward K. Spann for permission to quote from his book *Ideals and Politics* (Albany: State University of New York Press, 1972).

The Unitarian Church of All Souls for permission to reproduce pictures of the First Church Building, 1821, and the Reverend William Ware by Nathaniel Frothingham, and a woodcut of Dr. Charles Follen.

The Unitarian Universalist Association for permission to reproduce the portraits of William Parsons Lunt and William Henry Channing.

The University of Chicago Press for permission to quote from *The Life of Karl Follen* by George W. Spindler (Chicago: The University of Chicago Press, 1917).

Malcolm C. Ware for permission to reproduce the portrait of Mary Waterhouse Ware by Nathaniel Frothingham.

Yale University Press for permission to quote from *The Transcendentalist Ministers* by William R. Hutchison (New Haven: Yale University Press, 1959).

Index

269

C

E

East Lexington: and Follen, 235
Eckford, Henry: 72, *254,* 254–256
Eddowes, Ralph: 93
Eddy, Judge Samuel: 64
Eliot, Frederick May: death of, 8
Elliott, Daniel: 60
Emerson, Ralph Waldo: 93, 194,
    242, 243
Emerson, William: 93
Everett, Edward: 75, 76, 77, 80, *87;*
    dedication sermon, 86–88

F

Feltus, Henry James: controversy
    with, 105–108, 157
Fillmore, Millard: 49
Finances: 82, 116–118, 128, 135–
    136, 142, 219–220
The First Congregational Church in
    the City of New York: legal name,
    42
Fisk, Thaddeus: 124
Fitz-Randolph, Edward: 63
Flint, James: 77
Follen, Charles Christopher (son):
    212, 218, 238
Follen, Charles Theodore Christian:
    vi, 10, 179, 182, *206, 223;* and
    Brooklyn Church, 194; background
    of, 204–208; ministry of, 204–218;
    marriage of, 209–210; and Chan-
    ning, 210–211; enters ministry,
    210–211; and Christmas tree, 212;
    and slavery, 212, 215–216, 224,
    227–230; comes to All Souls,
    213–214; letter to Channing, 216;
    resignation of, 219–231, 233; lec-
    tures and sermons of, 220–221,
    227; letter to H. Martineau, 224–
    225; stubbornness of, 230–231;
    farewell sermon, 234–235; and East
    Lexington, 235; death of, 237;

comments on, 240–241; and Tran-
    scendentalism, 242–244
Follen, Eliza Cabot: 142, 157, 162,
    209, 213, 231, 238; letter from C.
    Sedgwick, 154; marriage of, 209–
    210
Follenius, Christoph: 204
Foote, Henry Wilder: 102
Forbes, Maria: 139
Founders of All Souls: described,
    45–73; and politics, 47–48; law-
    yers among, 49–53; artisans among,
    53–55; merchants among, 55–67;
    analysis of, 69–71
Fox, James: 141, 219
Francis, Charles: 199, 202, 256
Francis, Convers: 77
Francis, David: 256
Fraser, Mrs. Alexander V.: 7
Freedom: 12–13
Freeman, James: 27, 93
Free School: 139–140, 214
"Friend of Truth": 108
Frost, Captain John: 193
Frothingham of Boston: 152
Fuller, Margaret: 242
Furness, William: 154

G

Gannett, Ezra Stiles: 161
Gay, Ebenezer: 50
Gay, Mrs. Edward R.: 63n
Glaze, William: 24, 48, 63, 73; life
    of, 53–54; and Dummer, 56
Glover, Euphemia: 9
God, worship of: 13–14
Godwin, Parke: 48n
Goethe, Johann: 208
Goodhue, Benjamin: 256
Goodhue, Francis Richie: 257
Goodhue, Jonathan: 37, 105, 222,
    256–259, *257;* on Channing, 29–30;
    and founding, 33
Goodrich, A. T.: quoted, 83–84